Words of Praise for *Visionseeker*

"VISIONSEEKER is a fabulous exploration into the reaches of consciousness, a glimpse into the possible evolutionary future of the mind. Anthropologist Hank Wesselman is an expert guide who fully realizes he is playing with scientific and spiritual dynamite."
— **Larry Dossey, M.D.**, author of *Reinventing Medicine* and *Healing Words*

"Well written and suspenseful. Hank Wesselman's VISIONSEEKER rivals the works of Carlos Castaneda."
— **Michael Harner, Ph.D.**, author of *The Way of the Shaman* and director of the Foundation for Shamanic Studies

"Hank Wesselman's trilogy of his explorations in authentic shamanic time-travel represent an extraordinarily exciting contribution to the worldwide paradigm shift taking place in our time. Combining the sober objectivity of a trained scientist with a mystic's passionate search for deeper understanding, VISION-SEEKER contains further fascinating revelations of the generally secret teachings of the Hawaiian kahunas."
— **Ralph Metzner, Ph.D.**, author of *The Unfolding Self* and *Green Psychology*

"Hank Wesselman is a courageous anthropologist who explores the realms of spirit and consciousness to give us an expanded vision of the world. VISIONSEEKER will challenge the limits of reality."
— **Judith Orloff, M.D.**, author of *Dr. Judith Orloff's Guide to Intuitive Healing* and *Second Sight*

"VISIONSEEKER is an exhilarating, aesthetically lovely adventure, and a mind-expanding portent of our possible future. What raises the hair on the back of my neck is the flexible consciousness of this shamanic anthropologist, living life unconstrained by a local personality. Hank Wesselman's SPIRITWALKER trilogy has changed my way of living in time."
— **Gay Luce, Ph.D.**, director, the Nine Gates Mystery School

"Hank Wesselman shares his brilliance with us in VISIONSEEKER as he takes us on the intriguing journey of his own spiritual evolution."
— **Sandra Ingerman**, author of
Soul Retrieval: Mending the Fragmented Self

VISIONSEEKER

ALSO BY HANK WESSELMAN, PH.D.

SPIRITWALKER: Messages from the Future

MEDICINEMAKER: Mystic Encounters on the Shaman's Path

OTHER HAY HOUSE TITLES OF RELATED INTEREST

THE ALCHEMIST'S HANDBOOK, by John Randolph Price

AMERICAN INDIAN PROPHECIES:
Conversations with Chasing Deer,
by Kurt Kaltreider, Ph.D.

DREAM JOURNAL, by Leon Nacson

THE LIGHTWORKER'S WAY:
Awakening Your Spiritual Power to Know and Heal,
by Doreen Virtue, Ph.D.

THE LOVE AND POWER JOURNAL, by Lynn V. Andrews

7 PATHS TO GOD: The Ways of the Mystic,
by Joan Borysenko, Ph.D.

SIXTH SENSE: Including the Secrets
of the Etheric Subtle Body, by Stuart Wilde

(All of the above titles are available at your local bookstore.
Hay House titles can also be ordered by calling 760-431-7695
or 800-654-5126.)

Please visit the Hay House Website at: **hayhouse.com**
and Hank Wesselman's Website at: **sharedwisdom.com**

VISIONSEEKER

Shared Wisdom from
the Place of Refuge

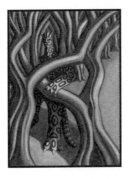

Hank Wesselman, Ph.D.

Hay House, Inc.
Carlsbad, California • Sydney, Australia

Published and distributed in the United States by:
Hay House, Inc., P.O. Box 5100, Carlsbad, CA 92018-5100
(800) 654-5126 • (800) 650-5115 (fax) • www.hayhouse.com

Editorial Supervision: Jill Kramer • *Design:* Summer McStravick
Leopard Man art: Hank Wesselman

Library of Congress Cataloging-in-Publication Data

Wesselman, Henry Barnard.
    Visionseeker : shared wisdom from the place of refuge / Hank Wesselman.
       p. cm.
    Includes bibliographical references (p.).
    ISBN 1-56170-753-8 (hardcover)
      1. Wesselman, Henry Barnard. 2. Ecstasy—Miscellanea.
3. Shamanism. I. Title: Visionseeker
  II. Title.

    BL626 .W47 A3 2001
    133.9'092—dc21
    [B]

                             00-047244

ISBN 1-56170-753-8

03 02 01 00   4 3 2 1
1st printing, March 2001

◊ ◊ ◊

To my family and friends,
To my teachers and students,
To my ancestors and descendants,
And to the gentle goddess,
Who gives us everything we have
And never asks for anything at all,
I offer this book with gratitude,
In reciprocation.

◊ ◊ ◊

C O N T E N T S

◊ ◊ ◊

What strange pleasure do they get who'd
wipe whole worlds out,
ANYTHING
to end our lives, our
wild idleness?

But we have charms against their rage—
(we) must go on saying, "Look,
if nobody tried to live this way,
all the work of the world would be in vain."

And now and then a son, a daughter, hears it.
Now and then a son, a daughter,
gets away.

— Lew Welch, author of *Ring of Bone*

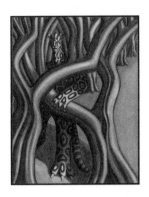

Introduction

I AM AN ANTHROPOLOGIST who works with an international team of scientists investigating the eroded, ancient landscapes of eastern Africa's Great Rift Valley in search of answers to the mystery of human origins. My academic training lies in the fields of environmental and evolutionary biology, geology, and anthropology, and much of my research involves reconstructing the paleoenvironments of prehistoric sites from which the fossilized remains of humanity's earliest ancestors have been recovered.

My first book, *Spiritwalker,* is an account of how my life took a decidedly different turn in the early 1980s. One foggy summer morning while I was finishing up my doctoral work at the University of California at Berkeley, I experienced a full-fledged altered state of consciousness just before dawn. This was a spontaneous event, achieved without the catalyst of any mind-altering substances or disciplined spiritual practice, and for its duration, my physical body was rendered paralyzed by ecstatic feelings of power or force that were quite formidable. Yet my mind was fully awake and hyper-aware, and it was in this expanded state that I had a direct encounter with what a tribal person might call a spirit.

This episode was followed by several others, all of which were accompanied by the same ecstatic feelings, as well as curious visual hallucinations of spots of light, wavy lines, and vortexes that seemed to be part of a huge filamentous grid or net. Nothing in my academic training as an anthropologist had prepared me for these experiences, and I responded to them with an intense curiosity. I was not one of those worthies who had spent decades studying at the knees of the wisdom masters, practicing meditation and yoga, hoping for visions and transcendent experiences, nor was I a member of the psychedelic explorers club. In those days, I worshiped solely at the altar of science.

Several years later, my family and I moved to a small farm on the Kona Coast of the island of Hawai'i, where I experienced another series of spontaneous altered states, all of which were accompanied by the same paralytic feelings of power and heralded by the strange visual hallucinations. In the first episode, my conscious awareness was brought into contact with the mind of another man in a most dramatic fashion. It was as if I were inside of him. I could see what he was seeing and hear what he was hearing. I could perceive his thoughts and emotions almost as if they were my own, and yet there were two separate personalities, his and mine, existing simultaneously within the one physical aspect.

When I recovered from my amazement, I discovered that I could tap into this man's memory banks, receiving information as a multilayered complex of thoughts, emotions, impressions, memories, and judgments. I learned that this man's name is Nainoa, and that he is an individual of Hawaiian ancestry who resides somewhere on the western coast of North America. And if this were not enough, he lives roughly 5,000 years from now in a world profoundly different from that of today. To say I was surprised would be an understatement of vast proportions.

I had heard about concepts such as telepathy, clairvoyance,

channeling, and trance-mediumship, but up until that moment, my reaction to these psychic phenomena had been one of amused skepticism. Now here I was, a trained scientist, experiencing the awesome jolt of the real thing myself. My initial response was one of confusion mixed with disbelief, and I shakily branded that first episode an extremely lucid dream. I say "shakily" because part of me suspected that what I had experienced was not a dream at all.

The altered states resumed, becoming an ongoing series of episodes that occurred roughly in sequence over the next four years. They continued to be spontaneous in that I could not deliberately induce them through my intentionality, yet in each, my conscious awareness was merged once again with that of Nainoa. Within these states, I learned a lot about him and his world, visually through his eyes, experientially through his actions in his level of reality and time, and cognitively through the veil of his culturally determined perceptions, judgments, interpretations, memories, and opinions. His thoughts and feelings had an alien quality, a foreignness, that was very distracting until I came to realize that this was due to the profoundly different "shape" of his mind, determined largely by his experiences since birth in his own slice of reality and within his own culture.

When I opened my eyes in Nainoa's body that first time, I tried to control his movements, and his body responded with confusion to two separate sets of mental commands. Somehow, despite my own confusion and excitement, I managed to figure out the problem and become completely passive. I merely "sat within" and observed. I believe that my limited experience with meditation proved invaluable, as I was able to discipline myself to become completely still, yet fully watchful. In the process, I discovered that if I wished to look at something, Nainoa would very shortly walk over and look at it. If I wanted to know something, it would obligingly appear in his mind . . . and in my own. Although Nainoa's language is different from any that exists today, I was able to receive the jist of meaning of his thoughts and words as the shape of his knowing was translated into mine, a process I still do not understand fully.

In response to this amazing experience, my carefully constructed scientific paradigm of reality began to come apart, and at that time, I had nothing with which to replace it. Although I didn't know it, I was in the throes of a classic initiation crisis, a mental and spiritual crossroads well known to the shamans of traditional tribal peoples and the mystics of our modern state-level societies. But unlike the tribal shaman or contemporary spiritual seeker, I was not prepared for such a life-changing and ego-shattering event.

Yet within my expanded-state connections with Nainoa, a most amazing story began to unfold. In the initial episode, I learned that his people are the descendants of Hawaiians who reached the North American coast in a fleet of double-hulled transoceanic voyaging canoes about 130 years before. Upon their arrival, they had found no people, no cities, and no evidence of the once-great American civilization. They had established a chain of settlements around the western edge of an inland sea, presumably a marine inundation of California's central valley. Like traditional Polynesian settlements of the past, these villages appeared to be large, planned, self-sufficient slices of landscape, with a fishing community on the coast and a farming community a day's travel inland.

From Nainoa's memories, I learned that the settlers' society is stratified by rank and priviledge, much like that of the precontact Hawaiians, with a political leadership derived largely from a ruling class, with various ranks of "commoners" below them in the hierarchy—laborers, farmers, fishermen, stockmen, artisans, servants, and so forth. If I was, in fact, seeing a slice of the future, it seemed that humanity's destiny lay in a system of balanced feudalism.

On that first day, Nainoa left his community to engage in a journey of geographic exploration of the largely unknown interior of the continent. But where were the oak-studded grasslands, pines, and evergreens of the California that I knew so well? The land I saw was covered with tropical rainforests, and the climate was most definitely tropical and "wet." If this was indeed California, a dramatic climatic shift had occurred, possibly on a planetary scale, bearing out contemporary science's worst-case predictions associated with the current greenhouse theory of global warming.

The adventure deepened as Nainoa crossed the inland sea and traversed the forested regions and the mountains beyond. During this solitary trek, he himself began to have expanded-state experiences—psychic episodes in which he started to receive his own initiation at the "hands of the spirits." It was also during this journey that Nainoa began to experience the time-shift phenomenon in reverse, on occasion finding his conscious awareness merged with mine in *my* level of reality and time. His reaction was to hypothesize that I was *his* ancestor, an insight that threw the whole affair into an entirely new light. As an invisible participant-observer to these incredible events, my own investigations began to extend far beyond the ordinary nature of reality into the inner realms of the human mind and spirit.

Upon reaching the comparatively drier wooded grasslands beyond the mountains, Nainoa found a group of indigenous hunter-gatherers of possible mixed Inuit French-Canadian descent called the Ennu, and spent most of a year living with them. During this interval, he became romantically involved with a woman named Kenojelak, whose father, William, functioned as shaman for his people when the need arose.

Toward the end of my stay in Kona, Nainoa's growing awareness of me and his wish to make contact was facilitated by William, who began to instruct him in the ways of the traditional shaman. The two men visited a place of power where Nainoa and I finally conversed directly for the first time. It was also in this place that we were taken on a visionary voyage into the heart of the great mystery of existence by an immensely powerful spirit known to the Ennu as a *dorajuadiok*.

Spiritwalker also contains relevant details of my own life during the four years I lived in Hawai'i, documenting my search for meaning behind these extraordinary experiences. During this time, I found myself drawn into a relationship with an animal spirit I call the "leopard man," an entity that I had known during my childhood as an imaginary friend. Much to my surprise, the leopard man reappeared during my visionary experiences, giving rise to the possibility that "he" was also connected to my descendant, Nainoa. Another avenue of possible connection was the "spirit stone," an object of great power that I first observed in Nainoa's time and which I subsequently found awash in the waves of Kealakekua Bay more than a year later. Quite suddenly, my life took on a kind of mythic resonance, drawing me ever deeper into spiritual dimensions of the mystic.

My second book, *Medicinemaker,* recounts the next stage in this ongoing chronicle, beginning with my return to California in 1989. For the better part of a year, I feared that my departure from the islands had severed my mysterious connection with Nainoa. Then early one morning, in May of 1990, my visionary experiences resumed. *Medicinemaker* documents the connections that occurred over the next five years, during which pieces of the puzzle of this strange contact across time and distance began to fall into place.

This second book also presents the account of how Nainoa returned to his own culture in the company of two Ennu hunters, one of whom is William the shaman. Nainoa's explorations and his discovery of the remnants of the lost American civilization brought him considerable recognition among his people, enabling him to ascend within the hierarchy of the ruling class. In addition, his emerging abilities as a medicine man, fostered by William, marked the beginning of his training as a *kahuna* (what we know as a shaman or mystic). When news of his accomplishments reached the ruler of all the Hawaiian land divisions around the inland sea, he was summoned to the capital, where he was brought into connection with a high chiefess, Maraea, the granddaughter of the Governor. A love relationship developed between them, and it was apparent that she would most likely become his wife.

Unfortunately, Nainoa's rapid rise into the hierarchy also earned him the jealousy of a politically well-connected priest, a man with a dark soul who had known him since childhood. This unsavory individual committed an act of spite that activated Nainoa's anger during a moment in which he was in connection with the spirit he calls the "spotted tiger man." This entity apparently took Nainoa's rage for a directive, and the priest's demise occurred that same day in the jaws of a tiger at the edge of the forest.

The use of spiritual power in a negative capacity is considered to be a serious error in judgment among Nainoa's people, and the visionary narrative in *Medicinemaker* concludes with Nainoa being sent to a place of refuge "to be purified of his sins" and to receive training from a well-known *kahuna* mystic. This fascinating story also contains much sacred knowledge derived from the Polynesian *kahuna* tradition, information that continues to be revealed in this third book in the series.

Interwoven with the visionary episodes recorded in *Medicinemaker* is the story of how I returned to my own people, resuming my former life as an academic teacher and researcher. This was a time during which the true purpose of the profound yet cryptic contact I have with Nainoa began to take shape.

When these visionary experiences began, I had no one to advise me—no honored, wise elder to provide guidance, counsel, or direction. I was very much alone and had to find my own road. As an anthropologist, I resisted the pathologizing of my experiences offered by the Western psychological paradigm and began instead to investigate the wisdom of the indigenous peoples—specifically, the practice and worldview of the traditional shaman. What I learned provided me with a meaningful cultural framework through which to order and understand what I was experiencing.

The shaman is a man or woman who is able to access altered states of consciousness utilizing focused intentionality in combination with repetitive percussive sound, rhythmic movement or song, and in some cultures, hallucinogens derived from psychotropic plants. While in the altered state, shamans are able to perceive in an expanded way, enabling them to enter ordinarily hidden realms of reality in which they interact with nonordinary beings that they typically categorize as spirits. Sanctified by their initiation, assisted by their helping spirits, and directed by strong, altruistic motivation, the shaman is the master of trance.

It was obvious to me that my visions were much like those of traditional shamans in that they were associated with abrupt, transient, altered states of consciousness. As spontaneous experiences, they often happened just before dawn when I was in that dreamy state between waking and sleeping, but through practice, I found that I could induce them during the day while very much awake, a fact that has led me to conclude that they are not hypnagogic hallucinations associated with sleep paralysis, nor are they dreams in the classic sense.

Within these visions, I sometimes find myself in that mystical geography that the traditional people have called the spirit world, but in many instances, my conscious awareness is once again drawn into connection with the mind of Nainoa. The monumental question of how such a phenomenon is even possible has been addressed in my previous books. *Spiritwalker* presents the story of my initiation crisis. *Medicinemaker* documents my recovery.

Visionseeker begins where *Medicinemaker* concludes, becoming the third in the series. It is about Nainoa's training as a *kahuna*, and contains much wisdom about the nature of the self as well as the nature of reality from the Polynesian perspective. It also presents aspects of my own training in core shamanism with anthropologist Michael Harner and his colleagues in the Foundation for Shamanic Studies. Taken together, these accounts reveal something about what it means to be an explorer of the mysterious interface between the edges of consciousness and the margins of reality.

Nainoa and I have learned that it can be lonely out there "in the bush," but like countless others before us, we have also discovered that this is the place where truth is found. And unexpectedly, we often find ourselves in very good company.

CHAPTER ONE

The Master Game

I N JANUARY OF 1995, I returned home from a month's fieldwork
in Ethiopia in a state of high excitement. Our multinational team
of scientists had made a major discovery, excavating about half
of a fossilized human skeleton from ancient sediments in the Middle Awash region of the Great Rift Valley that are about four and
a half million years old, making the bones considerably older than
any other human remains recovered at that time. The fossils pre-
served a complex of primitive features, giving rise to the possibility that we had found the earliest ancestor from which all of
humanity is descended.

While there, I had also experienced one of my deep visionary
episodes in which I had been able to connect with Nainoa and bring
his conscious awareness from his time and place into mine. This
event had included a direct encounter with a monumental spirit-
being of great power called a *dorajuadiok*, an entity without physical form, composed of a vast intelligence associated with a dense
concentration of energy. One of the many things I learned during

this interaction was that this spirit does not understand or identify with our human sense of individuation, but instead, expresses qualities that may represent some form of collective consciousness.[1]

During my "meeting" with this entity,[2] an enormous chunk of information was transferred into my memory banks from or through this awesome being, an experience that was simply overwhelming. I was very busy with my field research when this happened, and there was no opportunity to make notes. I was concerned that I might forget large parts of the information, but Nainoa had received "the program" as well, and with his highly trained skills of memory recall, the chances were good that I would be able to retrieve virtually all of it.

On the trip home from Africa, I felt Nainoa's conscious awareness come into connection with mine during a 20-hour plane flight from Italy to California. My attempts to retrieve some of the *dorajuadiok* data with his input were continually interrupted by discussions with colleagues about details of the field season, stops at airports, periodic meals, as well as on-flight films—all of which diverted my attention. There was also, of course, Nainoa's stunned amazement at directly experiencing these wonders, and I spent a good deal of the flight mentally reviewing what I knew about aircraft for his benefit—from their history and design, to the extraction of the fossil fuels and metal ores that made it all possible.

Nainoa's worldview is determined by the time and culture in which he lives, and his mind is shaped much like that of someone who lived during the Neolithic Period. Accordingly, he lacks a cultural frame of reference through which to comprehend our technology, and for much of the flight, I could feel his rising frustration as he sought unsuccessfully to assimilate much of what I simply regarded as the known.

I fell asleep somewhere over the western Atlantic, and when I awoke, the plane was landing in snowbound Newark to refuel. I focused my attention within, but Nainoa's awareness had disconnected. As a result, my attempts to retrieve the data remained in the initial phases of recovery.

Upon my return to my home in Northern California, I experienced severe jet lag for about a week and found myself waking at two or three in the morning, unable to get back to sleep. In those dark hours, I began to reconsider the issue of what it meant to become a mystic in an age of multinational corporations, super science, and high technology.

The majority of the time, my life was not very different from anyone else's. I was a married householder with children who made my living as a teacher and writer. At night, however, my life had taken on a kind of mythic quality in response to my ongoing visionary experiences.

When I considered the term *mythic,* Joseph Campbell, one of the preeminent mythologists of the 20th century, always came to mind. One of Campbell's great contributions was his revelation of the monomyth—the single, timeless, universal story found within all the rich and varied mythologies of humanity. Campbell called this story "the hero's journey," and in his book *Hero of a Thousand Faces*, he analyzed the major stages of the voyage, providing a grand synthesis and revealing the unity within humankind's incredible cultural and ethnic diversity.[3]

In the first stage in the journey, an ordinary citizen—someone like you or me—suddenly and unexpectedly receives "the call." This usually takes the form of an open invitation to embark on an adventurous quest into the unknown. As often as not, the person is quite comfortable with their life and is not particularly motivated to leave it all behind. In addition, society at large provides us with every conceivable reason for staying with the known, for not rocking the boat, for accepting its beliefs as real, for regarding its morals as appropriate, and for seeing its limits as valid.

The call can come in many forms. For some, it appears as a dream or vision, or as a visit from an ancestor or supernatural being who gives instructions or offers new directions. For others, it might come as a new job opportunity on the one hand, or being fired from their present job on the other—the end of a relationship or the beginning of a new one.

Whatever form it takes, the hero is the man or woman who recognizes it for what it is and awakens from the conventional slumber of culture at large. The individual then begins to penetrate the mystery beyond the edges of the known, enabling them to grow beyond the boundaries of the old self. As this amazing experience deepens, the second part of the journey begins—the stage of initiation.

This period inevitably includes tests, trials, and tribulations, one of which usually involves the search for a teacher who can guide the initiate in the right direction. Sometimes the teacher may appear as an internal one, a spirit guide or inner guru. Just as often it may be a teacher in the outer world, a Zen master, Rinpoche, or master shaman. When the teacher is found, the time of discipline and training commences.

As the tests continue, the law of karma has a way of speeding up, and the individual will often experience an increase in their personal problems. There are always failures in the beginning, and sometimes one's life can unravel in truly spectacular ways. The hero must persevere, proceeding onward toward the goal, heedless of their own well-being, comfort, or security, for this is also a time of purification in which certain negative aspects of the self must be faced and thrown off.

With the paying of these debts and the cleansing of the inner self, an additional factor usually enters the dynamic—help from the spirit world. This spiritual assistance provides the hero with supernatural power, protection, and support, and it is then that this individual is able to cross the threshhold into the inner worlds where they're granted access to the zone of magnified power, and entrance into the true visionary realms.

Everything changes at this point. Transformed by their initiation and assisted by their guardian spirits, the hero passes the tests, completes the quest, and achieves breakthroughs of life-changing proportions. The individual is utterly transfigured in the process, reemerging with great skills, profound knowledge, and new abilities.

In the third stage of the journey, the accomplished hero must then return to society, bearing their newfound gifts and functioning as one who has become the master of the two worlds, the inner and the outer. As such, the hero can now operate as a fully formed and fully initiated human being—as a warrior, protector, messenger, teacher, ruler, healer, and mystic. In short, the hero returns as a chief and a world redeemer.

At this point in the journey, the need to alleviate the confusion of the world and heal the suffering of others becomes the hero's major concern. To accomplish this, the hero must exercise compassionate thought, feeling, and action, transforming their newfound expertise and knowledge into wisdom. It is then that the authentically initiated and fully awakened hero becomes a sage.

Campbell has suggested that this mythic saga is universal, and that all of the world's stories, from classic literature to soap operas on afternoon television, are simply variations of this one great theme. He has also suggested that the monomyth is experienced to varying degrees by all of us as we pass through our lives—that each of us is living out our own, personal version of it. The inevitable conclusion: Each of us has the potential to become the hero in our own journey.

I spent many sleepless hours meditating on the nature of these insights as I recovered from my jet lag. My own experiences had precipitated an unprecedented personal transformation that, once started, was continuing to unfold, enabling an entirely new understanding of reality, the self, and the reason for living.

One morning soon after my return, I turned on the bedside light and speculatively looked over the pile of books and papers on the shelf within reach. My wife, Jill, awoke briefly and asked if I was okay, then turned away from the light and slipped back into her dreaming. I surveyed my sleeping mate with affection, then chose a book at random, one titled *The Spirit of Shamanism*, by Roger Walsh, a professor of psychiatry and philosophy who teaches at the University of California at Irvine.[4]

I scanned it quickly, getting an idea of the overall shape of the work, then settled down to read. To my delight, Walsh identifies the shaman as the world's premier mystic and culture hero—as the first in a long succession of cosmic explorers whose lifeway has stood for untold millennia as a monument to the untapped potentials within each of us. Unlike Campbell, however, Walsh makes clear distinctions between the different types of heroes, pointing out that while there are similarities between the lifeway of a mystic and that of a warrior or ruler, there are also major differences, especially in relation to the different journeys, goals, and games played by each.

Walsh uses the word *game* with deliberation, distinguishing between trivial or frivolous games played for amusement, entertainment, or distraction, and those serious and significant life games that present us with challenges and objectives that contribute to our personal growth and to the greater good of society and the world around us. It is in response to these life games that our constellation of survival skills and abilities is formed and sharpened, enabling each of us to succeed in becoming who and what we are. Walsh observes that without such "games-worth-playing," life becomes filled with repetition and boredom, giving rise to an ever-growing cycle of existential meaninglessness and disharmony, depression, and despair.

Within the first few chapters of Walsh's book, I came across several passages quoted directly from another book called *The Master Game,* by Robert De Ropp, a biochemist who carried out research in the fields of cancer and the biochemistry of the brain.[5] As I read the quotes with growing excitement, I recalled that I'd had this book in my own library for years but had never had the opportunity to read it. I got up, found the volume, and took it back to bed, where I resumed reading. By chance, I had found something of real interest and sent Walsh a mental message of gratitude.

De Ropp divides the life games that people play into two basic types: object games and meta games. Object games are those played to explore, master, and acquire the things of the outer world, especially the "physical foursome": money, power, sex, and status. Meta games are played to master the things of the inner world, intangibles such as knowledge, beauty, and the salvation of the soul. De Ropp points out that the different life games we choose to play are indicators of the type of individuals that we are, and also provide signs of our level of inner development.

De Ropp ranks the object games as hierarchically "lower" and describes them as more or less pathological in that the players who win emerge with little that they can truly call their own. For example, the businessman playing the Money Game may emerge as rich as Rockefeller, only to find himself embittered, unhappy, and empty—at a loss to know what to do with all his wealth. Those who play the Fame Game with the goal of becoming celebrities realize sooner or later that their fame is an illusion, a mere shadow designed to inflate their ego and keep it inflated, and that their public image ultimately has no relationship to the person they really are.

De Ropp portrays the Military Game as the deadliest of all object games, in that it is played by various grades of trained killers programmed to regard their craft as acceptable, even admirable, if those they kill believe in a different god or political system and can thus be collectively referred to as the enemy. History reveals that players of the Military Game can kill men, women, and children with boundless enthusiasm, destroying whole cities and devastating entire countries—in the process sacrificing the lives of tens of thousands of young people for the glittering dream of glory or victory, now more generally termed as "defense." So great is their power, exerted through various forms of political coercion and blackmail, that the thousands and thousands of young people involved make little or no protest as they go to their deaths. This fact has led De Ropp to conclude that there is a criminal element infusing most object games because they harm both the players and the society of which the players are a part.

De Ropp places the biological game on which the human species depends—the Householder Game—in a sort of neutral zone between the object games and the meta games. The aim of the player in the Householder Game is simply to raise a family and provide it with security and the necessities of life. Also found in this intermediate level are those nonplayers who are unable to find any game worth playing—often becoming chronic outsiders who are alienated from society—many of whom turn out to be antisocial loners with criminal tendencies.

De Ropp ranks the meta games as hierarchically "higher" in that they are played for intangibles and tend to be more subtle, yet even these games express both a positive and negative polarity. Those who play the Art Game, for example, are ideally searching for some inner awareness that can be defined and expressed as beauty. Yet many artists have no inner awareness at all and may only be proficient at imitating those who *do* have it. Others may become known for producing something that lacks beauty entirely but is acceptable by virtue of being new or startling.

In the same manner, those who play the Science Game are ideally searching for knowledge and meaning, but many players are little more than technicians with advanced degrees who, like many who play the Art Game, are primarily interested in status and fame. In addition, as all who play the Science Game discover sooner or later, projects that are truly original tend to be excluded by the array of committees that stand between the scientist and their funding, and the more or less routine projects are usually given preference.

The Religion Game is a meta game that is ideally played for the salvation of the soul. De Ropp points out that this game had fairly well-defined rules in the past, determined by a paid priesthood who made their livelihood by serving as intermediaries between the populace and various alternately wrathful or beneficent gods that they, or their predecessors, invented. Unfortunately, some of the players began to insist that *their* god was the only god, their truths the only truths. So eager were these priests to keep the game entirely in their own hands, that they did not hestitate to torture and kill all whom they viewed as outsiders, exhorting their followers to slaughter unbelievers as a sure way of gaining supernatural favor and guaranteeing entry into a hypothetically blissful afterlife state called "heaven" or "paradise."

Fortunately, there was, and is, another, quite different element to the Religion Game. In De Ropp's words:

> All the great religions offer examples of saints and mystics who obviously did not play the game for material gain, whose indifference to personal comfort, to wealth and to fame was so complete as to arouse our wonder and admiration. . . . They played the game by entirely different rules and for entirely different aims from those priestly con men who sold trips to heaven for hard cash and insisted on payment in advance. . . . [6]

These worthies were players of the Master Game that De Ropp places at the apex of all the meta games. This is the great game that has been played throughout time by the shamans and mystics, the saints and sages of all the world's cultures, who explored and mastered the inner world through the vehicle of their own mind and consciousness. The Master Game involves the quest for spiritual awakening, enlightenment, and liberation. The goal: to discover one's own true nature and to know from direct, empirical experience that this nature is both sacred and immortal. Roger Walsh writes:

> Different traditions express this [game] in different ways, but the message is clearly the same. Christianity tells us that "the Kingdom of Heaven is within you" or, in the words of Saint Clement, "He who knows himself knows God"; Buddhism says, "Look within. Thou art Buddha"; in Siddha Yoga the message is, "God dwells within you as you"; and in Islam, "He who knows himself knows his Lord." [7]

In De Ropp's eloquent words:

> The basic idea underlying all the great religions is that man is asleep, that he lives amid dreams and delusions [sic], that he cuts himself off from universal consciousness (the only meaningful definition of God) to crawl into the narrow shell of a personal ego.

To emerge from this narrow shell, to regain union with the universal consciousness, to pass from the darkness of the ego-centered illusion into the light of the non-ego, this was the real aim of the Religion game as defined by the great teachers, Jesus, Gautama, Krishna, Mahavira, Lao-tze and the Platonic Socrates. Among the Moslems, this teaching was promulgated by the Sufis, who praised in their poems the delights of reunion with the Friend. To all these players, it was obvious that the Religion Game as played by the paid priests, with its shabby confidence tricks, promises, threats, persecutions, and killings, was merely a hideous travesty of the real game. . . . [8]

[The Master Game] . . . remains the most demanding and difficult of games and, in our society, there are few who play. Contemporary man, hypnotized by the glitter of his own gadgets, has little contact with his inner world, concerns himself with outer, not inner space. But the Master Game is played entirely in the inner world, a vast and complex territory about which men know very little. The aim of the game is true awakening, full development of the powers latent in man. The game can be played only by people whose observations of themselves and others have led them to a certain conclusion, namely, *that man's ordinary state of consciousness, his so-called waking state, is not the highest level of consciousness of which he is capable.* In fact, this state is so far from real awakening that it could appropriately be called a form of somnambulism, a condition of waking sleep.[9]

As I thought about these ideas, I must confess that I felt a twinge of recognition. My spontaneous mystical experiences had served as "the call," and through the vehicle of my own consciousness, I had become a player—a living link in a long chain of players that stretched back across time to when the Master Game first appeared long before the rise of our state-level societies more than 5,000 years ago.

And when exactly did this great game take form? We don't know, but it is likely that the shamans of antiquity were the initial players, the first brave pioneers who began to explore the capabilities of the human body-mind-spirit complex. It is also possible that their courageous acts of exploration and discovery within the inner worlds may have propelled the human species into the next stage of its evolution—the evolution of consciousness.

The Master Game is still with us, and I suspect that it is being played by considerably more people today than when De Ropp wrote his book in the late 1960s. There is a general spiritual reawakening currently going on in the West, one in which an increasing number of individuals are seeking the direct, transformative experience of the sacred that defines the mystic.

Due to the relative ease with which the time-tested techniques of the shaman can be learned and practiced even by non-tribal urbanites, there is a resurgence of interest in the ancient shamanic methods for entering mystical states of consciousness. More and more contemporary Westerners are learning how to access the ordinarily hidden dimensions of reality to make contact with the inner sources of knowledge and power to facilitate healing and problem-solving. In the midst of a world obsessed with money, sex, power, and status, these heroes are quietly rediscovering the Master Game.

I found this knowledge deeply reassuring as I considered some of the truly awesome issues we face in our time—runaway overpopulation and environmental degradation; political, social, and economic instability; the rise of epidemic diseases such as the HIV virus and AIDS; issues of humanitarian concern and social justice; and the potentially devastating climatic shifts being generated by greenhouse warming, just to name a few.

In the face of these issues, the old stories, beliefs, values, and trends that collectively represent our cultural mythology aren't working so well anymore. It is clear that we must now create a new story, a new transmodern version of the monomyth. I smiled to myself with the realization that right at the core of this lurch toward the new is the Master Game. And there lies both the gateway and the key to the next stage of human evolution.

I picked up a yellow pad and a pencil and began to make some notes, when Jill turned in her dreaming and drew me into her sleepy embrace. We were still in recovery from our long separation while I was in Africa, and I felt a surge of primitive feelings in response. I put down my books and turned out the light. For long moments, I just held her in my arms, feeling the deep bond between us and experiencing the love I felt for her and the children we had created together. Then we played the Love Game at its most joyous level of intensity, and in the dreamy aftermath of that ancient ritual, a thought appeared in my mind.

Nainoa was also a player of the Master Game.

With that, the inner doorway cracked open, flooding my body with the sensations of power. As I began to vibrate uncontrollably, I glanced, by chance, toward the window, where my eyes could just make out the shape of the cotton tree I had grown from a seed in a large pot. It was the descendant of one of those rainforest giants from the tropics, and its crown of slender, palmate leaves was now six feet high, blotting out some stars shining through the window behind it.

As the trance state deepened, my body was overtaken by paralysis, and the strange phosphenic light show began. The stars flowed into the bedroom window, through the leaves, accompanied by the high-pitched roaring rush of sound that usually fills my ears at such moments. I watched, entranced, as the sparkling, swirling dots of light coalesced into lines that, in turn, seemed to weave themselves around the cotton tree like brightly colored vines. Then the room was gone, but the entwined lines of light surrounded by moving, firefly-like sparks remained, looking similar to the great mythical beanstalk that Jack climbed to get to the giant's castle in the clouds.

The vibration increased, and the glittering, twisted cable of light danced as if it were alive. I looked up its snakelike length and saw that it led outward into the lacy spider web of the great grid. Without thought or intention to do so, a sense of movement began, and I started to ascend along it, merging with it and rising faster and faster, as though I were spiraling upward on a brilliant, swirling escalator. Above me, I saw the curious crescent of light take form and begin to open. I rushed toward it and plummeted through in a blazing flash into the familiar darkness of the Hall of Silence.

My last thought was focused on Nainoa. Then thinking ceased and the shift occurred. . . .

CHAPTER TWO

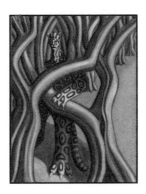

First Journey:
The Place of Refuge

I T WAS DAWN, and Nainoa had just taken an early swim in the lagoon that fronted the Place of Refuge in the Pukui land division. He was combing out his long hair, preparing to leave his sparse quarters for a meeting with the Kahuna Nui, the director of the center. He was humming a new chant that he was committing to memory when he suddenly felt the presence. He stopped chanting as his attention turned within and fastened on his inner guest. *A good moment to visit,* he thought, as he finished tying back his hair.

Nainoa waited, alert for any impulse or request for information, listening intently for the word-concepts expressed in Old English, but there was silence within.[1] He thought about what had just occurred. His *ku*, his body-mind, had picked up the arrival of his ancestor's consciousness, the one he thought of as the American, but unless he was also in the deep trance state, they could not communicate directly.

Well, not exactly, Nainoa thought. When those spontaneous mental reviews of recent events suddenly emerged from his memory banks for no apparent reason, he would watch their course carefully, a practice that sometimes allowed him to second-guess his invisible visitor. When he saw the direction of the drift, he would often contribute a few thoughts and memories that were outside the path being followed, and occasionally, he could dimly sense the other's response. It was a matter of increased sensitivity, an intuitive perception that had deepened and become a learned skill. As Nainoa had grown accustomed to hosting his ancestor's awareness, his own ability to detect the presence of this inner witness had become more acute.

He smiled, waiting for the flow to begin . . . and begin it did.

Nainoa had been in residence at the retreat center for the better part of three lunar cycles, immersed in the silent, monastic lifestyle of the resident *kahuna*-priests and their initiates. Every day, well before dawn, the rhythmic beat of the large wooden slit drum at the community's center would summon him from sleep. With the arrival of a student carrying a torch from which to light his oil lamp, Nainoa would rise from his bed and wrap himself in a cloak, shielding himself from the chill, damp air of the rainy season. After a visit to the *lua*, he would assume a cross-legged posture on the woven *hala* mats at one end of his small room.

The day's exercises began with *moe'uhane'ala*, the practice of subsiding once more into the dream state while remaining fully conscious, fully awake.[2] While immersed in this level of awareness, Nainoa was learning to explore the dream worlds, as well as the nature of the interface through which he accessed them. As he had become more proficient at this practice, he had discovered something truly interesting.

Everything that existed in the outer, everyday world had a dream aspect in the inner worlds. Places he knew well in his daily life, for example, had equivalents in the dream worlds, but they always looked different, discordant, or at variance, in ways that were strange and mysterious. He had no idea why this was so.

The early morning dreamwork was usually followed by a session of silent meditation in the Great Hall. During this period, Nainoa practiced *lokahi*, attempting to achieve balance and unity between and within the different aspects of himself, establishing a sense of inner peace and harmony that was then to be maintained throughout the day's schedule. He had gotten better at this with practice and could now achieve and maintain deep states of calm and focused concentration at will.

Nainoa smiled. The hours spent in solitude and silence had produced an interesting, unexpected side effect. During the periods of dreamwork and deep meditation in which he had examined the nature of himself, he had begun to discover the nature of everything else as well.

The meditation period was always followed by the morning meal, usually grilled fish, accompanied by steamed vegetables, starchy taro cooked in different ways, fruit, and coffee. He then spent the first half of the day working in the gardens with the other initiates, silently doing what needed to be done with focused attention, and with *lokahi*.

Nainoa's experience with estate management on the Kaneohe land division had provided him with a good working knowledge of agricultural practice, and it wasn't long before his expertise was noticed by Chief Hakai, the Kahuna Mala in charge of the center's gardens. When he confided to Hakai that he found the time spent weeding and working with the plants to be most nurturing, the older man had smiled knowingly, and a close friendship had formed between them.

Afternoons usually included time in which Nainoa worked on the written account of his long journey of the year before, recording his thoughts on long scrolls of fiber paper with ink and a fine-pointed brush. He looked at the stack of wooden tubes in the woven basket standing in one corner of the room and felt a sense of growing satisfaction. Each was fashioned from a section of timber bamboo, and each contained one long scroll of completed manuscript. On the outside of each container was a number, along with his written description detailing the contents. When the account was finished, copies would be made by clerks for distribution to all the libraries of the different ruling families in each land division. Then his originals would be sealed in their tubes, preserving them for generations to come.

Afternoons also provided free time for walks in the forest that surrounded the walled enclosure of the retreat center. It was out there among the trees that Nainoa felt his connection with nature reawaken, and it was then that he could perceive the living, conscious presence of the Great Mystery all around him. He recalled a line from an ancient poem written in classic Hawaiian: "*Au lilo mea punihei i na mea a'iwa'iwa o waho.*" In the *olelo* of the people, the phrase would translate as: "I have become a nature mystic."[3]

Nainoa loved his solitary walks among the great trees, and as often as not, he would slip into a light trance state in which the colors of the forest, its lights and darks, its sounds and its silences, would become exceedingly vivid. It was then that he made contact with his spirit ally, the one he thought of as the spotted tiger man. All it took now was his wish to connect, and he would feel that fierce presence appear. Most of the time, the spirit manifested an alert, neutral curiosity directed at him, but sometimes he would catch visual glimpses of it, and it was then that they would walk silently through the trees together, his spirit helper providing company, friendship, and protection.

Occasionally Nainoa would go more deeply into the trance and invite his spirit helper to merge with him, something he had learned to do quite by accident. The sensations that infused his body and mind during such connections were quite amazing. It was one thing to walk through the forest in the company of a spotted tiger; it was quite another thing to stride through the trees *as* a tiger.

Nainoa thought back to the episode that had brought him to the retreat center, to that day on the hilltop overlooking the Kaneohe land division when both the American and his spirit ally had been merged with him.[4] That was the morning when he learned of a great wrong that had been done to him and High Chiefess Maraea, his intended wife. Their dog, Ziku, an old friend and fellow traveler from his long journey to the Ennu lands beyond the mountains, had been poisoned, an act committed by a man who was his adversary. The deed had been done out of spite, and the dog had died. In those terrible moments when Nainoa learned of this crime, all the wrongs that he had endured during his lifetime had surfaced from their dark hiding places within him, accompanied by a deep, bitter anger. As his rage grew, his thoughts had included images of violence directed toward this man. It was in those fateful moments that he forgot about the presence of his spirit helper.

Nainoa smiled grimly. He would never forget what happened next. His spirit helper had apparently mistaken his rage and negative intentions for a directive. The tiger spirit's departure had been tangible, and Nainoa's adversary had been killed by a tiger at the edge of the forest that same day.

Among the *kahuna* mystics, the use of spiritual power to inflict harm was considered to be an error in judgment of the most serious proportions. It was clearly understood that the spirits who come into relationship with human beings to assist in alleviating pain and suffering are not at all interested in helping to inflict harm. To do so, even inadvertently, as Nainoa had done, was a critical turning point in the lifeway of the *kahuna*. If practitioners continued to use power for negative purposes, they became sorcerers, and their spirit helpers would inevitably abandon them. From that point on, the practitioner's power would begin to dissipate.

Sooner or later, the continued negative focus would begin to affect the sorcerer in an increasingly adverse fashion. Sometimes a string of bad luck would preclude the onset of an illness, a sure sign of the *kahuna's* fall from grace. Often the individual would succumb to the illness and die. But just as often, their end would come as a direct result of the magic that they had directed at someone in a negative way. When this force flowed back to them in their power-diminished state, it invariably killed them, often in an unpleasant fashion.

Such had been the case with Nainoa's own maternal grandfather, a powerful *kahuna* mystic and member of the Kaneohe lineage who became a sorcerer and whose name no one would speak. With the sudden death of his adversary, it appeared to many that Nainoa had inherited his grandfather's *ike*, his spiritual power, and that he had killed his enemy with sorcery.[5]

Much time had been spent reflecting on all this during his meditation practice at the center. In his mind, there was little doubt that his spirit helper had been involved. He understood quite clearly that the spotted tiger man was not some projected aspect of himself, nor was it a creation of his own mind. It was the composite, spiritual essence of a large variety of forest cat, and on that fateful day, this formidable predator had simply gone off to do what it does best, believing that it was operating in Nainoa's best interests.

And perhaps it had, he thought uneasily. He sensed that the swift removal of this enemy would make the next stages of his life considerably easier. But power had been inadvertently misused to achieve this end. The whole affair had been a lesson of considerable significance, and Nainoa understood now, as never before, the necessity of maintaining a clear, positive intentionality. To fail in this would be to place others in potential jeopardy, and himself as well.

Nainoa had been pondering all of this during one of his recent afternoon walks in the forest when he became aware that he was being watched by something—a something that was clearly not the American, nor was it the spotted tiger man. Initially, he had felt concern that it could be a real tiger, brought into this part of the forest by his ongoing focus on its spiritual aspect, but if so, he had seen no sign of it.

The feeling had persisted over the next several days, but Nainoa had not discovered what it was. Perhaps some other spirit had come to check on him to see how his practice was going, so to speak. He wished that Chief Wilipaki, Maraea's father, was still here so he could discuss this issue with him. Wilipaki was a powerful *kahuna la'au lapa'au*, a healing expert who was deeply knowledgeable about the plant medicines, and when his services had been required elsewhere, he had departed from the center, saying that he would return at some point.

Nainoa abruptly thought about a recent visionary experience he'd had while having a *lomi* (massage) session. He had gone into a deep trance in response to the body work, and his conscious awareness had traveled back across time to connect once again with the mind of the American. The man had been working with a group of prehistorians, searching for relics of humanity's earliest ancestors in an exceedingly dry part of the world known on the ancient maps as Africa.

At the peak of this episode, the two of them had once again found themselves in the presence of that enormously powerful spirit that the Ennu called a *dorajuadiok*. It had exhibited a somewhat different appearance on this occasion, looking more like a huge, dark triangle than the more linear, monolithic obelisk he had seen out at the Spirit Hills with William, but there was little doubt that it was the same kind of being.

As before, their merged-yet-separate consciousnesses had been drawn into direct connection with the spirit, an experience of mind-shattering immensity during which all sense of self had vanished. When both he and the American had regained a perception of their personal aspect sometime later, it became obvious that they had been given a large body of knowledge. They had also felt incredibly empowered.

Nainoa smiled as he monitored these memories. So that's what his ancestor was after—the knowledge received from that awesome spirit. He recalled the last time they had attempted to examine the nature of this experience. It had occurred during an exceedingly vivid dream in which he found himself in connection with his ancestor during a voyage on a flying machine. What a wonder that had been! As he began to excavate memories of that amazing encounter, his thoughtline abruptly shifted and returned to their meeting with the *dorajuadiok*. He smiled again, aware that his ancestor's intentionality was influencing his conscious flow, insisting that they pay attention to business.

Much of the shared wisdom he had received from the great spirit had seemed to be about the nature of the Universe, about its inception, growth, and development, as well as humanity's place within the glittering, diaphanous net his people called *koko'aka*, the energetic web of power within which everything in the Universe was connected to everything else.[6] The *dorajuadiok* had conveyed the knowledge that all life forms, including the spirits, are connected to each other and with the mysterious Source through this matrix, and that separation is merely an illusion.

The great spirit had also provided a clear sense that humanity had originally come out of another level of reality across the immensity of the Universe to connect with La, the sun. Humanity had originated as beings of light, as manifestations of the Source itself, to take up residence within primitive life forms on the surface of this planet that had been created by the sun to receive them. In association with humanity had come spirit guardians from deep within the Universe, *akua* of great power who possessed the secrets of life and the knowledge of humanity's destiny. The *dorajuadiok* had also revealed that in the remote past, some of these guardians had taken up residence on the planet in physical form in order to protect and guide the developing life forms. Having accomplished their goals, most had departed, but some returned to visit from time to time. The monolithic spirit had then identified itself as one such guardian.

From his subsequent conversations with others who knew more about spirits than himself, Nainoa had learned that the *kahuna* mystics knew about the existence of such spirit guardians who were of the highest energy and existed deep within realms of the Universe beyond the confines of planet Earth. It was known that such powers occasionally came into relationship with humans for whom they felt attraction, and for whom they would then function in a service capacity. It was generally felt that these spirits could then influence those with whom they made connection, providing knowledge about the true nature of existence and serving as conductors and activators of power.

Sometimes the presence of these guardians was detectable through the effects they were able to manifest in the everyday world. Often, they took up residence within an object, either natural or man-made, from which they could then act, manipulating the energy fields of the humans with whom they were in relationship to cause changes in their perception or create imagery within their consciousness, influencing their personal development—and by association—the course of human history.

A question suddenly appeared in Nainoa's mind, accompanied by an image. He smiled as he considered the idea. *Kapohaku'ki'ihele*, the spirit stone. Could it, in fact, house such a guardian? Nainoa paused in his thoughtline and pondered it at length. It was possible, he concluded, definitely possible. Perhaps he could ask the spirit in the stone at some future point and find out.

Nainoa's thoughts returned to the *dorajuadiok*. There had been more information, much more, some of which he simply didn't understand. He smiled again. Perhaps the American would.

TOK!

His attention shifted as he glanced out the window where the early morning fog was now illumined by the first light of the coming day. The drum was summoning the *kahunas* and their students to the main hall for the first period of meditation. This morning, he would vary his schedule to meet with Kahu Sala, the center's director. Further consideration of the *dorajuadiok* material would have to wait.

How amazing, Nainoa thought. This mental review with commentary had just taken place in a few long moments, yet there was the clear sense that a considerable distance had been traveled. He finished dressing, donning the simple pale-yellow loincloth and cloak favored at the center. His chief's necklace remained on its hook on the wall. Symbols of rank were not worn at the Place of Refuge.

As he left his room and walked out onto the broad lanai, Nainoa thought once more about the information the *dorajuadiok* had shared. His Ennu friend William had told him that these entities tended to come into relationship with humans who could serve as a bridge between the world of material concerns and the nonmaterial dimensions of thought, emotion, and spirit. Such humans were often assisted by these guardians in establishing relationships with other spirit helpers connected with their life goals and personal destiny.

He wondered if the *dorajuadiok* would still consider him worthy after his role in his adversary's sudden demise. And just as quickly, he knew that it would. The huge, shimmering obelisk lacked any sense of human feelings, emotions, or judgment. It was utterly neutral, impassive, and alien. It gave no directives or suggestions, but served instead as a source of information, experience, and power.

Nainoa thought back to the days of his arrival at the center. The *kahuna* priests had cleansed him with the Kala ceremony, removing any residual negative effects or attachments that might serve as blocks between his *ku* level of self and his *aumakua* (higher self). This was vitally important, because it was through the *ku* that connection with the personal spirit self was achieved.

In the process of his cleansing, an ancient chant had been sung, one that revealed the unity between the positive and the negative aspects of life and how the forces within them worked for growth, balance, and harmony on the one hand; and for destruction, imbalance, and things coming apart on the other. The role of the *kahuna* in learning to distinguish between the two and mediate between the forces within each had been made clear. Most important were the exercises designed to assist the evolving *kahuna* in learning to identify, understand, and control the negative aspects of their own nature. Nothing was to escape this search because the achievement of this realization was the only true means of assuring connection with the guardians who serve the Source.[7]

TOK!

As Nainoa descended the steps fom his lanai, he suddenly heard music, a curious stirring harmony of sound unlike anything he had ever heard before. He listened as he tied on his sandals, intently trying to determine where the music was coming from, whereupon it abruptly ceased.

CHAPTER THREE

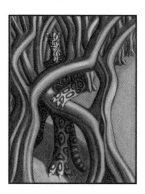

Depossession

I CRACKED AN EYE OPEN in my bed in Sacramento. The radio alarm
had gone off, terminating the visionary state and alerting me
that it was time to get the children up, dressed, fed, and off to
school. The music on the radio, by the way, was Aaron Copland's
Fanfare for the Common Man, the soul-stirring composition associated with the opening of the Olympic Games. It seemed that Nainoa
had briefly heard it, and I wondered what he had thought of it.

My irritation at losing the connection with him was intense but
short-lived. I had wanted to hear the conversation with the head
teacher. I wondered if I would be able to regain the contact and access
the dialogue, or the memory of it, at some future time. There was
also the *dorajuadiok* material. Nainoa was now aware of my interest, and I hoped that the moment would come when we would review
it together. There was no way of predicting when, or even if, this
would occur, so I resigned myself to being patient.

I was intrigued by Nainoa's mythic categorization of the *dorajuadiok* as a "higher" guardian spirit, possibly originating from

somewhere deep within the galaxy. In my own attempts to comprehend the nature of this strange entity and classify it in some sort of taxonomic way, I had tried to draw on my knowledge of science and thus go beyond mysticism. Because the nature of this spirit is clearly energetic, I had turned to fields of knowledge outside the biological sciences, entering the domains of advanced theoretical physics, fractal geometry, and nonlinear dynamics.

Insights derived from these disciplines suggest that the *dorajuadiok* "energy field" could be considered as a "phase space"—a sort of inorganic, yet living map that allows the condensation of space and time into a pattern of multiple dimensions. Seen from this perspective, the huge spirit might be considered as a "slice" through such a multidimensional pattern—an "emission" of some as-yet unknown phenomenon or being that demonstrates an underlying "attractor" that, in turn, could be likened to a hidden knot of coherence in the incoherent matrix of the Universe. In advanced theoretical physics, such phenomena have sometimes been called Poincare Maps.[1]

The *dorajuadiok* "attractor pattern" could thus be thought of as something like a high-energy bond in chemistry or a quantum hologram in physics, and the data that it transmitted to me and Nainoa in Africa would be carried in the phase resonance of the hologram. From the physicist's perspective, this information would be nonlocal in space and time, yet it could conceivably carry a "document" about the history of the Universe, the basic content of the data we seem to have received, which could be recoverable locally. The fact that the *dorajuadiok* also possesses a form of intelligence and awareness, and that it can communicate after a fashion, is truly startling and may reveal something about how both intelligence and consciousness evolved.

And just how did we receive this information? Recent changes to quantum theory and current discoveries in neurobiology reveal that the brain organizes information holographically and functions like a massively parallel quantum computer, with the microtubules in the neurons of the brain being the likely quantum hologram

28

receptors. It has been suggested that the quantum hologram is the wave portion of the wave-particle duality for macroscale objects. It has also been proposed that the quantum hologram may tie the phenomenal universe of quantum, micro, macro, and cosmic-sized phenomena together, and that the quantum hologram may be the mechanism through which nature learns.[2]

This knowledge implies that the quantum hologram may be the basis for all perception, including psychic awareness. It also suggests that true psychic sight is not a sixth sense, but rather the first, because it may very well have been around since the Big Bang. In fact, quantum physics is now seriously suggesting that consciousness itself may be the ground of all being.

Lest this strike the reader as fanciful, or falling into the category of *Star Trek* science, let me draw attention to a ten-year investigation conducted by anthropologist Jeremy Narby, one that correlates the tribal knowledge of indigenous peoples with the most recent revelations from the fields of molecular and neurobiology.[3] Until relatively recently, the scientific community has assumed that there is no direction in evolution—that life evolved purely by chance and that changes are entirely random in nature. But today, the more scientists are understanding about DNA, the template-text of encoded genetic information in the cells of every living thing on Earth, the harder it's becoming to believe that there is no intelligence involved in nature's design. It may be that the field of biology has a blind spot of historical origin.

Narby's study suggests that traditional peoples have known for millennia, and have even drawn, the twisted double helix structure of the DNA molecule, something Western science did not rediscover until 1953. His investigations reveal that this information is received by traditional shamans in "defocalized" altered states of consciousness in which they perceive in an expanded way.

Based on the most recent scientific evidence, Narby gathers courage and presents the startling hypothesis that the DNA molecule, and the life that it codes for at the cellular level in the natural world, are *minded* and are capable of transmitting information to the one whose consciousness is prepared to receive it. He has also shown that the shaman's ways of acquiring knowledge in expanded states of awareness are not only relevant to contemporary science, but they have clearly delineated the limits of rationalism as a scientific approach to such issues as the origin of life.

Could it be that shamans and scientists are converging on the same discoveries about life after centuries of following divergent paths? Could it be that the hard-core skeptics and professional debunkers of the existence of spiritual realities and the entities that can be found within them are, in fact, dead wrong?

A full semester of teaching followed, and it wasn't until late June that I had another connection with Nainoa across the dreamtime of inner space. This one happened while I was leading a shamanism workshop at a retreat center near New York called the Omega Institute.[4] The participants of this week-long experiential seminar reflected a diverse cross-section of the public at large, and included a dentist, a nuclear medicine specialist, an environmental activist, an oncologist, several counseling psychologists (including a Jungian analyst), a yoga and massage practitioner, a carpenter, a Red Cross worker, a musician, an economist, and an Umbanda chief from Brazil named Claudio, whose long hair was tied back with a colorful bandanna.

Umbanda is a New World spiritist tradition that combines elements of Roman Catholicism with the religion of the Yoruba people of West Africa, an animistic/polytheistic tradition that recognizes more than 300 *orisha,* or spirits—each expressing a definite personality, and each associated with some aspect of the natural world.[5] This tradition was brought to the New World with the slave trade and has evolved into many geographic variants, such as Vodoun, Macumba, Candomble, Santeria, Obeah, and Umbanda. In most of these, each *orisha* (called *orixa* in Brazil) has a Christian saint as counterpart/equivalent. Worshipers of Umbanda praying to the Virgin Mary, for example, are also connecting with Yemanja, a West African female deity whose element is the salt water; those focusing on Jesus of Nazareth are simultaneously addressing Obatala, the creator sky god of the Yoruba.

By chance, I had served as a U.S. Peace Corps volunteer from 1964 to 1966, and I had lived and worked among the Yoruba of Nigeria as a high school biology teacher for two years. I was sharing some stories from this time of my life with Claudio when something interesting happened. I suddenly knew who one of Claudio's primary spirit helpers was. The knowledge simply appeared in my mind. It was as though my subconscious had picked up the information while my intellect was otherwise involved. I wanted to test what I had just learned against reality, but how does one ask an Umbanda chief point-blank about the nature of his spirit helper? Ordinarily, such information is not shared.

As our conversation came to an end, I locked eyes with Claudio and casually mentioned the name of the Christian equivalent of the particular entity I had just perceived. Claudio's eyes grew large with surprise, then he smiled warmly. This particular saint is an obscure one not generally known to Norte-Americanos. The *orixa* it symbolizes is so powerful that Claudio would not even say its name aloud, but he graciously confirmed my insight by writing its name on a piece of paper.

I mention this brief episode because such experiences were now beginning to happen to me more and more often, and they never failed to reassure my inner scientist. It seemed that some of the abilities that were available to me at first only in my altered states of consciousness were now becoming increasingly accessible in my ordinary, everyday state of awareness, and this, I reflected, must be part of what it means to walk upon the shaman's path.

A dramatic confirmation of this ability took place more than a year later at another weekend workshop in Kansas City. At such gatherings, I usually give a public talk about some aspect of shamanism or the modern mystical movement on the first evening of the retreat, and on this occasion, a man approached me as soon as I arrived at the church where the presentation was to take place.

I'd had some connection with him by telephone over the past year, but I had never met him in person until this moment.

As I returned his greeting and formed a visual impression to connect with his now-familiar voice, something decidedly strange occurred. As I looked directly into his gaze, I was very much aware that there was something or someone else looking at me out of his eyes. This knowledge just came to me. Two other pieces of information were also apparent in those moments. First, it was quite clear that "it" was a separate being or entity from the man who stood before me; and second, it was aware that I could see it.

In the very next moment, I watched the man's demeanor shift out of affectionate warmth into an impassive neutrality as he informed me almost reluctantly that he didn't think he could attend the workshop. This struck me as exceedingly odd, as I had gotten a clear impression that this individual, whom I shall refer to as Jack, loved workshops and that he had been looking forward to this one for months. I smiled reassuringly to conceal my puzzlement and wondered to myself if perhaps the financial investment of the workshop "tuition" would be burdensome for him. The workshop was very reasonably priced, however, so my intuition suggested that finances were not the issue.

Jack launched into a long account of recent events in his life, reciting a long string of personal disasters while I stood quietly and watched him. When I saw an opening in his monologue, I injected an invitation for him to attend the weekend retreat as my guest, free of tuition, if he should change his mind, but this offer didn't appear to sway him, and he once again protested that he couldn't come.

As he rambled on with his depressing account, I was aware that I needed more information. I suddenly recalled Nainoa's ability to invite his spirit helper to merge with him. This memory just popped up in my conscious awareness, and on impulse, I decided to try it, right then and there. I knew that the leopard man, as I call him, does not like to be inside buildings, but I took a deep breath and put out the call anyway, forming a strongly focused mental intention—an invitation to that animal spirit to approach and merge with me. I had need of its eyes.

As I continued to listen to Jack, I held my focus, my intention icily clear, and after a few moments, my ears started to hiss with the familiar tension that the presence of this particular entity generates. There was a millisecond of delay during which I briefly saw a cluster of dark spots on a tawny field that coalesced around a set of pale eyes that I remembered well. And as those eyes met mine, my muscles began to vibrate, and the merge was accomplished. It went in through my eyes, much to my astonishment.

Instantly, I felt myself infused with an absolutely enormous sense of energy. Momentarily taken aback, I almost staggered, my breath catching in a gasp that I managed to conceal as an explosive cough behind my hand. I took a shuddering inhalation and managed to stabilize the energy into a flow that I could manage. As I hunched over, I greeted the alien, dispassionate mind now nested within my own. Within my inner visual field, the pale eyes closed, then opened, then closed again, conveying reassurance. When I straightened up and turned my gaze upon Jack, I immediately saw the nature of his problem. There was another man looking at me through his eyes. Jack was suffering from a classic case of spirit possession.[6]

Lest I give the impression that such states of expanded consciousness are always easily achieved and blissful to experience, allow me to point out that when this event occurred, I had been pursuing my apprenticeship of the shaman's craft for almost 15 years. Let me also suggest that authentic shamanic visionary states can actually be more like controlled nightmares, producing experiences that could be truly frightening to the uninitiated, the unprepared, or to someone with an unbalanced mind.

It is also quite obvious why the shaman is known as the master of spirits. At moments such as this, there can be absolutely no question as to who the boss is. In order to be able to control a spirit that has merged with you, the focused presence of your disciplined ego is essential. In the next moment, I got a dramatic example of why this must be so.

I was watching Jack closely, examining the curious double out-line of light around the perimeter of his body, when someone's child ran by to one side of me. My head swiveled involuntarily, and my eyes fastened on the boy as he was joined by another, the two of them running headlong out the door. They were playing tag or catch, as small boys do. In response, an extraordinary feeling gripped me, one that translated into an incredibly powerful urge.

My conscious ego was monitoring all this, and I realized that the leopard man had responded to the running children as if they were potential prey. Without conscious thought or intention to do so, my shoulders hunched, and the muscles of my legs coiled in preparation to lunge. And all of this happened in an instant, as some deep, innate feline releasing mechanism was triggered, one I could fully feel because of the merge.

My egoistic self immediately stepped forward and took control. This was not the moment to pounce on someone's children, nor was this the time to deal with Jack's problem. I was just about to give a public talk, so I mentally thanked my spirit helper, and using the full power of my ego's will forces, I politely invited it to detach. I waited, my body surging with energy and my mind grappling with another set of intentions, ones that were clearly not my own. In those moments, I sensed that I was having a glimpse into the nightmar-ish world of schizophrenia.

Then suddenly, I felt the release. It was as though I had been buffeted by a gust of hot air, and my sense of self was suddenly sin-gular once more. The spirit's departure was as palpable as its arrival had been, and a few moments later, I thanked Jack for his story, inviting him to come to the workshop once again, then walked toward the stage where the lectern was located. I felt incredibly energized by the experience of the merge, a feeling that lasted well into the night, making it difficult to sleep.

Having brought up this strange encounter, let me briefly out-line how it was resolved. I managed to get Jack to attend the workshop, and it turned out well for him. I often conclude such week-ends with a healing ritual for someone in the group, and on that occasion, there was no question in my mind as to who it would be. As the moment approached, I was also very much aware that spirit possession is not regarded as real by mainstream science yet, and that I, myself, knew next to nothing about depossession work.

I felt confident that the job could be done, however, because in the way of the shaman, it is really the spirits who do the work at the request of the one who can summon and control them. This suggested a plan. The only problem was that I didn't know if it would work or not until it actually happened.

In this case, I prevailed upon Jack to be on the receiving end of the healing ceremony—an honor, I might add, that he was most reluctant to accept. Although Jack had attended the workshop, he had slept through much of the weekend, almost as if the possessing entity was manifesting interference. It may be that whoever "it" was knew deep down that the jig was up. All this was running through my mind as I gently overrode Jack's protests and helped him to lie down in the middle of our circle.

There were several accomplished psychic healers in the group with whom I formed a tight inner circle around the prostrate man. I knew intuitively that when the entity was released, there would be no escape from these powerful women. I instructed the rest of the participants to form an outer circle and to shake their rattles in a fairly rapid, monotonous rhythm while inviting their spirit helpers to approach and provide them with energy. As each person felt themselves become power-filled, they were to channel it in toward the inner circle, whose members would then use the power in a healing capacity for Jack, continually replenishing their own supply from that incoming source. I was a member of the inner circle and would serve as the "catcher" when the entity was released— a risky procedure, especially for me—because it might very well leap into the nearest body—mine.

As the ritual began, I closed my eyes and settled into a light trance state in response to the rattles. For long moments, I just listened to the sound as I waited for the trance to deepen. I wasn't sure that the leopard man knew much about depossession, although it was superb at infusing me with power. As I felt myself shift into the deep state of shamanic consciousness, I put out the call for help, specifically asking for a helping spirit to approach and assist in the depossession of Jack.

Almost immediately, a large presence appeared. I could see it quite clearly without opening my eyes. I had heard about this spirit, an animal power whom I shall refer to as "the healing bear," from various shamans and medicinemakers, but I had never worked with this particular entity before. I greeted the spirit and expressed my deepest respect, apologizing for never having called upon it until now and explaining the nature of the current problem. I admitted that I knew next to nothing about depossession and that I desperately needed its help. In these moments, I recalled the marvels of merging with a power being and invited this healing bear spirit to merge with me now and to work though me, so to speak.

The next thing I knew, something struck me forceably between my shoulderblades, an experience reminiscent of the pillow fights of childhood. The blow literally knocked the wind out of me and projected me forward so that I almost ended up sprawled full length upon Jack. It was also at this point that everyone's spirits seemed to arrive in force, and the room suddenly felt saturated with energy, generating a hissing, scratchy drone of sound in my inner ears.

Recovering my balance, I looked up. In addition to the humans seated in the two circles, I perceived the room to be filled with other luminous things of various shapes and sizes. There also seemed to be crackling tracks of energy snaking wildly all over the place, weaving lines of colored lights whose movement seemed to be connected to variations in the drone of sound. As I watched, wonderstruck, this energy seemed to take form as woven strips of light radiating inward.

One of the inner-circle members was a young woman of partial Native American ancestry. She went into deep trance at this moment and started chanting in a language unknown to me. I glanced at her and saw an old woman sitting in her place and guessed that one of her ancestors had arrived to offer assistance, an insight that the woman later confirmed, revealing the language as Kiowa. All this happened in a flash as the enormous power of the healing bear merged with me. My inner scientist was monitoring all this, as always, and I perceived myself crouched on all fours like an animal, my body absolutely rigid as the power surged through and around me. I thought back to my traditional establishment upbringing on New York's Upper East Side and almost burst out laughing.

When I looked down at Jack, I controlled the impulse. I could now see the possessing spirit clearly. For one brief moment, it looked a little like the shriveled body of a very old human being, wrapped around and within Jack as though it was clinging to him desperately. Then it shifted, assuming a kind of ameoba-like, plasmic form that seemed to scuttle deep into Jack's thorax. In that moment of amazed incredulity, I knew intuitively that the possessing entity was the spirit of a deceased person that had attached itself to Jack as a "walk-in." I also perceived that it was very frightened.

It never had a chance, though, because this was the moment of power. I invited the healing bear spirit that was merged with me to take over. I glanced down at my hands and saw them flex as though of their own accord, my astonishment rising as long claws of light seemed to emerge from my fingertips. I recalled the healing Nainoa had done for his kinsman, Chief Kaneohe, and looked again at the possessing entity. Without conscious intention on my part, the spirit within me moved my arms, and those claws extended themselves into Jack's body. I watched, fascinated and horrified, as they clamped themselves around the possessing spirit and extracted it from Jack's body with a brief, truncated shriek. I then sat, stunned, as I observed my clawed hands clutching a writhing blob that now looked a little like free-form oatmeal. The extraction was done, but what was I going to do with the extractee?

I looked down at the candle burning beside me, and the path was revealed. I focused on the entity and mentally explained (gently) that it was supposed to go to the light, and that I would now send it on its way with a whispered prayer on its behalf—a prayer in which I put out the request for anyone in spirit who had loved this being in life to approach and assist in its transition from "here" to "there." With that brief directive, I slowly brought my hands down around the flame, constricting them in such a way that I literally fed the spirit into the light of the candle. I brought my hands together, closer and closer, until only the flame emerged from a tiny hole between my closed fists. When I opened them again, the spirit was gone.[7]

I then drew on the energy flowing in the room to augment Jack's personal supply of power in a healing capacity, my body shaking with the force of it while I transferred the power to him with my hands. That done, I invited the spirit to detach. Unlike my spotted ally who had definitely wanted to linger, it did so immediately. Jack looked quite different when the ceremony was done; his gloom had lifted, and when he smiled, the lightness in his demeanor was apparent to all. I heard from him shortly thereafter, and it seems that his life changed considerably in response to this brief ritual, and much for the better.

In deciding to share this rather unorthodox account, I am aware that most of the people in Western society know little about such things as spirit possession, and in their ignorance, they might regard this story as fanciful, even fictional. The few remaining traditional peoples, on the other hand, know a great deal about such phenomena and would understand precisely what I did. So did the more than two dozen participants of the workshop.

We live in an era of rapidly changing paradigms, a time in which increasing numbers of credentialed researchers, such as Michael Harner and Jeremy Narby, have become reinterested in the wisdom of the indigenous peoples. There is also a growing cross-section of the general public that is beginning to regard such accounts as worthy of serious consideration.

I have written about the modern mystical movement taking form in the West.[8] When I began to offer shamanism workshops, I became increasingly aware of the beliefs and values held dear by this rapidly-growing subculture. My inner scientist began to take notes, and over the next few years, I uncovered a closely-woven fabric of more than a dozen core beliefs, with threads of connection growing vigorously in many different directions.

As the pattern became clear, I began to suspect that I had stumbled into something that was not only interesting, but of vital importance to the continued well-being of Western society. For the reader's interest, I include here my partial listing of these core beliefs and values.

Core Beliefs

1. The belief that everything and everyone is part of a pattern and thus interconnected.

2. The belief in the existence of an alternate reality, often referred to as the spirit world or dreamtime by traditional peoples, or as nonordinary reality by modern mystics.

3. The belief in the ability of some individuals to achieve transcendent states of consciousness and enter the alternate reality for problem solving and healing of self and others; this belief is usually accompanied by a strong desire to personally experience the alternate reality.

4. The belief in the existence of spirit helpers and teachers who reside in the alternate reality. Although most modern mystics tend not to affiliate with organized religion, Jesus of Nazareth is regarded as a spirit teacher of great power, and most profess the belief in some form of supernatural godlike being or consciousness.

5. The belief that everything, both animate and inanimate, is imbued with a personal supernatural essence or soul; thus, everything everywhere is aware and thus "minded" to some degree.

6. The belief in the existence of an impersonal power or vital force that pervades all things and is expressed as life force in animate beings—the *mana* of the Polynesians, the *chi* of the Chinese, the *prana* of yoga, the *num* of the Kalahari Bushmen, or the *baraka* of the Muslims.

7. The belief in the existence of a personal energy body that can be perceived by some as an aura and can be enhanced through the energy centers within it—called *chakras* and *meridians* in Eastern thought.

Core Values

8. Strong concern for social justice and the quality of human life at all levels of society, both nationally and internationally.

9. Social tolerance, individualism, and spiritual freedom seen as highly valued ideals.

10. Strong support for women's issues, and concern for the safety and well-being of children and the elderly.

11. The rebuilding of families, neighborhoods, and communities seen as major areas of concern.

12. Human relationships being seen as more important than material gain.

13. Balance and harmony being seen as critical to the well-being of the individual, the family, the community, the business firm, the society, the nation-state, and the planet as a whole. Accordingly, it is understood that humans must live their lives in ways that contribute to this balance and harmony rather than following lifestyles and pursuing goals that create its opposite.

14. Strong regard for the survival of the environment, and by association, the human species, accompanied by a deep respect for nature. Modern mystics are seriously concerned with stopping corporate polluters, reversing greenhouse warming, and discovering the limits to short-term growth so that the world community can achieve the long-term ecological sustainability upon which the future of humanity depends.

15. Accordingly, the value of simple, natural living being seen as a high ideal.

16. Strong feelings of disaffection for Western allopathic medicine. These concerns are being greatly enhanced by the increasingly negative effects on the quality of health care being introduced by the business-oriented and profit-motivated Health Maintenance Organizations (HMOs).

17. Strong interest in alternative and preventative health-care modalities (holistic, shamanic, transpersonal, herbalist, ayurvedic, meditation, acupuncture, to name a few). These therapies are seen as adjuncts to, rather than as replacements for, Western medicine.

18. Strong awareness that the world's social, political, economic, and religious problems are reaching a critical mass. Virtually all feel that the ultimate solutions will be achieved through a general spiritual reawakening that progresses from the personal to the global, accompanied by the belief that this reawakening has the potential to change the directions of world history and propel humanity into the next phase of its evolution as a more aware life form with more expanded abilities.

19. Finally, virtually all who hold these beliefs and values are seekers of the direct, personal, transformative experience of transcendence, and it is really this that defines them as mystics—and as players of the Master Game.

Taken together, these beliefs and values constitute the core of a new worldview that is being shared by an ever-increasing number of people in the West. In the spring of 1996, the preliminary results of a national American Lives Survey, conducted by sociologist Paul Ray and sponsored by the Institute of Noetic Sciences and the Fetzer Institute,[9] revealed that in the United States alone, 44 million Americans fall into this category, representing about 24 percent of the adult population. According to Ray, this group represents a "larger population of socially concerned, environmentally aware, and spiritually focused creative people, who are carriers of more positive ideas, values, and trends than any previous renaissance period in history."

The sudden appearance of a subculture made up of individuals who are attempting to construct a whole new approach to the world is what anthropologists call a cultural revitalization movement. It's what a culture does when it is willing to face the fact that the old myths aren't working anymore and that we need to write a new story—one in which we explore a different way of seeing ourselves, our problems, and their solutions.

Ray points out that this "lurch toward the new" is a very unusual time in history because such a change in the dominant cultural pattern happens only once or twice in a thousand years. The millennium change is itself seen as significant in that it has apparently liberated people to try something entirely new at the societal level. Yet within our socially and ethnically complex society, the widespread acceptance of the new transmodern worldview with its awareness of spiritual realities and mystical power, and its concerns with social justice and ecological sustainability, depends on many factors.

One factor may have to do with the positions in society held by those who profess the new view. The educational level among these seekers tends to be high, and often they are in professional and social positions that make it possible for them to influence the values and attitudes of those around them.[10]

Like others who lead workshops, I've also discovered that more than half of the people who attend my retreats have children. This is a very hopeful sign. These mystical beliefs represent a different approach to life from the me-first competitive paradigm that most of us absorbed unconsciously as children from our parents, teachers, and friends. If children are acquiring these altruistic, spiritually based beliefs within their families, then they're already spreading rapidly throughout society, accelerating the shift.

Another reassuring fact: The prerequisite population base of modern mystics is already in place. Although there are a few more in places like California, Ray's study reveals that they are more or less evenly spread out throughout the population. This suggests that the modern mystical movement is not a fad, but a true transformational community in the process of generating a cluster of major values, beliefs, and trends that is already shifting the cultural norms of Western Society.

When I discuss this with the men and women in my workshops, they usually remain quiet for a while, silently considering the information I have just shared with them—the same information I have just shared with you, the reader. When they speak, inevitably each tells very much the same story—about how alone they have felt, of how they have lacked a clear sense of being part of this growing social movement.

Invariably, a feeling of release is triggered within the circle, and person after person then speaks up, confirming something I now know from countless testimonials—that modern mystics tend to develop in response to spiritual experiences that society at large has taught them to conceal. Faced with possible social ridicule from their peers, most learn to keep their experiences and belief systems to themselves.

These realizations were still taking form within me at that workshop back at the Omega Institute. It was on my fourth night there that my next contact with Nainoa occurred. I am greatly interested in causality with reference to these deep states, and it is possible that this one may have been elicited in response to one of the experiential exercises we had done that day, a shamanic journey outside of time to connect with the spirit of an ancestor. This attempt was done with a particular objective in mind, one that often produces surprising results, but it is worth noting that on that same evening, I had also visited the communal sauna before going to bed.

I mention this because my subconscious was undoubtedly impressed by the physicality of the intense heat, offset by the soothing dim lighting of the wooden room, in many ways a European equivalent to a Native American sweat lodge. I endured it as long as I could, my eyes closed, my mind focused within, and upon returning to my cabin, I dropped down into unconsciousness immediately.

I woke up in the middle of the night, unable to get back to sleep. I tossed and turned until dawn, listening to the silence of the hardwood forests that surround the retreat center. At around 4 o'clock, I experimentally tried to access the shamanic state of consciousness through my focused intentionality, and succeeded, much to my delight. As the state deepened, the woods seemed to exude a thick presence—a curious, rather dreamlike field that I could perceive, at least to some degree. There was also a sense of heightened power, one that seemed to be increasing by the moment, as though it was seeping under the door of the cabin and into my mind.

My body became quite aroused in response, and it was in this state of foment that I thought about my last connection with Nainoa. He had been at a retreat center surrounded by a forest. The similarity to my present situation was quite obvious, and I wondered with growing excitement if I could make a connection. I thought about the exercise we had done that afternoon. Perhaps I could do it now, but instead of going into the past to find an ancestor, I would go in the other direction toward one of my descendants.

I focused my intentionality one more time and tried to draw on the natural force that seemed to be flowing into my cabin from the forest. Abruptly, the sensations of power seized me in the invisible fist. I gasped with the effort of breathing as my body stiffened and the darkness of the room filled with sparkling lights. They merged into colorful, shimmering, snakelike trellises, and the luminous grid began to form. As the trance deepened and the thin crescent of light appeared, I heard a roaring rush of sound as though a stream was coursing by outside, or even through the cabin itself.

As the shift occurred, I heard a sound I remembered well—the sound of wood being struck by wood.

CHAPTER FOUR

Second Journey:
The Nature of the Self

T OK! NAINOA USED THE WOODEN BEATER to strike the carved plaque of wood hanging from one of the roof beams outside Kahu Sala's reception room. He hung the mallet back on its hook, then sat down on the polished wooden bench under the roof's overhang. As he waited for the *kahuna's* summons, he abruptly felt the presence once again. The contact was subtle, just there at the edge of his awareness. He glanced around but saw no one near him. He opened his mind fully and listened, but there was only silence.

His attention shifted to the meeting that was just about to happen, and he felt uneasy. Going eyebrow to eyebrow with a master *kahuna* mystic still made him nervous. He looked down at his hands. They were callused from working in the gardens. He had just walked through those gardens on his way to the director's house and felt a sudden sense of comfort knowing that he would spend the morning there, silently breaking and turning the soil with a digging stick, tending to the rows of crop plants interspersed with plots of decorative flowers and medicinal herbs. He glanced at the gardens and saw a flash of movement—a duck searching for large jungle slugs to eat.

TOK!

Kahu Sala had struck a similar wooden plaque within. Nainoa stood, took a deep breath to calm himself as he adjusted his cloak, and pushed through the bamboo curtain. The Kahuna Nui was dressed informally in a voluminous cotton dress dyed yellow without a pattern. A cloak of the same color was draped around her ample shoulders to ward off the morning chill. Her thick gray hair hung loosely down her back under the yellow flower lei wrapped around her head. She wore no emblem of rank. The smoke of incense hung in the air.

The director had opened the sliding screens that formed one wall of her small house and was seated facing outward toward the lagoon. The bell-like call of a bird floated in the misty stillness of the morning air. Nainoa knew precisely what type of bird it was, and his eyes involuntarily sought the dark green curtain of the forest beyond the stone wall, but it was still hidden in the warm fog. Kahu Sala glanced up at him and gestured toward the cushion beside her. Nainoa bowed and settled himself, folding his legs into the position he espoused in the great hall.

For long moments, the two simply sat and observed the palms, the sky, and the lagoon. The early morning haze shrouded everything, creating a dreamlike effect. He could not see the port of the Pukui land division although he knew it was there, just across the bay. A series of shrill whistles to his left betrayed the presence of small boys driving invading monkeys from the gardens. The smells of woodsmoke, roasting coffee, and cooking fish drifted across the compound from the kitchens, heralding the preparation of the morning meal. All was in order. The world was good.

A small, dark object appeared on the still, milky surface of the lagoon not far from the house. Nainoa recognized it as a turtle's head. The creature carefully observed the world above as it breathed deeply and thoughtfully before diving once again to eat the *limu* growing from the rocks. He had encountered this turtle often during his early morning swims. The Kahuna Nui had placed a *kapu* against the sacrifice of any living creature within the sanctuary boundaries, and all at the center knew this particular reptile as Honumakua—turtle father. Nainoa emulated the turtle now, breathing deeply and thoughtfully as he felt the harmony and balance take form within himself. The director of the center turned to him and smiled.

"*Heahea*, Chief Nainoa." Nainoa smiled and bowed once again at her words of welcome but said nothing, awaiting the first statement or question that would give him permission to speak.

"That turtle is said to have lived in this lagoon ever since the center was established here more than 100 years ago," Kahu Sala opened. "Maybe it is the same turtle, maybe not. Some believe it is a spirit." She fell silent for long moments, and when Nainoa still said nothing, she continued. "The *kahuna* mystic seeks connections to the spirits for many reasons. Most are directed toward the well-being of the community, but some are deeply personal."

Nainoa's eyes narrowed as he gathered his thoughts and replied, "William the Ennu used to say that it is through the spirits that all living things are connected with the energy that flows within everything as life force. For the Ennu, the land is intelligent, infused with supernatural power and vitality, at the same time expressing its own collective, mystical awareness. The Ennu mystics tap into that awareness through the spirits, and through them, with the power. For them, separation is an illusion."

The director appeared to reflect for long moments, then she suddenly cracked a grin. "I met William at the capital. That friend of yours certainly has a way with women." She suppressed a snort of amusement that suddenly escaped as a boisterous laugh. Her hilarity was infectious, and Nainoa joined her. The tension was broken. "William must have spent a lot of time in connection with his spirits," she went on, pointing at an unoccupied cushion, "because that man . . ." She left the phrase hanging as her laugh once again shook the room. Then her mirth subsided. Wiping her eyes, she continued.

"William's insight reveals something of great value. We can connect with power anywhere, anytime, once we have learned how, but there is little doubt that the power is most densely concentrated out in nature." Kahu Sala glanced out across the expanse of the sacred grounds whose temple platforms and residence buildings were scattered through the grove of palms bordering the wide lagoon.

"The townspeople think that the power resides here in these *heiaus*," she said, "and they come here in droves at festival times to increase their personal supply of *mana*. While it is true that our *heiaus* are repositories for *mana*, the *kahuna* mystics know that the power is everywhere, in everything." Her gesture took in the trees, the sky, and the lagoon.

"Sometimes we connect with this power spontaneously as you did on your long walk through the great forest, but paradoxically, the power always seems to emerge from within ourselves, specifically through those contacts we have in the inner worlds. In this sense, each of us is like a window, a walking portal, if you will. And when we discover the existence of that doorway within us, life becomes an incredibly enriched adventure. We learn then that existence is a patterned flowing of all life toward beauty, wisdom, and truth.

"Once contact with the hierarchy of spirits is accomplished and the initiate is seen as worthy by our esteemed colleagues on the other side of that doorway, they then begin to receive teachings and power directly from that source. These initial connections are usually intensely personal," she continued, returning to her original line of thought, "and from these connections, we learn a great deal about the nature of our selves as well as the nature of the reality in which our selves exist. Our awareness then begins to expand, providing us with a way of knowing that is beyond thinking. Please share your thoughts on this, Chief Nainoa, so that I may be enriched by your wisdom."

The answer took form within his mind immediately. "In considering the self," he began, "we must acknowledge that each of us is composed of three principal aspects. There is the lower self, which is known as *unihipili* in classic Hawaiian; or in the *olelo* of the people, the *ku*. This is the aspect of the mind closely associated with the physical body, and it is through this aspect that we can experience the everyday world, remember past experiences, and generate emotions. This lower self is motivated by whatever it feels it needs from moment to moment, and so it could be said that this level is the source of our desires."

Nainoa waited for a response from the director, and when none was forthcoming, he went on.

"The middle self was called the *uhane* in the old language, and it expresses the thinking function of the mind. This mental aspect of the self makes decisions and serves as the overall inner director through which our core personal essence expresses its will forces and its creativity. This level is the intellect, and it seems to be strongly attracted to order and understanding.

"The third part of the self is the *aumakua*, the higher spiritual, ancestral source-self. This is the part of ourselves that does not die. It is the immortal spirit to which each of us withdraws at the death of our physical bodies, and from which each of us is remanifested when we begin our path through life once again here on the physical plane of Earthly existence. I have come to think of the *aumakua* as an energy state of being, and it is through this aspect that each of us can connect with the universal power called *mana*, and even with the mysterious Source itself."

The Kahuna Nui cracked her knuckles and smiled in anticipation. "Let us consider each of these selves in turn, Chief Nainoa. How would you categorize the functions of the lower self, the *ku*?"

"In many ways, " Nainoa began, "the *ku* functions much like a servant, in that it does what it is told to do by the middle self. When our inner director decides to access information stored in our memories, for example, the *ku* is the aspect that retrieves those memories. The *ku* is also the source of our emotions and feelings . . ." Nainoa paused as one of the new initiates walked by the house— a tall young woman with a thick mane of long hair who was most attractive. Her arrival at the center several days before had caused quite a stir among the unmarried men. Although he himself was engaged to be married, a surge of primitive feelings emerged from his *ku* in response to her.

Kahu Sala didn't miss a beat. "The *ku* is also known to be very impressed with anything physical," she chuckled. "This aspect of ourselves responds positively to things that it likes, and negatively to things that it doesn't." She thought for a moment, then observed, "Have you noticed that when you ask someone what they think about some issue, then wait for a day and ask them how they feel about that same issue, you often get quite a different answer?"

Nainoa nodded and added, "It's almost as if the inner director is always thinking, analyzing, trying to figure things out, whereas the *ku* knows and will always tell you exactly how it feels. I've discovered that when I ask my *ku* how it feels about this or that, it never lies to me." He paused again, then shifted the conversation in a new direction.

"It is also known that the *ku* is in charge of our physical aspect. Our hearts continue to beat and we continue to breathe without thinking about it because our *ku* is in control of these functions. The *ku* is also the aspect of ourselves that repairs the body when we suffer a wound or become ill, functioning as the inner healer that restores us to a state of balance and harmony, allowing healing to take place. I used to have long talks with William about this amazing capacity of our bodies to heal, and he was very much in agreement with our own medicine *kahunas*. He used to say that in our own nature are all the things we need to heal ourselves. He also felt that the role of the healer is essentially to understand and assist nature. But there is another function of the *ku* that is equally amazing.

"The *ku* actively observes both the outer physical world in which we live and the inner worlds of thought, emotion, and feeling in which we dream. The *ku* is the aspect of ourselves that functions as the boundary between the inner and the outer dimensions of reality." Nainoa looked at Kahu Sala for her reaction to his bold statements. She watched him attentively but said nothing, so he went on.

"The *ku* is thus the sender and receiver of all psychic experience. It is through this level of myself that I am able to make connection to my esteemed ancestor across distance and time, for example, or to my spirit helper, the one I think of as the spotted tiger man. It is through my *ku* that I examine the nature of the dream worlds in my morning exercises."

Kahu Sala regarded Nainoa fondly as she responded. "My mother used to say that there is a *puka*, a doorway within the *ku*, that functions as a mirror for us most of the time, reflecting our own thoughts and creative imagery back at us until we are ready to penetrate the inner levels of reality, awareness, and experience. Then . . ." she paused dramatically, "for some of us, it opens, giving us access into the visionary realms."

Nainoa looked at the *kahuna* thoughtfully. "When I experience the opening of this inner doorway, when I connect with the mind of my ancestor in my dreaming across time and distance, I feel these enormous sensations of power in my body. It is almost impossible for me to continue breathing, and my body shakes uncontrollably. What is the source of these feelings, Kahuna Nui?"

The director was silent for long moments. "I can only speak from my own experience," she said carefully, "and in doing so, I should add that not everyone will agree with my thoughts on this issue. However, I am a dreamer, like you," she smiled, "and that gives us a certain advantage." Her gaze shifted away from him as she looked into distances that only she could see.

"When I was a small child," she began, "I often used to wake at night, unable to move, suffused with feelings of enormous force or power like a great weight resting upon me. When I overcame my fear of these experiences, I discovered that I was able to vision in these states, to dream vividly while my mind was very much awake. Often it was at these times that I was able to enter the different levels of Po, the spiritworld, and on several occasions, I, like you, found myself in someone else's body. As I said, it used to frighten me, and so I talked with my parents about these strange episodes.

"My father was a powerful chief who had great knowledge of many things, but he did not vision," she chuckled. "He used to say that such events were simply bad dreams—that they were due to my eating too much pork before sleeping. My grandmother, on the other hand, was a *kahuna* and a dreamer. She told me that the feelings of power were caused by the opening of the *puka,* the gateway into the spirit world. When I was an adolescent, I asked her the same question that you have just asked me. She told me that the power I felt was actually my own, but experienced in an expanded way. What do you think she meant by this, Chief Nainoa?"

Nainoa grinned. The director had neatly tossed the question back into his own lap. Something interesting happened almost immediately. The answer seemed to arise in his mind by itself. He spoke the words as they appeared, without thinking about them, and as he did, he wondered briefly who was speaking.

"Because the gateway is within us, within our *ku,* to be specific, the power that I feel when it opens must flow into my body from the other side. And what is on the other side? I suspect that it is my *aumakua,* and that the tremendous force that I perceive occurs in response to connecting with my spiritual aspect." A line from an ancient text appeared briefly in his mind, providing an old translation for the word *aumakua*—the spirit that hovers over me.

"If this is true," he continued, "it means that this spirit self is my *palena,* my interface with the spirit world, and that the power I feel through my *ku* is the *mana* that is carried by this aspect of my self. Or perhaps it would be more correct to say that my *aumakua* is carried by the *mana.*"

The Kahuna Nui smiled. "I have come to similar conclusions. My mother never gave me the answer, of course. She knew full well that my curiosity would eventually bring me to my own level of understanding of this amazing phenomenon. Let us now consider the *aumakua* self, Chief Nainoa. Share with me what you have learned about your immortal spirit."

"The *kahuna* mystics say that the *aumakua* is the source of our spiritual wisdom." Nainoa spoke with clarity, aware that the information was flowing from some deep source within him. "The *aumakua* functions for each of us as the spirit teacher, as the origin of all knowledge of which we ever might have need during our lives here on the Earthly plane. In this sense, it is the source of our intuition, communicating with us through ideas, dreams, and visions that it sends in response to our need to know.

"Often when I sit in silence in the great hall, practicing *lokahi* to achieve harmony and unity between my three selves, a sense of deep tranquility begins to pervade me, filling me with a sense of utter peace. I have noticed that if I consider some problem at such moments, the answer to the dilemma appears in my mind immediately. I believe that this information is coming to me from my *aumakua*. This would indicate that my spirit self is not somewhere else, but rather that it is right here, right now, in constant attendance, carefully watching everything I do, listening with concern to every word and thought, monitoring every choice and decision. My outer and inner life has changed quite dramatically in response to these realizations." He smiled as he listened to his own words.

"The *aumakua* is also the ultimate source of the self. It is from this aspect that we are manifested when we are born." He paused as a memory appeared within his mind. "My ancestor, the one I have spoken of as the American, is quite taken with the Hawaiian version of the *Pule Nui*, the great prayer of his people recorded in the earliest histories written just after the fall of the American civilization."

"Refresh my memory, Chief Nainoa."

"As you will recall," he began, "our historians have always debated the meaning of the initial phrases of the great prayer. Some feel that the Americans were addressing a remote creator deity of some sort, perhaps the mysterious Source itself. Others thought the Americans believed the sun to be a god and were attempting to access its power and protection with this ritual. Most of the *kahuna* mystics, on the other hand, felt that the prayer was addressed to one's personal spiritual aspect. As I recall, the *Pule Nui* was recorded with these words:

"Oh Aumakua, who exists in the Upper World,
Sacred is your symbol.
Let your wisdom and intentions be manifested here on Earth
As they are there in the spirit world.
Nourish me each day and assist me in being compassionate.
Help me to achieve right conduct and protect me from evil.
For you are the source of my power and my being.
Forever."

Kahu Sala remained lost in thought for long moments, then her eyes narrowed as she asked, "And what do you think about the line 'sacred is your symbol'?"

Nainoa's eyes dropped to a low table against one wall of the director's house. It was Kahu Sala's personal altar. In its center was a tray of sand in which stood a single upright stone. It was smooth and columnar, a water-shaped piece of rock brought from the home islands by the Kahuna Nui's ancestors.

"We use a standing stone to represent this aspect of the self," he said. "It is not recorded what symbol the Americans used for the *aumakua* . . ." His words drifted off as the comely initiate reappeared, bringing them wooden bowls brimming with freshly made coffee, sweetened with cane. There was also a wooden platter mounded with spicy bean fritters. Nainoa was very fond of them.

The director thanked the young woman by name, then turned to Nainoa with a grin and raised her hands over the platter, saying matter-of-factly, "The *kapu* against men and women eating together is temporarily lifted. Please join me in enjoying these fritters, Chief Nainoa."

As they chewed appreciatively, Kahu Sala looked at him and said, "The inner quest of the *kahuna* mystic involves the search for the *aumakua*. Within and around each of us exists that transcendent self, and when we become fully aware of its presence, we then know with certainty that the personality that we have developed in response to our lives, my Sala-ness or your Nainoa-ness, is merely a product of our middle and lower selves that is recreated in each lifetime."

She thought for a moment. "As I say this, I must add that aspects of the personality can be incorporated into the *aumakua* when we die. This means that the shape of our *aumakua* changes in response to what we do and become here during our Earthly existences.

"Sometimes, individuals who are unaware of the existence of their transcendent self will have a spontaneous mystical experience in which they find themselves in the presence of a powerful, beneficent spiritual being. The average person usually interprets the event as a visit from a deity or some mythic spiritual hero, and it may be that this is so. But most often, the visitor is that person's own *aumakua*, taking on a dream aspect that it knows to be of special meaning to us.

"As our awareness of this high self deepens and our quest for connection with it becomes more focused," Kahu Sala continued, "there comes a time when our *aumakua* may merge with us fully. It is almost as if the transcendent self descends from Ka Po'e Aumakua, the place of the Human Spirit in the Upper Worlds, as though it flies downward like some winged bird-being to take up residence within us. Then, it sits in deep repose within the sanctuary of our hearts, waiting . . ."

She paused and thought for a moment. "I have carried babies within my body, children that developed and grew within my womb until the time arrived when they could lead an existence free of the confines of the body that nourished them. It is much the same with our *aumakua*. It sits within, growing as we grow, maturing as we mature. From lifetime to lifetime, this process of personal evolution continues until the transcendent self is liberated from the physical plane of existence, free to remerge with the ultimate Source from which it originally came as a seed of light. Until that moment, it lives within us, patiently waiting for its liberation.

"This is the true meaning and purpose of our life. When we live our lives in life-enhancing ways, our spiritual aspect increases; when we act in ways detrimental to ourselves or to others, our *aumakua* is diminished. At each moment, we make decisions, whether to do this or that, whether to say this or that. The manner in which we live, in accordance with the decisions each of us makes, is what draws us further and further along the path of power and beauty, leading us inexorably toward wisdom and truth. And it is there, ultimately, that we rediscover the presence of *IAO,* the mysterious Source. We find it because our growing spiritual awareness allows the knower to become one with both the knowing and the known. It is at this point that perception, understanding, and action occur all at the same instant.

"This brings up the function of the middle self, the *uhane,* the source of our decisions and will forces. Allow me to ask, Chief Nainoa—can you make contact with the American directly, through your intentionality?"

Nainoa answered, "The mystical connections between myself and my ancestor still seem to occur spontaneously, with his awareness coming into this level of reality and time more often than mine is able to go into his." He thought about the recent contact in Africa and added, "But the American seems to be getting better at initiating the contact through his intentionality."

He paused in reflection, then said, "It is truly *kupaianaha—* most extraordinary. He has been dead for almost 5,000 years, yet I think of him as very much alive. When I am connected with his mind, I experience him and his world as if they are real."

"In a sense, they are real, and he is alive," replied the *kahuna.* "The key to understanding this paradox lies in achieving a comprehension of the true nature of reality."

TOK! Another student had struck the plaque outside the door.

"And this is obviously the subject of another discussion," Kahu Sala concluded with a broad smile. The fritters were finished. The interview was over. As Nainoa prepared to rise, the Kahuna Nui took him by the hand.

"It is not often that I have the opportunity to talk with someone with your level of experience. I feel greatly honored in knowing you, Chief Nainoa, and in being able to help you on your path. Several moments ago, we mentioned the *uhane,* the middle self that thinks, analyzes, integrates information, and makes decisions.

This part of ourselves is most important, because in learning how to master your thoughts, much that initially seems impossible becomes possible. Do not forget the enormous influence our *uhane* has in directing the activities of our *ku*. We will talk further about the relationship that exists between them. Until then, reflect on what we have discussed, and my blessings on you and your endeavors."

Nainoa uncoiled from his cushion and bowed deeply, prostrating himself until his forehead touched the floor. As he rose and turned to go, Kahu Sala said to him, "It is most interesting. I am aware of someone else's energy in your *aka* field, Chief Nainoa. I remember dimly perceiving this the first time we talked after your arrival here several months ago. This is the second time that this has happened, and the presence hovering around you is stronger this time. I suspect that whoever it is has been listening to our conversation. It is not your friend William. I know his energy well . . . perhaps a little too well." A throaty chuckle emerged from her massive chest.

"Now who else among your friends do you suppose would be interested in the knowledge of the *kahuna* mystics? If it is your ancestor, the American, I, Sala Kahalopuna, send him greetings." She watched an astonished expression flow briefly across Nainoa's face, and her amusement once again overflowed in a laugh of monumental proportions.

CHAPTER FIVE

Psychopomp

MY SURGE OF EMOTION at the *kahuna's* perception of my presence shifted my awareness, and I lost the connection. This had happened to me before, and I shook my head with chagrin. As I opened my eyes in my bed at Omega, the *kahuna's* closing words echoed in my mind. I, too, needed to learn how to master my thoughts.

I lay still in the darkness and considered the wisdom that I was acquiring through Nainoa. First and foremost, the aspect of the self that the *kahuna* tradition calls the *unihipili,* or more informally, the *ku,* seemed to be analogous to what we in the West call the subconscious mind. And this aspect was being revealed as the interface through which the mystic experience was achieved. The shaman's doorway into the nonordinary levels of reality was located in the *ku.*

Since my *ku* was also the source of the sudden surge of emotion that had disrupted the contact, it explained how the connection had been so easily severed. With more control over my lower self, I might be able to minimize such disconnections in the future. It was also quite clear that this control would come from my middle self, my conscious intellect and decision maker . . . my ego.

In that instant, I recalled all the well-meaning spiritual teachers who had said: "You've got to get rid of your ego. You've got to let go of your need to control." If the *kahuna* was right, and I very much suspected that she was, a strongly focused and well-disciplined ego was absolutely essential to the success of the endeavor. As the inner director, it was the source of our intentionality and will forces through which it directed the activities of the subconscious. Get rid of your ego? Absolutely not!

I switched on the bedside light and made some hasty notes on the vision and on the functions of the *ku*. As I looked at the list, I realized that the *ku* acts much like a computer, like a living, biological hard drive that has been programmed over immense amounts of time by the evolutionary process. The programs on this inner hard drive were coded for by the molecular alphabet of our DNA, and I suspected that my ability to see visions like the traditional shaman—or spiritwalk, as Nainoa would say—is one of these programs.

This insight is supported by molecular biology's discovery that the DNA in the nuclei of cells emits photons, or rather "biophotons," which are much like weak electromagnetic waves. Of interest is that the wavelength at which these photons are released corresponds exactly to the narrow band of visible light that we humans can see, from infrared at about 900 nanometers, to ultraviolet at about 200. Nuclear DNA apparently emits these photons with such regularity that various researchers have compared the phenomenon to an "ultraweak laser," one that can provide a source of light and can give the visual sensation of color, luminescence, and holographic depth to the one who can perceive it.[1]

I found these revelations very exciting. These scientific facts suggested a neural mechanism for visionary experience. Powerful physical stimuli, such as singing or dancing, the sonic driving produced by drums and rattles, or even the ingestion of a powerful plant hallucinogen, could produce a cascade of electrons within the neurons of the central nervous system leading to the stimulation of the DNA therein. And as this DNA began to emit visible photon-waves in response, this could well be perceivable by the shaman as so-called hallucinations in their expanded state of consciousness.

This mechanism also suggested a relationship between the photon emissions of molecular DNA and consciousness. Seen from this perspective, consciousness could, in neurological terms, be thought of as an electromagnetic field constituted by the sum total of these emissions. Since every organic life form on our planet, from bacteria and viruses to redwood trees and human beings, possesses the same DNA genetic code, written in the same molecular alphabet with the same four nucleic acids, the claim of traditional shamans that consciousness is universal within everything everywhere began to make very good sense.

In addition, the shaman's ability to communicate with nature in expanded states of awareness, and with animals and plants in particular, took on a whole new level of meaning. Since every living thing on Earth possesses DNA, the biosphere itself could be thought of as a single interlinked, multileveled unit of DNA-based life, with the DNA itself being the source of the knowledge and imagery perceivable to those mystics who could shamanize. Indeed, the indigenous peoples of Amazonia think of the great rainforest as a form of jungle television, with the shaman as the receiver once they are "turned on."[2]

As I thought about these extraordinary discoveries emerging from the interface of science and spirituality, I wondered, as always, about the *dorajuadiok*. It was most definitely not an organic being, and thus was not made of DNA, so just how was I able to see this "phase-space entity"? We cannot see, hear, or feel the energy flowing through an electric cord, but we can perceive the energy's effect when there is a suitable receiver like a television set or a light bulb. That the *dorajuadiok* became visible only in my deep expanded states was certain. If my DNA was involved, and I now suspected that it was, did this mean that I was actually perceiving this entity at the molecular or even the sub-atomic quantum level? Was this spirit really as huge as it seemed, or was it, in fact, extraordinarily small?

There seemed to be no way of answering these questions as yet, so on my return to California, I began to survey various anthropological ethnographies about traditional shamanism where I discovered something else of interest. Shamans tend to run in families, with related individuals expressing the visionary ability to varying degrees.[3]

Interestingly, my own family seemed to bear this out. I had discovered quite by accident that my father, dead now for 30 years, had also possessed "the spiritwalker program." He, like me, could spiritwalk across time, but whereas I tended to merge with a descendant in the future, he had merged with one of his ancestors who lived in the past.[4] And since he, like me, had grown up in an urban, Eastern establishment family background, the question came up: Why had the program been activated at all?

I discovered all this by chance from an old boyhood friend, Steve McAllister, who came to visit me in California in 1995. We hadn't seen each other since 1964, and as we filled each other in on all the major steps and missteps of our lives over a bottle of champagne in my backyard, Steve turned to me and said, "As you well know, our fathers were the very best of friends." I concurred, mentally excavating a long series of cherished memories of the two men from my childhood.

"Well, one night back in the late '50s or early '60s," he continued, "the two of them apparently had a long talk. It was at the end of one of those long summer evenings when everyone had had a lot to drink. It was very late, the time of night when close friends often do a lot of soul sharing, and on that particular evening, your father told mine about a series of strange visionary experiences he'd had—vivid, dreamlike memories of being a swordsman in the employ of one of the kings of France during the 17th century."

Steve went on. "Your father was very explicit about both the nature and the content of these experiences, even describing the kind of sword the man possessed, and revealing his family name and his wife's family name, as well as the name of the town where he was living at that time. I don't remember those technicalities now, of course," Steve told me, "but I do recall that he described the most recent episode in some detail to my father. He was somewhat freaked out because he was apparently merged with this man when he was killed in a duel. He was even able to describe the sword his opponent had used to do the deed. Your father had been through the death experience and was very shaken.

"My father," Steve concluded, "was very impressed at both the intensity and obvious sincerity with which your father revealed this unusual story to him. He told me of this conversation many years after your father died when he was reminiscing about him one evening. I've never forgotten it."

This strange account has given me much food for thought. My father was a New York corporate attorney, a very private man who had never shared this part of his life with me, or perhaps with any-one else, but here's something interesting. In his youth, he attended Harvard University, where he studied English before going on to Har-vard Law School. While there, he took up the sport of fencing. He was so good at it that in short order, he was made captain of the fencing team. He pursued this new obsession with considerable fer-vor, much to the puzzlement of his family, becoming an East Coast champion and eventually a member of the U.S. fencing team at the Olympic Games in Berlin in 1936.

As I thought about this now, a series of questions appeared in my mind. Why had my father been motivated toward fencing in the first place? Why had he become a champion so quickly? Could the physicality of the sport have opened the doorway in his *ku*, con-necting him across space and time with his "ancestral self," in the same way that I had connected with Nainoa through the physicality of my living on the island of Hawai'i, not to mention the proxim-ity of the spirit stone? The answers to these questions were, of neces-sity, intuitive rather that factual, but the similarity between my father's experience and my own suggested that there was a genetic predisposition in my lineage toward visionary experience, one that included time traveling.

I considered the spontaneous way in which my experiences had begun. The spiritwalker program had suddenly appeared on the screen of my mind, enabled, if you will, by the exquisite physicality of lovemaking with my wife. In my case, sexuality had functioned as "the mouse" that "double-clicked" the program on my inner hard drive. The relationship between sexuality and spirituality was so obvious to me in those moments that I wondered how so many of the world's religious hierarchies had managed to get away with suppressing it. I also realized as never before that there is one vow that the Universe will not accept: the vow of celibacy.

At the time of this writing, with more than 15 years of visionary experience to draw on, I have begun to bring the program under some degree of conscious control. I can now intentionally induce the altered state in which my body is suffused with the power sensations, and if I am listening to a drum or rattle, it is much easier. Where I go and what I am able to accomplish in this state is determined by my intentions combined with my will forces.

This has led me to suspect that once the existence of the program and the inner portal become consciously known, the *ku* can be trained to open the doorway at any time—that it can be conditioned or programmed by the conscious mind/ego, much like a computer, to use any number of physical stimuli as cues. It follows that with continued training and discipline, this initially extraordinary experience can become more and more familiar, so that the time will eventually come when the physical stimulus is no longer needed, and the accomplished shaman, or *kahuna* mystic, can open the inner gateway though intentionality alone.

I was still figuring all this out when I got an interesting taste of just how spontaneous and unexpected the experience can continue to be. This episode is also of particular interest because it suggests the existence of a "hidden agenda," of which I, initially, was completely unaware.

My wife and I were attending the annual summer conference of the Institute of Noetic Sciences, held that year in San Diego.[5] The unifying theme of the conference was about service, and the list of presenters featured an impressive assemblage of worthies, most of whom seemed to be actively involved with integrating their gifts of inner wisdom with the ongoing work of the world.

Between the scheduled sessions, I also got to know many of the participants, discovering in the process that most, like me, had been young, socially conscious idealists in the 1960s, who joined the system in the 1970s, and achieved material and professional success in the 1980s. Most were now in their 50s, and somewhere along the line, many of us had rediscovered the Master Game.

Early one afternoon, Jill and I found ourselves in a 90-minute workshop offered by Dr. Belleruth Naparstek, a nationally known psychotherapist who integrates imagery and intuition into her practice for facilitating healing. It was during the experiential part of her presentation that something completely unexpected occurred.

Belleruth had guided our group into a healing visualization in the darkened room. I was sitting next to Jill, my eyes closed, following Belleruth's words, all the while sinking deeper and deeper into the imagery. There followed a longish period of silent meditation, accompanied only by soothing and melodious music. Quite suddenly, I felt myself settle into the deep shamanic state of consciousness in which I vision. This had not been my intent, but I didn't have time to think about it because the inner doorway abruptly opened.

The accompanying rush of power sensations was immediate, and my breath caught as my body stiffened in response to the rapture. As the light show began behind my closed eyelids, my inner director kicked in. I was in a public gathering. I had to remain silent and still . . . silent and still. My *ku* responded, and the sensations stabilized at a workable level. I remained sitting rigidly upright in my chair.

My vision came up quickly, and I found myself seated on a flat rock under a dense stand of trees along the edge of a steep hillside.

I glanced down and out across a lush green pasture with a sprinkling of cattle in the distance. My eyes sought the horizon, whereupon I got quite a shock. There was the vast blue ocean stretching away in all directions. I glanced up at the woods behind me. There were *koa* trees and tree ferns, and deeper in, I could see a flowering *ohia* tree. In some unknown fashion, my conscious awareness had been drawn back to the island of Hawai'i.

This was not what I was supposed to be doing in Belleruth's exercise, so it hadn't been my intentionality that had double-clicked the program. So what had? And if there was a hidden agenda in this case, what was it?

I wondered about these questions as I continued to study the scene before me. Years before, I had been invited by the directors of the Kona Historical Society to join them on a drive across some of the ranch lands at higher elevations along the slopes of the volcano Mauna Loa. Great swaths of forest had been cleared to create long, steep grazing areas that ran from the mountain down toward the ocean. As I looked around me, I understood quite clearly that I was on that mountainslope "up *mauka*" (up country) in Kona. The question returned. Why?

I saw movement in the pasture and discerned a human figure walking across the hillside at some distant downslope. Whoever it was seemed to be wandering aimlessly as though they were lost. I felt concern mixed with curiosity, and activating my will forces, I stood up and began to walk down the mountainside. Paradoxically, I could still hear the music in the workshop room and was very much aware that I was operating on more than one level of consciousness at the same time, an ability typical of the traditional shaman.

I approached the person below me who appeared to be an older man with thick white hair. As I came closer, much to my astonishment, I recognized him. He saw me just at that moment, and it was obvious from his look of surprise that he recognized me as well. He rushed up to me, his eyes rather wild, and grabbed me by the shoulders. I could feel his emotional state vividly. He was frightened. His words came out in a burst of feeling.

"Hank! I'm so glad I found you. I don't know where I am . . ."
He looked around quickly, then qualified his words. "Actually, I think
I know where I am, but I don't know how I got here or how the hell
to find my way back home!" I greeted him by name and gave him
a robust hug. This seemed to reassure him. I looked him over carefully. This man had been a significant elder in my life back in the
late 1960s and early 1970s. He had also been dead for more than
20 years.

It was at moments like this that my experience with shamanism was worth absolute gold. I realized immediately that he, or rather
his soul, was still here on the physical plane, but in its dream aspect,
not far from where he had lived in life. Like many who die unexpectedly, he had not been prepared for his death. It was even possible that he did not know he was dead.

I peeled his hands from my shoulders with some effort, then managed to get him to sit down. I talked with him for what seemed like
hours, gently reassuring him as I briefed him on his present state
of existence. This was not an easy experience. The man was
extremely agitated at first, finally calming down as the effect of my
words sank in.

It was now apparent to me that my consciousness had been
drawn into the level of the spirit world in which we dream—the same
level in which the soul finds itself after death. This is the postmortem
state described as the *Bardo* in the Tibetan Buddhist tradition, and
I sensed that I had been brought here to help convey this man's soul
across the threshhold into the *aumakua* realm of existence. This
was obviously the hidden agenda in this case, but who or what had
made this decision? Not me. I hadn't thought about this man in
years.[6]

The conveyance of the souls of the dead into the spirit realm is
what is known as classic psychopomp work, and among the world's
traditional peoples, this task normally falls within the expertise of the
shaman. I'd had no experience working with the dead, but from my
ongoing studies of shamanism, I had a sense of how to proceed. Like
shamans everywhere, I decided to call on the spirits to ask for help.

This presented an interesting challenge in this particular case, because the man whose soul was now with me had been a card-carrying atheist in life, and he had hated organized religion with a passion. How could I get him to cooperate? I decided that I would ask for a shamanic spirit helper to convey this soul to where it was supposed to go in the upper worlds, and I hoped that the spirit would be both impressive as well as acceptable to my old friend. The success of the endeavor hinged on it.

I prepared the ground, informing my friend where he was supposed to go as I mentally put out the call. I told him that I was going to summon someone to help him cross over. He seemed to calm down as I described what I knew of the vast cosmic regions of the upper worlds. I had done some fieldwork in these levels of experience and awareness, and I kept glancing at the sky as I talked. I had asked for a spiritual being that could fly.

An indistinct speck finally appeared above us, growing rapidly as if it were engaged in a precipitous descent. My friend looked up, following my gaze, his eyes widening as the speck grew larger and larger by the moment. A shrill shriek shattered the silence as the creature finally opened a set of mighty wings and banked, narrowly missing the hillside and circling in a wide arc. It was absolutely enormous. My friend and I stood open-mouthed as it flew over us once more, then landed lightly on the hillside above.

My scientist's mind immediately tried to impose meaning on what I was seeing by pigeonholing the being into some known taxonomic category—and failed. It appeared to be one of those mythological creatures combining an interesting mix of different animal species. Built on the scale of a dinosaur, its powerful body resembled that of a mammal—an immense lion or tiger, perhaps—but its comparatively smaller head, easily 15 feet above the ground on a columnar, tapering neck, betrayed large, black, almond-shaped eyes and a long, hooked beak. It folded its huge wings with a loud rustling sound and settled into a distinctly sphinxlike pose in the grass, coiling its rather snakelike, prehensile tail around one of its haunches.

It appeared to be a griffin—an honest-to-God griffin.

I stood awestruck as I studied the creature carefully. Most of its body seemed to be covered by large overlapping scales or feathers about a yard long. These were an off-white color, with pale peach undertones near their base, contributing to the creature's otherworldly, somewhat dragonlike appearance. The small head on its impossibly long neck suddenly tipped downward, and I found the creature's attention focused fully upon me. I looked into those fathomless black lenses and wondered how it communicated.

"Greetings, great griffin," I called out tentatively. "My profound thanks for your response to my call." I waited uneasily, projecting feelings of welcome and good intention. I will never forget its response.

A "soft voice," if it could be called that, whispered in my mind's ear with a delicate, almost feminine, melody of sound. "Greetings, immortal." These startling words were accompanied by warm feelings, filled with polite curiosity.

I asked permission to approach, and its head tipped forward once again, seemingly to signify assent. I walked slowly up the hill, explaining who I was, who my friend was, and the nature of our need in this strange but vivid dynamic. The dark eyes never left me until I requested the griffin's assistance in conveying my friend to where he was supposed to go. The creature shifted his gaze then and fastened those dark mirrors on my friend. "He knows where he is supposed to go," chimed the music in my mind. "He just doesn't remember . . ." There was a long pause, followed by a feeling of assent. "I will assist him in returning home," whispered the words.

"Home?" I asked.

"Home!" came the reply.

No further explanation was offered. My friend had remained rooted to his spot some distance away, so I went over to him and took his hand, drawing him with me toward the luminous, white being. I didn't know if he could hear the griffin's voice, so I talked calmly and steadily, assuaging my friend's fear with reassurance and projected good feelings. The griffin continued to repose quietly, so

I walked boldly up to it and gently took hold of one of its long scales. It felt soft, yet strong. Maybe it was a feather. I drew it forward, then let it go. It snapped back into place with a soft smack. A sense of amusement appeared in my mind, and looking up, I found the griffin regarding me with a neutral, detached stare.

"Help him to settle on my shoulders, behind my neck and before my wings," came the thought. "Show him how to hold on." This was accomplished quickly.

As I climbed down again using the scale-feathers like a ladder, I sensed the creature's imminent departure and sent a last thought-question toward it. "How is it that you were the one who came? Have we been in relationship before?"

"We have, immortal, but you don't remember." Imagery began to move in my mind then . . . scenes of gray stone buildings and a city street wet with rain. I was projected into a memory from my childhood, a dream image of walking up East 78th Street in New York toward my apartment building on Fifth Avenue. I could hear the sounds of traffic mixed with the etheric music of the workshop room.

As I trudged through the rainy twilight, I looked up at an ornate entrance to a building, and there, flanking a dark doorway, were two griffins carved in stone. I recalled wondering in my childhood fantasies what it would be like to have a pet griffin for a friend. What would my friends say if I arrived at school every day riding on a griffin instead of a city bus?

"So you do remember . . ." purred the words.

I was stunned. "But those were fantasies," I protested. "Those were imaginary daydream images."

"They seemed real to you then," came the breathy response, "and they were real to me. Now you know something interesting about the reality of dreams."

My friend had remained curiously silent during this dialogue, and I looked at him now. He was sitting on the griffin in a rather wooden pose, right where I had ridden in my childhood dreams. I thought again of the stone griffins on the building above the rainy city street. "You mean that you could see me through the stone eyes of those statues so long ago?"

There was no response. Perhaps it was deemed unnecessary. The great being suddenly unfolded its long wings with a snap, spread them to catch the wind, and rose gracefully into the sky. I waved to my friend, but he seemed not to see me. It was as if he was already being drawn into the realm to which he was heading. The griffin gained altitude quickly, circling like an eagle, higher and higher into the sky. Once again, I heard that soft, melodious flow of song within my mind's ear. "Farewell, immortal. Until we meet again . . ."

Abruptly, the music in the workshop room came to a close, and in the ensuing silence, my awareness shifted. The scene before me simply evaporated as I opened my eyes and looked at my wife with confusion. Jill doesn't miss much. She regarded me evenly for long moments, then smiled and asked cheerily, "Been having an interesting time?"

Our children were visiting with Jill's parents for the duration of the conference, so she and I had the opportunity to enjoy several days together, submerged in the adult world of meetings, workshops, and conversations with other modern mystics. We were also alone together in our hotel room for several nights, something that didn't happen very often, being as we were in the married-householder-with-children stage of our lives.

It was on the evening of the same day that I managed to convey the soul of my old friend into the spirit world that I had my next connection with Nainoa, and as so often happens, it occurred in response to a joyous marital encounter. There was also my intentionality, of course. As I drifted in that peaceful, dreamy aftermath that lovemaking creates, I remembered Kahu Sala's words, and my inner director clicked on. I began to think about the possibility of making a journey to my esteemed descendant.

I found it intriguing that my last two encounters with Nainoa had happened in sequence on the same day in his time frame, while months had elapsed in between those same contacts in my own.

About three weeks had passed since my connection with him at the Omega Institute. I wondered if I could make contact now.

I glanced at Jill. She seemed to be asleep. I turned my attention to my *ku*. It was sparkling happily, impressed beyond measure by what it had just experienced. The timing seemed good. I activated my will forces and thought again about making connection with Nainoa, and as I did, I redefined the intention.

My goal was to reconnect with him a bit later on that same day that he'd had that conversation with the Kahuna Nui. I waited in the darkness, concentrating fiercely on my objective, but nothing happened. I held the thought, but after a half hour, still nothing. I decided to abandon the attempt and slipped into dreaming, into that shallow state where imagery appears in the mind spontaneously. I dimly recalled Nainoa's exercise of dreaming while awake. My mind watched as the dream images emerged, but I must have passed into deep unconsciousness, because when I surfaced briefly to look at the clock, it was four in the morning.

I subsided once more into dreaming, and as I headed for the drop-off point where we pass into the depths, it was as if I suddenly woke up. I didn't fully awaken in the normal sense, but my conscious mind became fully awake while my *ku* continued to dream. I recalled my intention of the night before—to journey to Nainoa later in that same day. I held the thought . . . held the thought . . . and much to my amazement, it happened.

The power sensations surged into me as the doorway opened, activating the light show of phosphenic visuals almost immediately. My body felt like it was inflating with force as the invisible fist squeezed me almost breathless. My hands felt huge, and I couldn't close them. The blast of feeling was not unlike the tantric ecstasy I had enjoyed with Jill only hours before, but this time, it was simply overwhelming, as though someone or something was turning up a rheostat.

The grid appeared behind my tightly closed eyes, reminding me of Australian Aboriginal paintings I had seen in books. I wondered if the grid was a psychic-energetic map that one could follow across the dreamtime. I didn't have time to think about it because the transition was swift. I passed through the dark hall of silence and then . . .

I heard the bell-like call of a bird, my senses simultaneously registering the rich smells of wet earth and the sweet scent of flowering coffee. I could feel the warmth of the sun on my skin and perceived the sweat trickling down my face. My vision came up then, as though I had opened my eyes. I glanced down at my hands. They were strong, brown hands holding a thick wooden pole. I was there.

CHAPTER SIX

Third Journey: The Garden

T HE SONG OF THE FOREST BIRD floated in the warm, humid air. Nainoa paused in his work and looked toward the trees beyond the wall. That bird had been singing all morning, almost as though it were calling to him. His eyes searched among the shadows of the great buttress roots, rising higher and higher along the massive vine-entangled trunks until he was scanning the forest canopy far above. He did not see it.

He leaned on his digging stick and looked out across the gardens. The other students were working in silence, turning composted manure into the reddish soil with their sticks, pulling weeds and doing what needed to be done with focused attention. No one was looking in his direction. He scanned the forest again. There was definitely a sense of something sending a communication. *Be patient,* he thought. He would walk in the forest in the afternoon.

He resumed his work, humming a chant that he was learning as he bent forward to jam the fire-hardened point of his stick into the ground between the swollen bases of the large *taro* plants. These were dry-land *taro* unlike the other varieties that grew in flooded paddies. He broke off the *keikis*, the baby plants spontaneously generated from the corms, and placed them gently in a basket for replanting elsewhere in the gardens. He caught movement out of the corner of his eye.

Chief Hakai, the Kahuna Mala in charge of the gardens, appeared among the luxuriant green rows of the gourd vines held up by bamboo trellises. The gray-haired older man was carrying a digging stick and was wearing a *malo*. He came from one of the most powerful ruling families, but aside from his tattoos, he appeared no different from any commoner working in the fields.

Hakai stopped to talk with two recent arrivals who were still very much in awe of everything and everyone around them. Nainoa saw the students relax in response to Hakai's words. The master gardener had a way of valuing people, no matter how elevated or lowly their status, and he was much beloved by everyone who knew him. Nainoa bowed to the *kahuna* as he approached, waiting respectfully for permission to speak.

"*A me ke aloha pumehana*—warm greetings, Chief Nainoa." Hakai smiled, observing the gigantic *taro* leaves with interest. "Our green friends are honored by your attention."

"*E ku'u haku aloha kakahiaka*," Nainoa answered, using the classic Hawaiian phrase in return. "Good morning, sir. Your words about green friends have prompted a memory of something that happened on my long walk of last year. It occurred during my passage through the great forest, a dreamlike encounter with a tall, green leafy being who seemed to guide me on a journey through the dream worlds. I have often wondered if it was the forest spirit well known to the hunters and timbercutters."

"Ahh, Nahelemakua . . . so you have been honored by a glimpse of the green one," the *kahuna* murmured, nodding knowingly. "Tell me, did it look male or female to you?"

Nainoa recalled the vertical green shape that had appeared on the forest floor before him on that fateful night in the forest. It had trembled slightly, giving the impression that it was a densely foliated bush, considerably taller than himself. Abruptly, a face had appeared within the foliage—a green visage that observed him with an alert intelligence. It was as if a part of the forest had assumed a vaguely human shape to communicate its awareness to him. Was it male or female? Hard to say. It had flickered constantly, changing shape from one moment to the next. Initially, it had appeared to be made of leaves. When Nainoa blinked his eyes, it shifted, becoming more geometric, as if it were made of irregular shards of green glass that allowed light to shine through it.

"I don't recall perceiving it as being either male or female," Nainoa answered, giving a brief description of what he had seen.

"Just wondered," said Hakai. " I've noted over the years that men tend to see it as masculine, women as feminine, revealing something of interest about the human mind and how it perceives. I suspect that each of us has been trained since birth by our parents, teachers, and friends to see reality in a certain way. As a result, we see these plants before us as *taro,* and those over there as *ipu,* as gourds. Along the way, men learn to apply a male shape to the reality that they see, while women perceive that same reality through female eyes. It is possible that this way of perceiving may also extend into our spirit vision as well."

The *kahuna* was silent for a moment as though reflecting on something. "Long ago," he continued, "I had an experience much like yours. When I was a child, my friends and I used to play in the forest, and one day I became aware of a tall, wild humanoid creature of some sort, one that seemed to be made of leaves and vines. It appeared in a particular place where there were lots of huge cotton trees deep in the woods. The being was not frightening, nor was it particularly friendly. It was just there, a watchful presence that belied curiosity more than anything else. I was quite amazed that my friends could not see it. Until that time, I thought that everyone could see what I could. This served to alert me to the fact that not everyone can vision.

"In my own mind, I classified this entity as a magical spirit-friend, a sort of tree man whose awareness I could feel fastened upon me whenever I was out in the forest. Being a boy, I always experienced it as male. Interestingly, my mother's land division was bordered along one side by a river, and I recall perceiving the flowing water as female—as the waterwoman counterpart of the tree man, so to speak."

Nainoa recalled the spirit who had appeared in dream to William's daughter, Kenojelak, shortly before his departure from the Ennu lands beyond the mountains. She had called this spirit the Riverwoman, describing it as a blue humanlike figure that had come out of the water near the camp to give her information and to prophecy the future.[1]

Nainoa gave the *kahuna* a brief description of Kenojelak's vision, then asked, "Chief Hakai, why would an elemental waterspirit, or the spirit of a particular kind of tree or animal, look human to us? Is it because we humans look out into nature and expect nature to look back at us with a human face?"

"Good question," the older man replied with a grin. "I have come to believe that the spirits of nature often appear to us in human or near-human form so that we can interact with them more easily. Being spirits, they are energetic, and by assuming a shape like our own, they know that we will be more inclined to come into relationship with them and talk with them. In time, the accomplished *kahuna* mystic can learn to see them as they really are.

"The spirits usually serve as teachers when they first come into relationship with us, conveying power and knowledge that allows us to accomplish various things—healing work, for example. There is a plant over there that we use for healing . . ." The *kahuna* gestured with his stick, pointing across the garden to a section in which medicinal herbs were growing. Along one side could be seen the rounded dark green shapes of a small grove of *noni* trees. "When I connected with the spirit of the *noni* for the first time, I saw it as a small human—a friendly, muscular little man with a gnarly, bulbous shape much like the fruit of the tree itself. The spirit looked a little like the cross between a human and a potato, and curiously, it had a set of wings sprouting from its shoulders so that it could fly. This spirit was the first of the plant helpers who came into relationship with me, instructing me in the use of its juice for healing purposes."

Nainoa slowly looked around the garden surrounding them. "Each plant has its own spiritual essence, doesn't it?"

The *kahuna* nodded, then added, "In order to make contact with them, we must learn to enter the level of consciousness in which they can be seen. It's the same level in which we dream at night while asleep, so the ability to access this state is easy. The accomplished *kahuna* mystic learns to inhabit this level of awareness more and more deeply, but we do this while very much awake, all the while keeping in mind what it is that we wish to accomplish.

"At first, the goal is simply to catch a glimpse of the spirits. Once this is accomplished, one's *ku* has a sense of what it is looking for and how to achieve it. Then comes the time of training in which we learn to deepen and stabilize those initial glimpses into a permanent visionary capacity in which the spirits and the reality they inhabit can be summoned and seen at will. Through practice, the mystic eventually acquires the ability to see the spirits all the time, even in their everyday waking state of mind.

"Many of us discover that we have this ability by accident, as you did in the forest," Hakai continued. "Others learn about it and try to achieve it through training. Many succeed, especially if they are deemed worthy by the spirits. This suggests that most of us can vision, at least to some degree."

"What of those people who the spirits deem unworthy?" Nainoa asked.

"Another interesting question," murmured the master gardener. "It seems that those who become spiritually powerful are chosen far more often than they do the choosing. This means that the spirits have a hand in things right from the beginning, and that no amount of praying, begging, bargaining, or training will get someone chosen if the spirits deem them unready.

"There is also the matter of lineage," Hakai went on. "It is well known that *kahuna* mystics tend to run in families, suggesting that there is an inherited transmission of *ike*, the spiritual power that conveys the ability to vision, among other things. This transmission occurs through the *aka* body, through the energetic aspect of ourselves that travels through time in direct relationship with our personal *aumakua*, our spiritual aspect."

The *kahuna* fell silent and considered Nainoa thoughtfully before continuing. "It is generally known that your maternal grandfather was a great visionary and mystic." Hakai paused, then added grimly, "No one will speak his name today because of a serious flaw in his character, one that motivated him to use his power in negative ways. There is only one sin, Chief Nainoa: to intentionally inflict harm on another, whether by word or thought or deed, and ultimately, his propensity to do so led to his untimely demise. The spirits are everywhere, in everything. They miss nothing, and they never forget."

The *kahuna's* eyes shifted to regard the *taro* leaves once again. "I might add that all of us, at one time or another, have transgressed in ways that are of grave concern to our invisible friends. This is always a critical turning point. If we continue to misuse our abilities, the spirits supporting us withdraw, and we lose our *ike*. We are stripped of our spiritual power and dumped back into life as an ordinary person. This is a very sad thing. Often, the disempowered and unprotected *kahuna* loses a large part of their soul in the process, an event that opens them up to physical illness and mental suffering. Sometimes, as in the case of your grandfather, the disgraced individual dies."

Hakai abruptly drove the point of his digging stick into the earth, vigorously loosening the soil around a large corm. Then he paused and added, "There are other ways to fall from grace, of course. When I was a boy, there was a young woman in my land division who fancied herself quite the healer. In fact, she did have an impressive record of successful healings for one so young. Things came to a head when she did a healing for the high chiefess who was the paramount ruler of the whole land division, a wonderful woman who also happened to be my grandmother." He paused, then added wistfully,

"We were very fond of each other, my grandmother and me.

"Anyway, this young woman helped my grandmother recover from a dreadful illness. We had actually given up hope for her survival when the ritual was done. As a result of this success, the young medicine *kahuna* developed quite an inflated sense of herself and went around proclaiming her abilities as a healer. Unfortunately, she had taken a shortcut in her training somewhere along the line, and she failed to understand a matter of critical importance: *No one heals anyone else.* Afflicted people actually heal themselves. The *ku* of the sufferer accomplishes the task in response to a powerful assist from the spirits who work with the *kahuna* healer.

"We should also observe that humility is highly regarded by the spirits," he went on. "For a person to become too taken with themselves is dangerous, the first step to their eventual undoing. Such was the case of that young woman. She abruptly lost her power, and when that happened, she could no longer cure. I don't believe she ever got her power back. She eventually married and had children, but none of her offspring had the power either. We'll have to wait and see about her grandchildren. Sometimes the power skips a generation or two and reappears somewhere down the line.

"Thirsty work, gardening . . ." Hakai grinned at Nainoa. "Let's go get a drink." The two men walked along the rows of plants to a shaded corner of the garden where a goatskin bag filled with water hung from a post. They drank deeply, then sat down on a bench under a stand of pandanus, from where they could see out across the garden. Hakai resumed his discussion.

"Let me share something interesting with you, Chief Nainoa. My work sometimes takes me away from this center, and while I'm away, I am often asked to do healing work on behalf of others. As you know, everything that exists here in the physical level of reality also has a spiritual aspect in the dream world." The *kahuna* broke off, his eyes roving across his plantation with obvious affection.

"This garden, for example, has a dream equivalent in the spirit world. When I'm away, I can connect with this garden by going into its dream aspect while in the visionary state of consciousness. I have been doing this for years now and have come to think of this place as my *hunamala*, my secret garden.

"I have discovered that I can work in this inner garden, changing or altering the place according to how I want it to be. If I want a grove of sweet mangos, I just create them with my imagination and there are mangos in my garden." He broke into a wide smile as he added, "There are many breadfruit trees in my garden, many *ulu*, and they bear all year." Nainoa joined him in laughter. Breadfruit were a strong favorite among the Hawaiians, and like mangos, one of the few crop plants that were seasonal.

The *kahuna* explained, "I noticed early on that I could communicate with the plants in this secret garden. But here's something really interesting. I have discovered that when I change my inner garden, something in my outer life shifts in response. It is almost as though everything in my garden is a symbolic aspect of myself or some area of my life, and when I change the garden in the dream world, my everyday reality changes, too."

Hakai laughed with delight. "This is true *ho'okalakupua*—the making of magic. When we use our creative imagination to make a thoughtform of something we strongly desire to have or experience, it is the first step to manifesting this idea or need into our everyday reality.

"This creative aspect of ourselves is a function of the middle self, the *uhane*, the thinker and decision maker, and when this inner director repeatedly concentrates on the thoughtform it has created, it increases the amount of *mana* that the inner image receives. When you pay close attention to something, *mana* flows in that direction. As we do this day after day, a strong *mana* field forms within and around the image—a field that has the power to attract or assemble the nearest available equivalent experience in the everyday world. It is in this way that true magic works, and the more *mana* one has, the more one can accomplish using this method."

Hakai was quite aroused by the subject matter under discussion, and continued with rising enthusiasm. "I have also noted from time to time that my secret garden has the ability to change spontaneously, and it seems to do so completely independent of my intentionality. I was quite surprised the first several times this happened. My astonishment increased when I studied my outer life carefully and discovered that I could almost always find the part that had shifted in response. It's really amazing when you think of it. This inner garden in the dream world is a place of power to which I have instant access, whenever there is a need. The fact that it can change on its own confirms that it has an existence separate from myself and that I am not just making it all up."

"My ancestor has such a place," murmured Nainoa thoughtfully. "The one I call the American . . ."

Hakai went dead silent with this revelation. After a long pause, he offered, "I heard your talk at the capital. There have always been a few who could access the inner worlds and connect with the spiritual essence of their ancestors."

"I have come to believe that the phenomenon is possible because both he and I are embodiments of the same *aumakua*," Nainoa replied. "We are both physical manifestations of the same spiritual aspect. What this really means is that the connection is possible because part of my *kino'aka*, my energy body, is derived from his. There is no way to prove this, of course, as the genealogical threads between us are lost in the mists of time. But I have discussed this at length with my mentor, Chief Kaneohe, and he believes that this is so. So does the American. When I am in the state of *akaku*, the deep dreaming-while-awake, I can sometimes achieve connection with the mind of this ancestor, and then I can access his memories, his vast knowledge . . ." Nainoa's words drifted into silence as he considered the wonder of this endeavor.

"And he has a secret garden?" Hakai's curiosity was piqued.

"He does. Or perhaps I should say that he *did*. He passed away almost 5,000 years ago, and yet it seems as though he is very much alive, very much aware . . ." Nainoa paused as he sought terms to describe the indescribable and failed. "We have come to know each other rather well," he finished lamely. Hakai grinned and prompted him once again.

"His secret garden?"

"Ah, yes. It is the dream aspect of a place he knows on the home island of Hawai'i, where he lived for many years on a small farm holding. His garden is actually a place on the coast that he used to visit with his family. When he left the island, he discovered that he could visit the island in his dreaming by going to this place."

Nainoa looked at the older man. He had Hakai's full attention. "The American always seems to use this place as a point of arrival and return in his visioning. He uses it for other tasks as well. He is skilled at journeying into the spirit worlds, down into Kai, into the Lower Worlds of Milu, as well as to Uka, the Upper Worlds of Lanikeha. His secret garden seems to be in between these great cosmic regions, existing in Waena, the middle level of dream."

Chief Hakai's eyes gleamed. "This American ancestor of yours was a *kahuna* mystic. Was he also a *kahuna kupua*, a master of spirits?"

"He was. He had many spirits in his personal service. My friend William the Ennu describes those who can master spirits and travel beyond the confines of the body as *spiritwalkers*. The American calls them *shamans*."

Nainoa broke off and thought for a moment as he considered Hakai closely. Yes, the man would understand. He came to a decision.

"The American and I actually share a very powerful spirit helper, the same one who helped me in the healing of Chief Kaneohe after my return. I sometimes suspect that this spirit was partially responsible for bringing the two of us together. There is also the stone . . ."

Hakai regarded the younger man closely. "I have heard of your relationship with the *pohaku kupua*, the spirit stone of Chief Kaneohe. Your ancestor was the stone's first *kahu*, was he not?"

Nainoa marveled at the Kahuna Mala's intuitive ability. Only Chief Kaneohe and himself knew this story in its entirety.

"Yes," he replied. "The American was the stone's first caretaker. In fact, he was the one who found it in nature, recognized it for what it was, and subsequently carved it, bringing out its inner form. He found the spirit stone in the waves of a wide bay on the west side of the island, and actually placed it in the ordinary aspect of his secret garden for a time. I discovered before I left the Kaneohe land division that the spirit in the stone remembers that place. This has allowed me to see this garden both through the American's mind and through the stone."

Hakai looked at him closely. "I suspect that we all have such a place within our dreaming. Often, as in this case, it is the dream aspect of some place that we know in the everyday world. But I believe it can also be a purely personal place that we make for ourselves. We can simply dream it into existence, using our intentions in tandem with our creative imagination to produce the desired result."

TOK! The wooden slit drum at the community's center sounded the end of the morning work period. It was time for the midday meal. Nainoa's stomach growled. Hakai heard the sound and laughed.

"Your *ku* is hungry, Chief Nainoa. Let us take our discussion to the men's house for some food." The two men stood and began to walk. "Did your ancestor use his garden for healing work by any chance? Sooner or later he must have discovered that there is a very powerful spirit that lives in the garden."

CHAPTER SEVEN

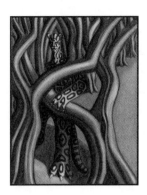

The Place of Power

I THOUGHT A GREAT DEAL about this episode and the one before it.
I was receiving a body of esoteric wisdom from the hidden teachings of the *kahuna* mystics through Nainoa. Interestingly,
Nainoa was involved in a similar experience, extracting knowledge
from my investigations of the shamanic tradition when he was in
connection with me in my slice of reality and time.

I was somewhat startled, to say the least, when he disclosed information about my method of shamanic journeying to Chief Hakai.
I was also amazed that he knew about my stopping-off place in the
dream world from which I access nonordinary reality. I had never
categorized this place in any particular framework, but the whole
idea of having a "secret garden" appealed to me immensely. An
opportunity to further explore this personal place of power presented
itself in the fall.

Several years had passed since I had participated in any formal
training in shamanic practice, and in the interim, I had become aware
that Michael Harner had created an advanced program in which an

ongoing, established group of individuals would meet for a week twice each year for three years. I had run into Harner at some anthropology meetings the previous March, and he had told me that a new group was being formed, encouraging me to call up his Foundation for Shamanic Studies to enroll.[1] I followed his advice and was accepted into the new group.

It is not my intention to discuss the nature of the foundation's training program or the exercises we engaged in because these are best discovered for oneself through direct experience, much in the way initiates once acquired knowledge and training from accomplished teachers in the old mystery schools of the past. I did, however, have some amazing personal experiences during the next three years, some of which I *can* share, as they relate to the ongoing series of mystic encounters that are recorded in my books.

On a bright October day, I drove over to the Westerbeke Ranch in the wine country of northern California where the training would be held. The sky was the deep blue of Indian turquoise, and the afternoon light had achieved that soft tawny quality I always associate with the harvest season. Local produce stands along the country roads were overflowing with colorful squash, pumpkins, and Indian corn; and the vineyards carpeting the rolling hills were tinted with yellow, rose, and rust.

The shadows were long when I arrived at the ranch tucked into the hills west of Sonoma shortly before sunset. I was greeted on the veranda of the main building by Christina Stack, an East Coast artist and one of the foundation teachers who would be assisting Harner with the program. We introduced ourselves to each other and chatted about logistics, then I walked up the path under spreading oaks and found my bed in the communal men's cabin. Five years had passed since I had participated in a workshop with Sandra Ingerman at this place, and I was pleased to be back.

We had our first gathering after dinner. Most of the 45 participants sat on big cushions on the floor around the edge of the large meeting room, although a few with back problems sat in chairs. I looked the group over with interest. Most of us were midlifers in our 30s and 40s, with a few elders and near elders in their 50s and early 60s. The majority were women. All were modern mystics trained in the way of the shaman. All were players of the Master Game.

The room quieted as Michael Harner arrived and took his place in the circle. He lit a candle and placed it on the floor in the open center of the room, then greeted us warmly and invited each of us to say a few words about ourselves. When all had spoken, he began the training by sharing some information about two important discoveries that he had made. First, traditional shamans learn to draw on compassionate spirits who want to come into relationship with humanity in order to help us in various ways. And second, these sympathetic spirits are not all powerful and need our help in opening up a bridge or channel between their reality and ours. The shaman has always served as the bridge, as the one who moves into the transcendent realms to connect with these spirits and bring the power back to accomplish various things, usually on behalf of others. When the bridge is formed, the miraculous happens. And this is true magic.

I was reflecting on this statement as I took a walk through the wooded hills above the ranch early the next morning. I strode up the dirt road past the buckeyes and oaks, bay trees and madrones, my passage spooking the deer in the thickets and the quail who scuttled across the road. The occasional hawk or vulture soared over me curiously, and my *ku* began to sparkle happily, impressed with this wild California countryside. I recalled Kahu Sala's ruminations about nature as the primordial source of power. Goosebumps formed in response to this thought. There was no question. I could feel it all around me.

Abruptly, my awareness expanded and I became aware of a presence. It was just there at the edge of my consciousness, and it had a most powerful tinge to it. It felt familiar, but it wasn't Nainoa, nor was it my spirit helper, the leopard man. I knew what they felt like. I suddenly recalled that I'd had this same feeling the last time I was here, but I had never found out who or what it was. Maybe this time . . .

The road rose and fell along the wooded hillsides, then abruptly descended through the trees to a rocky stream bed. I walked pensively among the boulders along its banks, pausing to admire a large buckeye whose knobby branches were loaded with fuzzy, gray baseballs that were splitting open to reveal the gleaming brown seeds within.

I sat down on a large stone near the water beneath the steep hillside covered with a grove of bushy bay trees. Across the stream before me was a majestic willow. The floor of the canyon was carpeted with leaves, and the silence was broken only by the chuckle of the water gurgling among the stones at my feet. Always the scientist, I noted that the rocks in the stream seemed to be mostly volcanics, porous lavas and finer-grained basalts and quartzites.

I was absolutely enchanted with this marvelous place and went into light meditation, letting my mind merge with the locale. Only moments passed before something once again interrupted my concentration. I was being watched, of that I was absolutely certain, but whatever it was eluded detection. I waited, but nothing unusual occurred. As I walked back to the center for breakfast, the sense of presence remained, almost as though it was following me. My curiosity was piqued, and later that morning during one of the experiential sessions involving goal-oriented shamanic journeywork, I decided to see if I could discover who it was.

I lay down on my back in our darkened workshop room on an old Navajo rug I sometimes use in ritual circumstances. Most of my fellow participants had taken up similar positions all around me, although some sat upright in the position favored for meditation. Each of us had practiced shamanism for many years, and each accessed the transcendent realms in the way that worked best for them.

In the center of the room, Michael Harner and Christina Stack began to drum, establishing the monotonous, rapid beat used by traditional shamans as a powerful assist in shifting awareness. I closed my eyes and sank into the sound. The familiar dreamy state of the light trance descended immediately. I knew what I was looking for in this experience now, and I just let my awareness flow with the sound for a few minutes. Then I instructed my *ku* to open the inner doorway and invited the presence I had sensed that morning to approach. Several things happened virtually simultaneously.

My body was seized by the overwheming sensations of force as the doorway opened, flooding me with power. I felt some concern as I began to shake uncontrollably. I didn't wish to disturb the person journeying next to me, but I didn't have time to think about it because in that moment, my awareness expanded and the presence arrived.

It felt absolutely huge—larger by magnitudes than any of my spirit helpers. I thought briefly of the *dorajuadiok*, but in the same moment, I knew it was not that dark obelisk. This presence felt similar in that there was an enormous field of energy associated with it. But within it, or carried by it perhaps, was a personality that expressed a distinctly feminine quality, combined with an awareness that was quite formidable. And in those moments of power, there was absolutely no question that that awareness was focused on me. It was definitely a moment for diplomacy.

I extended a polite greeting combined with good intentions and a question. The power surged in response, and my face suddenly became blazing hot, as though someone had placed a cloth dipped in scalding water over my mouth and chin. My eyes snapped open as my body shot upright in reaction. Michael Harner gave me a startled look. The pain had catapulted me out of the shamanic state of consciousness. I looked around the darkened room but saw only my colleagues spread out around me. I gave Harner and Christina a reassuring gesture and lay down again on my rug.

I closed my eyes, wondering at the pain in my face. I tried to relax, allowing myself to settle down, and as the dreamy state descended once more, a soft breathy tone of sound whispered a word in Hawaiian in my ear: "*Vaaayyy-leee-naaahhh . . .*" Astonishment swept through me as recognition hit. It was Pele, the great spirit that resides in the active volcanoes of the island of Hawai'i. I realized in a flash that she had come into this room at my invitation, and as my awareness refocused on my scorched face, I concluded tentatively that she had just kissed me.

My previous encounters with this spirit rose unbidden in my consciousness. Before leaving the island in 1989, I had requested that she visit me from time to time. I was now 3,000 miles from Hawai'i, but the hills around Westerbeke were all made of volcanic stone, so perhaps her realm includes all such geological deposits. I surmised that when she had become aware of my presence in proximity to her domain earlier this morning, she had emerged from the rocks and had followed me back to the center. As the burning sensation in my face began to subside somewhat, I gathered my scattered wits to respond.

"Tutu Pele," I began tentatively. *"A me ke aloha pumehana . . .* I greet you with warmhearted *aloha."* I waited for a response, my body vibrating once again with the enormous force surrounding and penetrating me, fervently wishing that Nainoa was in connection so that he could share this extraordinary moment.

My visionary ability came up at this point, and the workshop room evaporated. I briefly perceived a figure of monumental proportions. She had a human configuration, yet she was not. She was so tall that I couldn't see her face. It was as though I was looking up at one of the titans of Greek mythology, and as I thought about this, I admitted to myself that this was a valid perception, for Pele could be categorized as one of the immortal, primordial forces associated with the earth—as a power that had come into existence billions of years ago as the planet itself had taken form.

A shift of some sort occurred, and she seemed to become more human, or perhaps it was my own mind imposing a culturally determined stereotype upon what I was seeing. I abruptly perceived Pele as an extraordinarily tall, dark-complexioned woman whose long, somewhat reddish-tinted hair seemed to reach right down to her feet. Did she have feet? I couldn't tell, nor do I recall what she was wearing because my attention was captured by her luminous eyes that looked directly into my own. Once again, I heard the ancient Hawaiian greeting whisper in my ear:

"Vaaayyy-leee-naaahhh. . . . ," and for the first time, I saw her smile.[2]

At this point, I gathered my courage and offered her an account of all that had passed since I had left the island. I presented the information in bursts of thought-feeling interspersed with remembered imagery of places seen and things accomplished. I included an account of my meeting with the *kahuna* Nelita Anderson and mentioned that she'd told me that Pele often came into relationship with those who were *kaula*—visionaries who could perceive the future. I revealed that Nelita had given me a piece of lava from the district of Ka'u on the Big Island and that she had said, "This is one of Pele's stones. This is for you."

Throughout, the heroic figure stood before me and listened. This was somewhat unnerving, as I understood quite clearly that nothing could be concealed from those eyes—that she could see everything. I concluded my story by saying that I had cared for the stones that she had given me permission to take from the island—the spirit stone in particular—and enhanced my account by bringing up a visual memory of each.

As I mentioned the spirit stone, I became aware that my *ku* perceived this awesome being before me as quite different from the presence that infused the stone—that she might fall into a different taxonomic status, so to speak. As if in answer to my unasked question, an impression arose in my mind, an intuitive understanding that Pele is a nature spirit whose elements are fire and volcanic stone, and that the power-with-awareness in the spirit stone is distinct and particular to that single object.

At this point, the rhythm of the drumming changed, summoning the workshop participants to return, so I didn't have the opportunity to proceed more deeply into this fascinating issue. As my awareness began to shift, I offered my *aloha* once again to the great spirit before me. I valued her for honoring me with her presence, requested that she visit with me from time to time, and asked that she continue to watch over me and bless my family and me with her power and protection. Once again, I saw her smile.

Then the drumming stopped, and I opened my eyes in the

workshop room. I could no longer see her, but I could still feel her presence. I went to the bathroom during the break and looked in the mirror. My face was red from the nose down, as though I were sunburned. By the end of the day, it had faded.

It was also during this first training session that I was able to further explore my personal place of power, my secret garden in the dream world, and once again, I received some real surprises.

In my shamanic journeywork, I experience the spirit worlds as a great three-leveled system with worlds above this one and worlds below. These realities are dreamlike and subjective in nature, and are simultaneously levels of awareness and levels of experience. By shifting my awareness, I effectively change my level of experience, in the process shifting from one level of reality to another. This reveals that these realities can also be understood as levels of conscious-ness, including, of course, the level of ordinary reality in which we live our lives on an ongoing day-to-day basis.

In the classic Upper Worlds are found the luminous levels inhabited by the gods and goddesses, the spiritual heroes and heroines of the past, and those higher powers beyond solar and plan-etary development. The Upper Worlds are the source of the Judeo-Christian-Islamic concept of Heaven or Paradise. If a shaman wishes to access Jesus of Nazareth or connect with the spiritual essence of the Buddha, they would journey to the Upper Worlds. There seem to be many different levels, and as shamans of all tra-ditions and all times have discovered, the Upper Worlds are where the spirit teachers reside.

Below the physical plane of everyday existence are the mythic Lower Worlds—the great cosmic regions visited by shamans for tens of millennia in order to access the spirits of nature and to connect with mystical power, among other things. To find the wolf or the bear spirit or make contact with the spirit of the oak or a medicinal herb, one would go to the Lower Worlds, and as vision-aries across time have learned, this is where the spirit helpers tend to be found.

The Place of Power

In between the Lower and Upper Worlds are the Middle Worlds of human dreaming. These are the places we go into when we dream at night, and many cultures believe that these are also the levels in which we find ourselves immediately after the death experience—the Bardo states of the Tibetan Buddhists, or the Purgatory/Kamaloca of the Christian mystics. It is in these levels that my secret garden is located.

As Nainoa had revealed to Hakai, the ordinary-reality aspect of this place is on the island of Hawai'i, a site at Kealakekua Bay where I used to go with my family on a daily basis when we lived in the islands. An opportunity to visit its dream aspect appeared later in the week. Once again, I was lying on my Navajo rug, with Michael and Christina providing the powerful assist with the drum. I merged with the sound, instructed my *ku* to open the inner doorway, and as the power sensations swept into me, the primary focus of my conscious awareness shifted from here to there. It was very fast, like changing channels on a television.

My vision came up as I arrived on the massive stone platform of the *heiau*—a prehistoric Hawaiian temple that overlies a dense concentration of *mana* in the earth below it. In my dreaming, the surface of this *heiau* includes a *hale mana*—a house of power in which I keep various things. There is also an altar of fine-grained black basalt, a separate altar (or *lele*) for offerings to my spirit helpers, and various carved post images representing the major Hawaiian deities—Lono, the fruitful; Ku, the powerful; Kane, the creator (symbolized by a standing stone); and Kanaloa, the spirit of the deep ocean and the sustainer of life. There is also a smaller vertical stone, a water-smooth *ku'ula* that stands on the *heiau* today.

To me, these images also represent aspects of the human soul cluster—Lono, the conscious *uhane* soul/self and inner director; Ku, the subconscious *unihipili* soul/self and inner servant; Kane, the creative *aumakua* oversoul; and Kanaloa, the enlightened state when all three souls are in balance—fully formed, fully experienced, and fully awake.

I looked around me and took in the full experience of this

marvelous place. To the west lay Kealakekua Bay and beyond, the vast expanse of the Pacific where Kanaloa lives. I walked to the edge of the *heiau* and looked down at the crescent of sandy beach backed by a broad terrace of water-shaped boulders out of which coconut palms and red-leafed *kamani* trees were growing. This was where I had found Kapohaku'ki'ihele, the spirit stone, many years before. A short distance inland, I saw the pond of fresh water inhabited by the *mo'o*, a water spirit. The ordinary-reality aspect of this pond is called Wailokoali'i, and it is one of the gateways that I often use to go to the Lower World. I looked up and saw the huge cliff that wraps around the bay. To the east, the monumental mass of the volcano Mauna Loa rose into the clouds.

All of my senses were kicking in so that my experience of this place was becoming increasingly vivid. I could smell the salt of the ocean and the celery-like scent of the trees from the forest behind the *heiau*. I could hear the light sea breeze rattling the palms, as well as the ceaseless pulse of the waves breaking on the beach. I could feel the sun on my skin and the roughness of the lava stones under my feet. I thought about Hakai's revelations concerning his own secret garden, specifically about how he could change his garden to suit his needs. As I looked around at the surface of the *heiau*, I realized that I had done that very thing. As far as I knew, the ordinary aspect of the site lacked the *hale mana*, the altars, the standing stone, and the post images I had created with my intentionality.

An idea appeared within my mind. It would be nice to have a house in my garden. I had always wanted to have a place at the beach, and this seemed like a perfect opportunity. I went over to the slab of smooth black basalt that served me as an altar and lay down on it. I closed my eyes and erased my thoughts. Then I created a visualization—an image of the house just as I would like it to be. I began with a stone house platform much like the *heiau* but smaller. I imagined a crew of workers constructing it under the direction of a master stone worker at the edge of the pond near a big tamarind I knew was growing there. Then I proceeded to design the house on the platform, and as the thoughtform was transformed into reality by the same construction crew, I drew on the *mana* of the *heiau* to invest the image with power.

For long moments, I dreamed my house into existence, crowning the edifice with a tall thatched roof in the Hawaiian style. Then another thought appeared. I would need a caretaker to live in my house when I was not there. At this instant, I recalled Hakai saying that there was a powerful spirit that lived in his garden. I cleared my mind and put out a request to the spirit in my garden—that it provide a caretaker for my house. Then I opened my eyes, rose from the altar, and walked over to the edge of the *heiau*.

There, beyond the pond, was another smaller stone platform surmounted by my house, partially concealed by the trees. I could clearly see part of its tall, thatched roof as well as a section of a broad lanai. Excitement rose within me. The magic seemed to have worked. This would be my personal getaway place in the Middle World of dream where I could go to restore myself. I recalled Hakai saying that the garden could also be a useful place in which to do healing work for others.

I descended the stone steps of the *heiau* and walked around the pond, noting that there were a few orange flowers from the *kou* trees floating on its surface. I paused and plucked a scarlet hibiscus blossom from a bush and placed it on the water, an offering to the water-spirit. Then I strode into the shade of the trees and approached my house for the first time.

I climbed the stone steps and unlatched the gate, surveying the house with satisfaction. It was just as I had imagined it. I crossed the lanai and opened the door. My eyes roved with delight over the details of the central room, from the smooth hardwood floor to the exposed, carved wooden beams holding up the roof. Along one side was a raised sleeping platform covered with finely woven pandanus mats, and in the floor's center was a rectangular, recessed firepit for cooking, and heating oneself on cool nights. I walked over to look out one of the windows, and there, on a smaller stone platform near the house, I saw the dream aspect of the spirit stone, its pointed end crowned with several white shell *leis*. On a low altar before it

was a scarlet hibiscus blossom. Surprise surged through me. I
hadn't put it there . . . then who . . .?

At this moment, I became aware of a presence, and turning, I
saw a woman standing backlit in the doorway behind me. She was
holding a large, flat wooden bowl or tray filled with what appeared
to be fresh lychees. I had never met another human being in my
spirit garden before, and my first take was to wonder if someone
else had found their way into this place in their dreaming.

I made a gesture of welcome, and she moved gracefully into the
room. Now I could see her clearly. Before me stood a woman of
medium height with a *lei* of ferns and orange flowers from the *kou*
trees wrapped around her head. Her dark hair was worn long, con-
cealing most of her shoulders and chest. A colorful *pareu* was
wrapped around her lower body in the Tahitian style. Her dark eyes
were regardingly me solemnly. She was not a young girl, nor was
she old. She was quite beautiful, with classic Polynesian features.
There was something vaguely familiar about her. It was as though
we had met before, but I couldn't recall when or where.

"Welcome," I said, somewhat formally. "My name is Hank
Wesselman, and I think of this place as my secret garden, as my personal place of power in the dream world to which I come from time
to time to accomplish various things. Might I inquire as to who you
are and how you found your way here?" As I said these words, a
memory from my childhood suddenly emerged from my *ku*, a recollection of a visit to the Metropolitan Museum of Art in New York.
This was (and is) one of my favorite places. As a boy, I was capti-
vated by its antiquities, especially the Egyptian collections.

I must have been about eight or nine years old when my
mother and I found ourselves upstairs in the section of the
museum that holds the paintings of the French Impressionists
and Post-Impressionists. My mother was a painter, and she
introduced me that afternoon to Renoir and Monet, Pissarro and
Van Gogh. But there was one painting in that great collection that
drew me beyond all the others—Paul Gauguin's image of two Tahitian women. One of them was standing, barebreasted, holding a

large, flat platter of fruit or flowers.

All this passed through my mind in an instant as I realized that the woman standing before me strongly resembled the girl in Gauguin's painting. Then the moment passed as she stooped and placed her bowl on a low table, her motion parting her hair and revealing her breasts. Like the girl in the painting, her nipples were almost the same color as the fruit. Then she stood once more, her dark eyes regarding me with gravity.

"*Bonjour, monsieur. Je m'appelle Tehura,*" she replied in French, reinforcing my growing conviction that this was indeed a Tahitian woman and that she could well be the woman from the painting. "My name is Tehura, and I have come at your request. How may I be of service to you?" I was stunned. I had momentarily forgotten my request to the spirit of my garden. *The caretaker of my property had arrived.* I accessed my limited knowldge of French and asked her if she spoke English. For the first time, she smiled, her face filling with light.

"But of course. Long ago, when I was young girl," she began in somewhat broken English, "I had a lover, an American sailor who came to my island. He taught me to speak the English." She paused and looked around the room approvingly. "*Quelle belle maison*—what a beautiful house."

I reached down and took one of the lychees from her tray. I cracked its thin, spikey shell, exposing the glistening white fruit within. I popped it into my mouth, savoring its slightly astringent, grapefruit-like flavor before spitting out the shining black seed and tossing it out the window. I reached down again and took a handful. I am very fond of fresh-picked lychees.

"Where did you get these delicious lychees, Tehura?" I asked.

"Come, I show you," she replied, taking my hand. We left the house, crossed the lanai, and descended the steps. As we passed the spirit stone, Tehura paused and bowed, holding her hands palms outward toward the stone in a gesture of reverence. Then she walked on, gaily picking a hibiscus blossom from a bush and placing it in her hair.

She took me inland on a trail through the ancient forest that ascends the slopes of the mountain to the east. This woodland is filled with *keawe* and *opiuma* trees, coconut palms and monkey-pods. Many of the tree trunks are blanketed with the huge leaves of monstera vines, and *taro* grows in the low places. There are *ti* plants everywhere, and as I paused to smell the spike of some flowering white ginger, I saw the buttress-rooted trunk of a towering cotton tree, its branches high above loaded with green pods.

I looked around me with wonder. Here I was in the dream world walking through an enchanted forest with an equally enchanting woman, an exotic Tahitian who seemed to have come to life out of a painting I had seen as a boy. I was suddenly aware that I could still hear Michael and Christina drumming. I looked at the woman walking with me and wondered if she could hear it, too.

I never found out because Tehura suddenly pointed with delight. There ahead of us was a dark green lychee tree loaded with clusters of the dusky, rose-colored fruit. She picked some and gave them to me. My mind filled with questions as I sat down on a broad stone below the tree.

"Tehura . . . where did you come from and how did you get here?"

Her eyes regarded me levelly for long moments, then she said, "I came from my island far to the south. I was summoned. I came on a canoe. The crew dropped me on the beach below the *marae*. Then they left." She stopped speaking as though her answer was complete. I was aware that she had used the Tahitian word *marae* instead of the Hawaiian word *heiau*, reinforcing her statement of her place of origin.

"Tehura," I persisted, "who summoned you? And have we ever met before?" Once again, she regarded me with gravity. Then she spoke, her words a mixture of French and English.

"I was born long ago and lived my life on the island of Tahiti, far to the south across the ocean. I had a good life filled with friends and family, joys and sorrows. At the end of my life, I went into a dream and didn't wake up." Her eyes squinted with effort, as though she were trying to express something she understood well but for which she lacked concepts in English. "I have been in the dream ever since," she continued. "I live in the dreaming of my island, for islands dream, too, you know, just as we humans do."

Then Tehura looked at me strangely and said something totally unexpected. "Sometimes in my dreaming, I can see into a room. It is as though I can look through a window into this very big room with many paintings on the walls. There is nothing else in this room, only paintings. Sometimes the room is empty, but often, I can see many people walking around in the room. They come and look through the window at me, as though they can see me, but when I try to talk with them, they never answer. I found this frightening at first, but I have gotten used to it. It is a very strange dream."

For long moments, I was simply speechless at the implications of what she had just revealed. "Tehura," I finally said, "did you ever meet a painter on your island, a Frenchman who came from Paris?"

"Ahh, but of course . . . it was Monsieur Paul. He used to make paintings of me and my friends. He was my lover until he went away and didn't return." Her eyes turned sad. "He was a very unhappy man. That one had many sorrows inside him. I tried to make him happy . . ." Her words drifted off as her eyes filled with tears.

For long moments, her eyes flowed freely, the tears coursing down her brown face. My thoughts were filled with questions, but this didn't seem an appropriate moment. Instead, I got up from the stone and took her hand, drawing her back down the trail toward the beach. We walked in silence until we could see the pond through the trees. To one side rose the stone wall of the *heiau*. Tehura dried her tears then and turned to me.

"I was summoned to come to this place in my dreaming. I did not know who was calling me or why, but the request was so strong that I had to come. Now that I am here, I know who called me, but I still don't know why."

"Who called you, Tehura?"

Her eyes turned to regard the massive shape of Mauna Loa rising like a dark wall to the east. "There is a powerful spirit that lives in this mountain. Like me, she came from the south long ago. It was she who called me."

Pele! Of course . . . she was the spirit of this place. I thought about my meeting with her only days before and understood. But how had she known of my boyhood attraction for the girl in the painting? It was at this moment that I heard the rhythm of the drumming change, calling me back.

"Tehura, would you like to be the caretaker of my garden? Would you like to live here in my house and care for it in my absence?" Her eyes began to sparkle as I said this, and she smiled broadly in response. I took this as a yes. The drum was beckoning, and I had no time to continue.

"You are welcome here. Please stay. I will return soon," I promised, "but for now, I must go." I turned to climb the steps of the *heiau*, then paused and plucked one more scarlet hibiscus blossom. I ascended quickly to the top, then walked across the platform and placed the flower on the altar, an offering to the spirit who lives in the mountain. Then I closed my eyes as the drumming ceased, and my primary focus shifted back to the workshop room.

I thought about this journey a great deal as the week came to a close. I was very much aware that a Western-trained psychiatrist might categorize what I had experienced as a fantasy or daydream, and conclude that I was just simply making the whole thing up with my creative imagination. When I created the thoughtform of my house, I was indeed using my creative imagination in combination with my focused intentionality, but what of Tehura? What about the things she said that I *hadn't* created?

Once again, the cognitive investigator might be inclined to say that in these instances, it was my subconscious at work, filling in details, making the whole illusion more interesting, and here is where I beg to differ.

Through my investigations of the inner worlds over the past 15 years, I have come to understand that the creative imagination is a function of the conscious mind/ego. The subconscious *ku* is not creative, but like the inner hard drive of a computer, one of its primary functions is memory. In this sense, it is incapable of making anything up—it can only inform the egoic inner director of what it already knows. But it can observe and send what it perceives to the conscious ego.

In my shamanic journeywork, I often begin the session by instructing my *ku* to bring up the memory of a place I have experienced in either ordinary or nonordinary reality. Then I become the bridge between my here and my there. I simply instruct my *ku* to open the inner doorway, and I then go through it to that place. My *ku* is the aspect of myself through which the journey is both experienced and perceived, yet while I am in these subjective dream environments, my inner director can still make decisions.

This means that I can determine the course of the action to a certain extent, but there comes a point when things begin to happen that I am not creating with my intentionality, and it is then that I understand quite clearly that I have shifted into a level of reality and experience that has its own existence separate from myself. This is what it means to *vision*.

I have discovered through repeated visits to my secret garden that all the elements that make it up, both animate and inanimate, are conscious and alive to some degree, and all can be communicated with for greater understanding. Like Hakai in Nainoa's time and place, I have learned through direct experience that when I change my garden, my life changes in response. This is a place of extraordinary power and beauty in which I now do much of my spiritual work, and so I frequently invite my spirit helpers, as well as my spirit teacher, to meet with me there in order to accomplish various things. When I do healing work for others, for example, I sometimes invite their spiritual essences to come into my garden, where my spirit helpers and I can work on them.

Tehura continues to live in my garden as its *kahu*, or honored caretaker. I would like to add that she is not some dream lover or manifested fantasy from childhood. I have come to accept that she is the soul-spirit of a wise Polynesian woman who lived over a hundred years ago and who has become a close and trusted friend. Often when I am overly stressed or my physical body is in pain from held tension, I go to my garden, and Tehura works on me, relieving the pain by releasing the tension with her strong hands.

Like Hakai, I have come to suspect that all of us have such a personal place of power in the inner worlds of dream, and in sharing this information with you, the reader, I encourage each of you to find it.

I wondered if I would have a connection with Nainoa during that week, but the time was full and the next contact didn't happen until later in the fall. I have a favorite place along the American River near Sacramento where Jill and I are fond of walking with our children. It is a wild place, an "island" of grassy riverine woodlands surrounded by an ocean of sprawling suburbs—an island populated by deer and wild turkeys, woodpeckers and owls, and dominated by grasses and majestic valley oaks. When my family and I walk there, along the stony terraces next to the rushing river, I think about the waterspirit that lives in the pond in my spirit garden, and I almost always find a flower to offer.

Perhaps it was in response to being out in this slice of nature that inspired the next journey to Nainoa. Then again, perhaps it was in response to Jill.

CHAPTER EIGHT

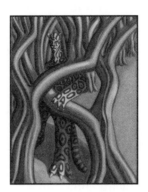

Fourth Journey: The Spirit in the Forest

IT WAS EARLY AFTERNOON, and Nainoa was walking in the forest beyond the walls of the center. The bell-like call of a bird floated in the still air. His eyes scanned the green roof of the canopy high above, and he saw movement—a group of red monkeys eating leaves. They took note of his passage, and the deafening roar of the males reverberated through the dim light. He calculated the distance and smiled. If he'd had his bow, there would have been monkey meat for dinner.

As he walked on, he suddenly felt the presence. He had been aware of it to varying degrees throughout the day. He waited for the flow of thoughts he knew would begin, his eyes following a flock of green parrots as they rocketed by. *The* dorajuadiok *material,* he thought—this might be a good time to review some of that amazing information.

He thought about the concept of *nohona*—existence. When he

and the American had been drawn into connection with the *dora-juadiok*, that awesome power-being had shown them the birth of existence through the partitioning of *aka*, the universal, promordial stuff out of which everything, everywhere, was formed—into *ao holo'okoa*, the realm of the manifested Universe; into *mana*, the universal power; and into *ike*, the awareness of each for the other. The patterned flowing of these three elements—matter, energy, and awareness—could be a good way to define existence, and according to the American, this flow had been going on for truly immense amounts of time.

The *dorajuadiok* had also revealed that the appearance of life was part of this patterned flowing, and they had been taken on a journey in which they were shown that living beings of varying degrees of complexity exist everywhere in the Universe. The implication had been clear: The creation of life is what the Universe is designed to do, and it is through the medium of living beings that the Universe is creating its own mind-spirit, a process that is going on everywhere.

Nainoa recalled his first connection with the *dorajuadiok* out at the Spirit Hills in the Ennu lands to the east of the mountains. The American's consciousness had been merged with his during that dramatic encounter, and he had asked the powerful entity whether a creator existed, one whose intentionality had brought all existence into being. There had been a response that conveyed a clear sense that the towering spirit didn't know—that this was and is the great mystery of existence.

Nainoa crossed a fern-covered hillside, then paused as he entered a sunlit glade. One of the gigantic forest trees had toppled recently, blown down by a storm, creating a hole in the canopy through which the sun streamed downwards. The huge tree lay prostrate on the downhill side of the trail, its massive trunk still embraced by a strangler fig. Its fall had cleared a swath of smaller trees, and Nainoa could see down and out across the sloping terrain to another hillside beyond.

He approached the tree's huge root ball and studied the twisted mass carefully. It was more than three times his height. The sunlight gleamed off a piece of dark green glass protruding from the earth among the roots. Nainoa used a stick to excavate around the shard, revealing that it was part of a bottle. As he worked it free from the roots' grip, he found to his delight that it was an unbroken one, filled with soil.

He turned the bottle over and over in his hands, marveling at its symmetrical shape. It was an artifact of the once-great American civilization, its surface frosted by its long burial in the ground. The Americans had been here, right where he was standing now. Perhaps there had been a town in this very place. He looked around at the forest. There was no other evidence of human occupation. The forest had covered everything. He looked at the bottle again and felt a sense of contact with the long-gone people of this place. He wondered what the bottle had once contained.

An indistinct track meandering downhill away from the main trail attracted his attention. It probably led to a stream where the forest animals went to drink. He worked the stick into the bottle, but the earth was too compacted to extract easily. Perhaps he would walk down to the stream to wash it out. The call of the bird sounded again from that direction. Nainoa smiled as he took the track. It was almost as if he were being summoned.

By the time he got to the bottom of the hill, he had slipped in the moist earth twice, and his yellow cloak and *malo* were stained with mud. He grinned ruefully and looked up and down the rushing stream. Perhaps he could find a spot to wash his clothing articles and dry them in the sun before he returned to the center. He made a decision and turned upstream, walking along the track that followed the watercourse.

The land ascended steeply, and Nainoa found himself enclosed in a narrow canyon with steep walls that had been cut by the stream. The track continued along one side, and before long, the canyon opened into a place where the terrain flattened out. There, he discovered a long pool with a dense grove of bamboo growing out of the rocky slope along one side and a sandbar along the other. A small waterfall cascaded into the upper end of the pool, and next to it, he saw a wide shelf of stone that had been scoured smooth by the stream and which was now exposed above the water level. Trees overhung the lower end of the pool, creating deep shade, but the ledge was in the sun, so it was dry and warm. It was just what he was looking for.

Nainoa had never been to this place before, and he studied the scene before him carefully. There were fish in the deep end of the pool, but he saw no sign of crocodiles, nor did there seem to be any of the giant water serpents. He walked along the sandbar, and his trained eye picked out the prints of pigs, deer, monkeys, large forest rodents, and various birds. Near the stone shelf he saw the unmistakable pugmarks of a tiger. The prints were many days old, overlaid by the tracks of other forest creatures. His eyes scanned the surrounding forest carefully. If the tiger was there, it was highly unlikely that he would see it.

He closed his eyes and allowed his consciousness to expand, searching his surroundings for the mindshape he had come to know so well. Within his mind's eye, he formed an image of his spirit helper and put out the request—for protection and support . . . protection and support. Then he invited the spirit to approach, to join him and enjoy the locale.

Nothing in particular appeared in his thoughts in response, so he opened his eyes and looked around, observing the pool and the forest closely once again. The crown of one of the trees overhanging the water was filled with yellow flowers. The place had a dreamlike quality to it, somewhat like the American's secret garden. He wondered briefly if he had stumbled through some doorway into his own enchanted place in the inner worlds of dream.

He stripped off his cloak and loincloth and waded into the pool where he cleaned the earth from his clothing. Then he spread the clothing articles out on the sun-warmed ledge to dry, and attempted to wash out the bottle. The earth within it was hard, so he put it in the water to soak, wedging it securely between some stones.

On impulse, Nainoa took a swim in the pool, wondering if there was a waterspirit in residence. He was very much in his ordinary state of consciousness and felt no response to the thought, so he climbed onto the ledge and stretched out in the afternoon sun. A cloud of blue butterflies arrived to drink from the sand at the water's edge. He watched them hover in the sunlight, then closed his eyes and listened to sound of the waterfall. The warm stone under his body relaxed him, and he felt the familiar dreamy state descending. He was almost asleep when something alerted him, and he opened his eyes.

To his amazement, there, on the other end of the ledge near the cataract, were two figures. One of them was a short, rather stocky old man dressed in shabby, patched clothing, his long gray hair gathered into an unkempt topknot at the crown of his head. Next to him was a spotted tiger stretched out in the sun. The man was sitting crosslegged with his eyes closed and appeared to be in deep meditation. The large cat's eyes were closed as well, and it seemed to be asleep.

Nainoa felt his astonishment increase. He had not heard them arrive, but then, maybe the sound of the waterfall had masked their passage. Was he dreaming, or was this for real? Should he speak or maintain silence? As these questions moved through his mind, he was startled to find that the man's eyes were now open and regarding him with alert interest. They were similar to William's eyes, but even longer. The man's flat, rather moon-shaped face was covered with a sparse, untrimmed beard. Nainoa could see that he was smiling.

Nainoa wondered uneasily if the man was a spirit, and much to his surprise, the wild-looking individual suddenly burst out laughing. Nainoa recalled that he was naked and assumed that this was the source of the man's mirth. As if in response to this thought, the old man slowly stood up and gracefully divested himself of his patched clothing. His jacket had curious wide sleeves, and he was wearing pants. When the old man was naked, he stretched his arms high over his head, let out a loud fart, and jumped into the pool with a joyous whoop.

The man surfaced, blew a mouthful of water at the tiger, who looked vaguely annoyed, then swam strongly down the length of the pool, executing a leaping turn before churning back again, fish scattering before his energetic progess. The spotted cat watched his antics with a flat, bored stare, then glanced at Nainoa and closed its eyes.

There was no question in Nainoa's mind. The animal was his spirit helper, and he had come with company.

The old man hauled himself up on the ledge again, shook himself like an animal, pointedly dripping water on the tiger, then sat down naked on the rock again. He glanced at Nainoa as if noticing him for the first time. "Nice day," he observed offhandedly, using the speech of the common people. Nainoa gathered his wits and offered a somewhat formal reply.

"My greetings to you in return, esteemed sir. My name is Nainoa Kaneohe, and I am currently a guest at the monastery in the Place of Refuge located in the Pukui land division. I am fond of walking in the forest during the afternoons, but I have never been to this place before. I hope I am not intruding. You seem quite at home here." As he spoke, he carefully looked the old man over once again. He was not a chief, of that he was certain. He had never seen him before. Perhaps he was a hunter or an artisan who worked in the marketplace in town.

"My greetings in return to you, esteemed sir," the old man offered cheerfully, mimicking him. "And my name?" He leaned over and scratched his rear end vigorously, then seemed to come to a conclusion. "I have had many names. Some people have called me Crazyhead, some called me Stupid. My mother had her own pet name for me, of course." He gave Nainoa a knowing look and grinned. "Then there were the girls in town. They had some pretty descriptive terms for good old me." He broke off into another gale of wild laughter that sounded just a little over the edge.

When he had recovered from his burst of emotion, he wiped the tears of mirth from his long eyes and said, "You can call me anything you like. Or you could call me Palianu. It means 'cold cliff' in the old language of your people and is similar to one of my names of long ago when I lived among my own people. The name suits me well, as I no longer live in the world of men, but prefer living in wild, mountanous places like this one. Most just shorten my name to Pali. What are you doing at the monastery?"

Nainoa was completely taken aback by this unexpected response. Could it be that he had stumbled across another indigenous American? "To what people are you referring, if I may ask?" The old man simply shrugged and gestured vaguely toward the west. When no further explanation was forthcoming, Nainoa concluded that the man was probably a forest recluse who had gone a bit crazy living in isolation.

Nainoa came to a decision and gave the old man a short description of his background, including a brief account of his long walk the year before. He concluded by telling him about the unfortunate incident that had led to the death of his kinsman and enemy and how that had led to his current extended stay at the center, where he was being cleansed of his unknowing contribution to the whole affair.

At the beginning of this account, as if sensing that the story would be lengthy, Pali had leaned back and reclined upon the tiger, crossing his arms behind his head and using the large carnivore much as one would use a pillow. The spotted cat seemed to take this as a given, and simply closed its eyes and went back to sleep.

When Nainoa summed up his tale with a description of his spirit helper's role in his enemy's demise, the old man hooted with delight and vigorously scratched the top of the big cat's head. Then he turned to Nainoa and said knowingly, "You have to be very careful with tigers. They make wonderful companions, especially in the forest, but if someone crosses you and you get pissed off at them . . ." He left the thought hanging and glanced warily at his feline companion.

Nainoa then gave Pali an account of how he himself had come into relationship with the spirit of the spotted tiger, concluding by asking the old man about his own obvious connection with the beast. Pali glanced again at the tiger, then looked wistful as he replied,

"Many years ago, maybe hundreds, maybe thousands of years, I dunno . . ." He looked uncertain, then shrugged again and went on. "I used to work occasionally in a monastery in the mountains, in the kitchens where a friend of mine had a job. I used to do chores for the monks, washing rice bowls, sweeping floors, carrying water, chopping wood, that sort of thing. They often asked me if I wanted to live at the monastery, but I declined their invitation. They were awfully stuffy with their altars and robes and ceremonies and such. I lived in a cave in the cliffs not too far away, which suited me just fine, but it was great having the monastery nearby. The monks gave me things I needed, useful things like candles, needles and thread, occasionally ink for writing poems or a bowl of rice—"

"Rice?" Nainoa interrupted.

Pali looked at him with uncertainty, as though he were thick-headed, then shrugged once again and continued. "The Governor of the region where the monastery was located was a well-known spiritual master of high degree. We became friends, and it was through him that I came into relationship with the tiger." He squinted his eyes as though seeking the information from some vast inner trove. "It was a striped tiger, a big one, but today, a spotted tiger came to my cave and invited me to come for a walk in the forest. I assume that it was to meet with you."

Nainoa's pulse quickened at this revelation, and he pinched himself to see if he was dreaming, which he suspected he was, yet the pinch had no effect. The old man noticed his gesture and exploded into crazy laughter once again. This seemed to annoy the tiger, which opened its eyes wide, then abruptly got up and walked off into the forest, leaving the two of them alone on the ledge above the pool.

"So what else are you doing at the monastery?" old Pali asked.

Nainoa thought about the question, then offered a summary of his conversation with the Kahuna Nui that morning.

"So you are studying the nature of your self, and particularly the immortal, transcendent self, the aspect that you call *aumakua*?" Pali inquired.

Nainoa nodded, and the old man recrossed his legs, settling once again into a meditative posture. All traces of his erratic behavior abruptly ceased. The fact that he was still naked seemed completely immaterial. Nainoa was aware that the old recluse, if that's what he indeed was, had suddenly taken on his aspect of power.

"This is a worthy subject for discussion," Pali began. "Most worthy." He closed his eyes and remained immobile for a short period. Then he reemerged and began to speak.

"In my experience, most formal religious orders tend to create sets of rules and regulations that students have to follow rigorously. I have observed that such practices can indeed lead to realization of the true nature of the self, *but . . .*" he broke off with a dramatic gesture, "such practice usually leads to an intellectual appreciation of what illumination is all about, rather than an actual experiencing of the process itself.

"If the student takes refuge in this intellectual acceptance of what is, then they have already lost the way. We cannot achieve the deep mystic illumination by memorizing sacred texts or practicing lengthy rituals. We must *experience* life, and as your bigshot *kahuna* said to you this morning, this experiencing is intensely personal. When I used to go to the monastery, I would see all those young initiates looking detached and oh so holy, and I always wanted to tear their robes off and take them down to the bordello in town. Now that's where you can begin study of *the way.*" Pali made a lewd gesture and broke into another wild laugh before settling down and continuing his train of thought.

"True realization cannot be achieved through cutting ourselves off from the flow of life by joining some grand poobah religious order. This actually damages us. It deadens us by restricting the flow and narrowing our personal experience. By doing this, we distance ourselves from the universal within us. There is no value in withdrawing from the world and becoming some holy so-and-so.

"To the contrary," Pali continued, his hand slicing though the air like a knife, "we must discover the true nature of ourselves through total immersion in the world around us, in its labors and pleasures, its joys and sorrows, its hopes and dreams. It is then that we begin to understand the nature of the great pattern, as well as our place within it, and *that* is when true illumination begins."

Pali paused in his thoughtline to admire some orange dragonflies patrolling the air above him. "Each of us must merge; we must fit ourselves into the universal that exists all around us. When our consciousness and lifeway find their place within this universality, we begin to discover the universality within ourselves. And that is when the inward search for the self commences.

"You see," he turned to look directly into Nainoa's eyes, "our growing understanding of the nature of everything around us refines us; it sensitizes us, and it is then that we begin to develop standards of personal behavior consistent with our increasing realization."

As Nainoa listened openmouthed to the older man, the awareness grew within him that this was not some deluded commoner who had taken up residence in the forest. To the contrary, Pali spoke like a master *kahuna* mystic.

"My friend the Governor used to say that there can be no realization without action," Pali went on, stabbing the air with a finger, "and there can be no action without realization. The Governor was a highly illuminated person, but he didn't withdraw from the world. He served his people by being an exceptional administrator. He expressed a sensitivity, a gentleness, and a simplicity in all his actions. Because of this, he was highly successful in his dealings with people, a fact that used to frustrate his fellow politicians at court to no end."

Nainoa was about to interrupt the old man to ask *what* governor, *what* court, *what* politicians, when Pali suddenly grinned at him mischeviously and added, "His relationship with the tiger used to scare the shit out of the monks. Whenever the Governor came to visit the monastery, the tiger would come out of the forest. We would find its footprints in the morning." His words drifted off again as he became lost in reminiscence. Then he shrugged, adding, "That's how I came into relationship with the tiger." The old man's demeanor shifted again as he returned to his thoughtline.

"The Governor used to say that realization is a way of seeing, a way of being in the world. As realization grows within us, it creates this natural sensitivity, one that encourages us to look within and discover the nature of our different selves. As our realization grows, it doesn't require that those around us change for the better, but it does insist upon certain standards for ourselves—qualities such as thoughtfulness, kindness, an appreciation for everything and everyone around us, and above all, an understanding that everything is holy, from the smallest ant to the mightiest mountain.

"When the inward search for the self begins, when we become aware of the different aspects that make up what we think of as our personality, we begin to have those spontaneous flashes of insight that the Governor used to call the blinking of the dragon's eye. These episodes of expanded understanding lead us to become aware of the flaws in our own character, enabling us to have a good look at our own shit."

Pali laughed boisterously, then continued, "And when we do, we begin to develop away from our negative tendencies and start to live a lifeway directed toward the greater good. This, of course, is usually beyond the understanding of most of our friends and associates, and they begin to think we have gone crazy. When you step onto the spiritual path, you can expect very little in the way of support from those around you." More laughter.

The old man then squinted his long eyes until they were mere slits, and observed with mock piety, "Of course, we occasionally fail in our quest. There are always the girls in town, you know . . ." Wild laughter. "But our growing realization helps us to accept our inevitable backslidings without personal condemnation or despair. And sometimes a good screw is exactly what you need to help sort things out." Pali cackled lustily.

"But let us return to the beginning of our talk, to our concern with the transcendent self. The inner search inevitably brings us to the point where we become aware of the spiritual source from which our current personality is derived. And as your *kahuna* friend

117

said, once we become aware of our *aumakua* aspect, our increasing realization actually attracts it, and it begins to grow within us. The Governor used to refer to it as the adept self, or the Maitreya self, and as such, he told me that it is the true meaning of the universal Messiah that people throughout history keep waiting around for. The coming savior *is* the transcendent self."

"*Adept? Maitreya? Messiah?* These terms are not familiar to me—" Nainoa broke in.

"They're just words," Pali gestured with impatience. "What's important is that once this contact has been established, the growing bond with the transcendent self gives us access to universal power and unlimited knowledge, as you have begun to discover. And this combination of power and knowledge has the potential to project us into undreamed-of levels of awareness and experience."

Nainoa was silent as he considered the implications of what the old man had just revealed. Then he came to a decision and told Pali about his spontaneous mystic connections across time and distance with the consciousness of one of his ancestors.

"That's exactly what I mean by undreamed-of levels of experience," the old man chortled gleefully. "In each lifetime, we develop a new multileveled personality, one that we tend to think of as a singularity. But in reality, each new personality is a collective entity that includes the impulses gathered or created in different lives, in different times. We are not one; we are many, and we can make contact with any numbers of past personalities simply through practice combined with sustained concentration. But first we must understand and accept that such an experience is possible. *And,* we must discover the nature of our inner spirit being.

"Within each of us can be found the universality of the transcendent self. This is the personal spiritual aspect through which it is possible to connect with the greater universality of everything, everywhere. As you have found, it is through your transcendent self that connection with your ancestor is possible."

"My ancestor," Nainoa put in, "is interested in human origins. He said to me once that humanity began existence as a shambling, bipedal ape much like an atom in space."

"Ape? Atom?" inquired the old man curiously.

"Just words," Nainoa gestured with impatience, mimicking Pali's earlier reluctance to explain. "What's important is that my ancestor says it is through the *aumakua*, through the transcendent being, as you call it, that we as individuals can actually achieve space. Our consciousness is identified with space. And through spirit-walking, it becomes space."

Pali laughed his crazy laugh and responded, "Your ancestor knows. And so, apparently, do you, my young friend. The presence that we sometimes become aware of, but cannot see, is the transcendent self. Once it has been realized, it lives within us. It rarely speaks. It never criticizes or judges or makes demands. It never tells us what to do. It merely sits within us, through countless lifetimes, waiting for the moment of its liberation.

"There was a great spiritual teacher who lived in a fabled land called India long ago," Pali went on. "His name was Gautama, but most refer to him as the Buddha."

"We have stories about such a man," Nainoa said. "We call him Kotama and sometimes refer to him as the Puka Nui, the great gate."

"Sounds like the same guy," Pali observed matter-of-factly. "Anyway, in this man's teachings, each individual's potential for realization expresses itself into the world as two principal soul forces. One is called *Manjusri*. This is the intellectual function of the mind. It includes our urge to know, and as such, it is the aspect of the self that actively investigates the great mystery of existence. Manjusri is the symbol for the spiritual seeker who walks the Universe alone, and it represents motion from the self outward toward wisdom, beauty, and truth.

"Gautama called the other soul force *Avalokiteshvara*, although the governor used to refer to it as *Kwan Yin*. This is the heart force, the emotional aspect of realization, and as such, it represents the self as the thing sought. Kwan Yin is the compassionate force within the self, the urge to be of service to everything and everyone around us. As we grow in wisdom and beauty through our searching as Manjusri, it is through our experience of Kwan Yin that we achieve unity with all of life.

"These two soul forces are actually two halves of a whole. Manjusri expresses motion outward into the world around us through the power of thought. Kwan Yin produces motion inward into the worlds within us through the power of feeling and emotion. And in the middle, between these two polarities, sits the mystic. The ancient image of the Buddha, seated in deep meditation, has come to symbolize complete realization in which both the Manjusri and Kwan Yin soul forces are in balance and harmony with the transcendent self. It's really through this inner spiritual aspect of ourselves that all experience is integrated into a singularity of meaning." Pali finished, looking pleased with himself.

"We Hawaiians call this state of unity *lokahi*," Nainoa contributed. "It represents the full expression and interconnection of our three principal self aspects. What you call Manjusri sounds like what we call *uhane* or *lono*; in the same manner, the Kwan Yin force that you have mentioned seems to be a function of what we call *unihipili* or the *ku*."

Both fell silent at this point, considering the shape of what had just been said. Nainoa harbored a growing suspicion that the old man was a spirit, or rather the spirit of some old nature mystic from long ago and far away. He wondered how he had understood what Pali had said so clearly. It had seemed as if the old man had been speaking in the language of his own people.

Pali turned to him with a smile and said, "My friend the Governor used to say that the motion outward from the self as mind, and the motion inward toward the self as heart, is actually the breathing-out and the breathing-in of the transcendent self. He also told me that realization is actually a progressive infusion of universal energy through one's three selves. These infusions are sometimes perceived as surges of mystical power accompanied by sudden expansions in our awareness and our understanding. He was very wise, that man. His name was Vengan," he concluded wistfully.

Nainoa looked at the sky and became aware of the passage of

the afternoon. Clouds were building on the hillsides to the west, revealing that it was almost time for the afternoon deluge, a predictable, almost daily occurrence during the rainy season. Pali followed his gaze and observed dryly, "You better get dressed. You can still make it back to your monastery before it rains if you hurry. And don't forget your bottle."

Nainoa rose, quickly tied on his now dry *malo* and donned his cloak, then went to the place he had stashed the bottle. The earth within it was soft now, and he began to pour it out, sloshing the water back and forth. "I would like to come here and talk with you further, Pali," he said over his shoulder as he finished rinsing the bottle.

"You will be welcome, Nainoa," came the old recluse's response. "Now that you know the way to this place, you will be able to come here anytime you want. And don't forget to give my regards to the ladies of your settlement." Pali let out another burst of wild laughter as the first peal of thunder rumbled in the distance. Nainoa looked up a moment later and found, much to his astonishment, that the ledge above the pool was empty. There was no sign of the old man. He was alone.

The thunder rumbled again. He called out a hasty good-bye, but there was no response, so he headed back downstream, clutching the bottle. As he ascended the hillside and reached the higher ground near the fallen tree, he broke into the trot espoused by the Ennu when they wanted to cover a long distance across country. The air was thick with the approaching storm.

When he emerged from the forest near the center, he could see the wall of rain approaching across the lagoon. He dashed across the small outdoor market and through the gate, giving a quick greeting to his friend the gatekeeper, then loped across the compound and entered his small room as the first fat drops began to rattle off the thatch of the roof.

As he caught his breath and watched the rain begin to come down in earnest, an interesting thought appeared in his mind.

He had found his secret garden.

CHAPTER NINE

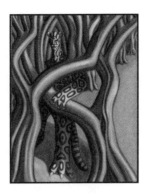

Ganduli

IN THE DAYS THAT FOLLOWED, I was able to excavate various fragments of this extraordinary dialogue from my memory banks,
recalling the conversation in chunks until I had reconstructed
it in its entirety on paper. This took time, but I eventually reached
a point where I was satisfied with the shape of what I had written.
The conceptual content of the long conversation between the two
men, including Pali's essentially Buddhist worldview, is entirely theirs.
The grammatical choice of words, syntax, and morphology is, of
course, entirely mine.

It is my custom to make detailed notes of these amazing visionary experiences as soon as possible. The very next evening, I was
lying in bed at the end of a long work day with my yellow pad across
my knees, reflecting on what I'd learned about the nature of the *transcendent self*, or as some would call it, the *higher self*. Jill was still
up, watching the late-night news in the living room, when my weari-
ness overcame me, so I turned out my bedside light and descended
into that shallow zone between waking and sleeping, where I

suddenly found myself in a state of utter bliss. The marvelous, unde-scribable ecstasy of the mystic trance state was there, but without the overwhelming sensations of power.

While in this state of rapture, I perceived something extraor-dinarily beautiful—a "something" that clearly seemed to be within myself. "It" appeared to be both geometric and organic, both fig-urative and abstract, both solid and lattice-like, both symmetrical and asymmetrical. I could see it with clarity as an objective form composed of curved, overlapping planes that were translucent with light against a misty, golden field of color. I was also very much aware that it was conscious and cognizant of my watchfulness.

My state of bliss increased into a deep, abiding tranquility, and I watched, enthralled, as the luminous object began to move, unfolding slowly in exquisite simplicity, like a flower opening. I sud-denly understood why the lotus has been chosen as a symbol for illumination. The form that I witnessed looked somewhat like this flower, a white one with off-white planes and edges. I lay there in my bed simply wonderstuck by the beauty of what I was seeing as it shifted and changed. There was absolutely no doubt in my mind that it was alive.

Jill came to bed shortly after and wrapped her long body around mine in an embrace filled with love. I slowly began to emerge from this deep state of mystic rapture, but it took 30 minutes to fully return, and when it was accomplished, she was asleep. I lay awake in the dark, reviewing what I had perceived. *What else,* I thought, *but a glimpse of my own transcendent self?* But inter-estingly, its shape was not human, nor did it look like some winged angelic being. Perhaps I was beginning to see it as it really was.[1]

It was shortly after this episode that I left my family at Christ-mastime and headed off to Ethiopia once again to rejoin the expe-dition with which I was doing research. In my hasty departure, I forgot to consult with the spirit stone in the garden, something I always did before leaving for the field. Throughout the first long day of travel across the United States, I felt chagrin and some self-criticism at my failure to do so. That evening, I transferred to a night flight to London and took some melatonin to help induce the sleep state. It was during my fitful rest on this flight that I felt something merge with me and abruptly found myself suffused by the sensations of power. I woke up in the grip of the energy and asked my *ku* who or what it was. The answer was immediate. It was the spirit stone.

As the ecstatic force held me rigid in my seat on the aircraft, I was able to achieve connection with the stone and accomplish my ritual in a long-distance manner at 35,000 feet, while heading east over the Atlantic. And during this "meeting," I had a clear sense that I was being infused with a strong injection of *mana*, power that was coming, without a doubt, through the stone. For an extended period, I simply soared on the feelings, taking them in and storing them in my body. As I emerged from this state, I recalled the card I had picked from one of several decks that Jill uses for divination work—the card for power.

I have written about my fieldwork with the international group of scientists currently working in the Middle Awash region of the Ethiopian Rift Valley, and have also reported on the nature of the discoveries that are being made there.[2] This year, before heading for the field, it seemed appropriate to express gratitude and respect by bringing a ritual offering for the spirits of this place, and especially for the spirit of all humanity. For this place, in all likelihood, was the region where humankind may have been born.

In keeping with this intention, I had extended an invitation to the members of my three-year training program, medicine people all, to send along a small personal offering. Most of them did, and in my luggage was a shopping bag of power bundles with the names and the good intentions of their makers attached to each.

When I arrived at the field camp in the remote desert country of the Afar people several days later, I discovered that it was located once again near the fossil sites along the dry sand river flanked with thorn trees and tamarisks called Ganduli. As I greeted my fellow investigators and set up my tent in the shade, I was aware that I was once again among hard-core scientists who knew nothing about shamanism and who generally held negative feelings in response to things spiritual.

I noted that there was also a lot of tension in the camp, and I realized that I had no desire to become a spectacle or activate their feelings of disdain. Indeed, the creation of negativity would have been contrary to what I was trying to achieve. I decided to "journey" to determine how to proceed in making our offerings.

My spirit helper, the leopard man, didn't wait, but approached me on that first night in my dreaming, looking very feline and fierce. In the dream, I was sitting outside my tent when the leopard materialized among the trees and went down to the waterhole we had dug in the bed of the sand river. I remained motionless while he had a drink in the moonlight, and when he was through, he strolled toward me and lay down an arm's length away with a low, guttural rattle—more of a growl than a purr. I was delighted, and as I glanced sideways into his pale eyes, I reflected that he was truly in his element here, for this was also the place where the leopards had evolved.[3]

I looked at my spotted friend and formulated a general request for assistance with the placement of the offerings, and the response was immediate. The leopard got up and walked away from the camp, and I followed. We strolled together for some distance, proceeding down the sand river until we reached a place where there was a long sandbar below a magnificent flat-topped thorn tree surrounded by tamarisks. The leopard lay down on the bar and closed his eyes. I assumed that this was to be the place, so I joined him, adopting a cross-legged posture.

I entered the deep meditation state, which, in retrospect, was precisely what I needed to do to restore my inner harmony, disrupted by jetlag and the arduous nature of getting into the field. When I emerged from meditation sometime later, I discovered that my spirit helper had shapeshifted, assuming the humanoid form from which the term "leopard man" is derived. And much to my surprise, he was emulating me, sitting in the half-lotus posture with his eyes closed and his back straight, with his clawed hands in his lap. This was not the first time I have sat *zazen* in my dreaming, but it was the first time that I witnessed my spirit ally in such a situation.

I emerged from the dream state back in my tent at dawn, amazed at what had just occurred. I pulled on my clothes and boots, then set off alone down the sand river, curious to see if the place I had been shown in my dream state actually existed in ordinary reality. After walking about a half mile, I was ready to return to camp when a male dik-dik, a small rabbit-sized antelope, emerged from the thorn scrub along the river's edge. He looked at me with a startled expression, his longish, prehensile nose questing in my direction, and then he dashed off down the sandy wash.

I decided to take this as a sign, and followed. There, another quarter mile along, was the place I had seen in my dreaming—and there was no mistaking it. There was the same sandbar below the same thorn tree. Confirmations like this are always reassuring, and each morning during the month I was in the field, I walked to that place and sat in meditation for an hour at dawn.

On Christmas morning, I took all of our offerings to this thorn tree, saying the name of each person out loud as I tied them into the lower branches, with the exception of one bundle whose maker specifically requested that it be buried in the earth. I then sang the power song that I had received in Hawai'i many years before and lay down under the tree, attempting to access the shamanic state of consciousness without the aid of the drum. When I had achieved moderate success, I activated my connections to my circle at Westerbeke, trying to visualize each person as I remembered them around the workshop room's perimeter. Then I put out the call to the leopard man and to the spirits of this place.

In my mind, I could feel presences gathering, slowly and tentatively at first, and then with more and more directness. I could feel them approaching from above and below, from within and without, each new arrival producing surges of feeling in my physical body. I could feel the shape of their awarenesses and could sense their curiosity. Many were perceived as distinctly neutral, others as benevolent and mild—the trees, for example, conveyed a collective dreamlike consciousness almost like singing. But there was also a presence that was huge and whose power was truly intimidating.

An Afar elder named Ali Gafu had told me the year before that there is a genie who lives along this dry river (their word for *genie* is "ginn," pronounced with a hard *g*), and it may be that this was what this fearsome presence was. I felt very grateful for the protecting presence of my spirit helper at that moment because, quite frankly, the proximity of this enormous powerbeing unnerved me, and I suddenly felt overwhelmed. It was as though an immense boulder was hovering over me, actually resting on me so that I could feel it threatening to squash me like an ant at any minute. I hadn't expected this, and gathering my wits, I drew on my spirit helper's protection and support as I pulled myself together, feeling myself calm down slowly and my inner state stabilize.

At this moment, I understood once again why the shaman is called the master of spirits in virtually all traditional societies. In dealing with beings such as the one I could feel right now, there simply could be no question about who was the chief. As Ali Gafu later told me, you have to be very careful dealing with the *ginn*, because if you cannot control them, they will control you—and then you're in trouble.

When I felt safe once more, I addressed the assembled spirits, taking the opportunity to say something about who I was and what I was doing here. I formed an image in my mind of the circle at Westerbeke and revealed that I had brought offerings from this gathering of shamans to honor the spirits of this place. I then proffered our power bundles with our good intentions attached, mentally wrapping our gifts with ritual propriety and respect. In addition, I honored the ancient, ancestral spiritual source from which humankind had evolved in this place, and I conveyed our gratitude to the powers that had accompanied and molded us on our long evolutionary journey across time.

I finished the ritual by doing something I always do when in connection with power. I shifted my focus and let my mind drift across those I knew to be suffering . . . and sent each of them a strong surge of this power in a healing capacity.

I emerged from the deep state feeling incredibly energized, my body shaking uncontrollably as the power was released. At that moment, the first gentle, rhythmic call of a tinker bird floated through the trees; and a chorus of high, shrill jackal songs greeted the dawn from somewhere down the wash. For some time, I just sat below the tree, moved beyond words by what I had just experienced. Then the world became ordinary once again, and I slowly walked back to camp.

Long hot days of survey, excavation, and discovery followed, during which, at odd times, I would detect unseen awarenesses fastened upon me. Sometimes I would glance around to find a jackal watching me, or something big would pass overhead, and I would look up to find an Egyptian vulture observing me closely. In the evenings in camp, wildcats would drift by just beyond the light, pausing to look at me before disappearing into the darkness. And virtually every night at dinner, a large praying mantis landed on my shoulder or on the back of my arm and looked speculatively into my eyes for long moments before snatching a moth out of the air.

There was also that sense of presence that clearly came from within. I knew what it was now.

On the last evening before breaking camp, there was a full moon. After dinner, I took a flashlight and walked alone down the empty riverbed to the place of power under the thorn tree. I had decided to do an exercise that Michael Harner had given me on this spot. As I took up position on the sandbar under the tree, the landscape was drenched in moonlight, and the desert night was completely and utterly silent.

I began the exercise, which involved a specific shamanic procedure, and let my eyes unfocus into the monochromatic patterns of light and dark surrounding me. When I had settled, I decided to see if I could use the procedure to help me have a visionary look into the dim recesses of human prehistory. I closed my eyes and directed my mind toward the past, instructing my *ku* to search for the ancestral thread of humanity that extended across the thousands of millennia that separated our time from that of the earliest ancestors who had lived here.

For a long while there was nothing, then slowly, imagery began to move through my consciousness, and the night air seemed to become noticeably warmer and more humid. Quite suddenly, I could definitely smell a new odor and was reminded of the rich aroma generated by the tropical forest of Nainoa's time. I wondered briefly if I was reconnecting with him, but my focus lay in the past, not the future.

As murky images of a moonlit, jungly river bank emerged, I heard an owl call, one that I recognized as distinctively African, and there were frogs chorusing and tree crickets singing. I looked up at the moon and saw that I was sitting under a different tree. I had no idea what kind of tree it was, but it was huge, and it wasn't the thorn tree. I heard the unmistakable sound of water, and looking down, I saw that the river before me was flowing. I was no longer in the arid, stony deserts of the Rift.

My excitement soared as I looked around, trying to accurately observe my surroundings. Unfortunately, it was pitch dark, and I could see virtually nothing beyond major shapes and landforms. If I had indeed managed to shift my awareness four and a half million years into the past, could I connect with the consciousness of our primordial ancestors? Once again, I instructed my *ku* to search for them in the tall black wall of tropical forest that bracketed the moonlit river before me. And then I heard the unmistakable grating cough of a leopard from somewhere upstream.

At that moment, I began to pick up the consciousness of something else, or rather "some things." They were there, all around me, or rather above me, and I realized that they were up in the trees. They were sleeping up in the trees in the dark. This was completely new territory for me, but I decided to see if I could establish connection with them.

Interestingly, I did not perceive any of these mindshapes as "human," and could sense only dreamlike shadows that felt totally unfamiliar. The more I probed, the less familiar they seemed. In retrospect, this was probably an accurate perception, as these four and a half million-year-old protohominids may have looked more like apes than humans, and their minds, associated with a brain a quarter the size of ours, must have been at a totally different level of complexity and organization.

Again I heard the leopard's call, a peculiar sound much like somebody sawing wood. In response, I felt a flow of fear swirl through the mindshapes I was in connection with—a contagious surge I suddenly internalized within myself, producing a metallic taste in my mouth. The prince of darkness was out there, the spotted carnivore who came in the night to eat us—and I was sitting on the ground!

This strong jolt of emotion caused me to falter in the exercise, and I momentarily lost my concentration. My awareness shifted in response, and I was suddenly back under the thorn tree above the dry river, heart pounding, my ears listening intently. The question was, had I heard the leopard in my visioning, or had the call penetrated into the vision state from my immediate surroundings?

Despite my interesting bond with the leopard spirit, I was very much aware that dealing with ordinary-reality leopards is quite another matter. The Afars had told me that they were still around, taking the occasional goat or cow. All they needed was a little cover from which to operate, and here I was, sitting in prime leopard habitat, three quarters of a mile from camp, with only a flashlight. I continued to listen intently, my awareness focused fully in ordinary reality now, my eyes watching for any movement along the sand river.

The warm night wind took this moment to sigh in the thorny branches above me. Our power bundles danced with an interesting rhythm in the moonlight, swaying like the tassels on a belly dancer's costume. I glanced at my watch. An hour and a half had passed as though in an instant. I waited for another 20 minutes but heard no further leopard coughs.

I reached out toward my spirit helper's presence and invoked its protection, then recommenced the exercise, but I continued to feel uneasy. My conscious mind was very much on alert, concerned about large carnivores on the one hand, and thinking about and analyzing what I had just experienced on the other. I was too worked up, and I was unable to shift back into the shamanic state of consciousness. Toward midnight, I decided to call it quits and return to camp.

We broke camp the next morning. I rose before dawn and went back to the place of power for one last journey. Once again, I lay down under the thorn tree and reestablished connection with the spirits of this place to bid them farewell. The *ginn* felt less intimidating on this occasion. I finished by expressing the hope that the good intentions and ongoing efforts of the medicinemakers of our world would contribute to the greater good of the Universe, assisting it to function for us in life-enhancing ways.

I also put forward my hope that humankind would continue to evolve and grow until we had achieved our destiny and taken our place within the great pattern of the universal mind-spirit. I didn't ask for anything specific for myself or for my three-year group, but as I emerged from the deep state, I returned with a strong feeling that we had made medicine together—good medicine.

The moment I opened my eyes, I got a jolt. There were seven jackals silently observing me from the other side of the tree no more than 20 feet away. They seemed not the least bit startled by my presence, and given the circumstances, I began to suspect that they had come for a reason.

At that same moment, the blazing crescent of the sun appeared over the edge of the world, its rays bathing the wild dogs in a pink glow. The jackals immediately raised their heads and burst into song, keening their incredibly high, shrill voices in unison straight up into the canopy of the thorn tree. Directly above them hung our power bundles, and as I lay there on the sand, completely enchanted, the strong conviction arose in my mind that our bundles were being sung to power, and that this act was an affirmation, a gift from the spirits of the place. On impulse, I asked a question, and a strong conviction arose in my conscious awareness. I was supposed to bring them back. I was being directed to return the bundles to their makers with the power they had acquired here.

I sat up slowly, keeping an eye on the jackals with my peripheral vision. I glanced toward the east, where the great red orb of our star continued to rise through a gap in the trees. I felt momentary confusion. I hadn't intended to bring the bundles back. I had meant to leave them. I decided to ask for another sign. I needed confirmation of this change of plan.

As the sun cleared the horizon, something landed on my lap with a plop, and I looked down to find a small, dry seed pod coiled up into a tight loop. I glanced up to find that the tree's upper branches were loaded with them. Another landed next to me with a dry click— and then another. As I looked around, I saw that the ground was littered with them. The thorn tree knew that the rainy season was approaching, and it was giving birth. I noticed that some of our bundles resembled these pods, and I sensed that this was the sign I had asked for.

I looked over at the jackals, but they had vanished, their mission accomplished. A wonderful sense of inner peace pervaded me as I slowly got up and stood under the tree, running my hands with affection across its rough bark. I quietly sang my power song as I gently detached our bundles and slipped them into my shirt.

I then took two stones from the dry river bed, a large, flat, round one and a smaller long one with one flat end, and placed them between two of the trees exposed roots, the small one upright on top of the larger as though sitting in Zen meditation. Then I bade final farewell to the place and returned to the field camp, profoundly moved by all that had occurred there.

I had no connections with Nainoa in the field camp that year, nor did I see the *dorajuadiok*, although, as I have said, the sense of being watched was often felt. My fieldwork was most successful, however, and I returned to the cold, wet, rainy season of northern California in mid-January.

I was just as jetlagged as the year before, and I was lying

awake in the dark one morning, listening to the rain pouring down outside and reviewing the past several contacts with my esteemed descendant. All my transtemporal journeys over the past year had, amazingly, reconnected me with him on a single day in his time frame. It was kind of like seeing "A Day in the Life of Nainoa at the Place of Refuge." I had no idea why these journeys had happened in this way, unless it was my own subconscious curiosity about his monastic existence and what he was learning from his training while there. As a married householder whose daily life was filled with responsibilities and jobs, such an existence was beyond my reach— well beyond it.

Perhaps it was the sound of the rain. Perhaps it was my thoughts. But the inner doorway opened, and the sensations of power abruptly swept into me, filling my body with the overwhelming feelings of force, while the phosphenic light show flooded my brain with luminous visuals. As my excitement rose, I recalled the time and place of my last connection with Nainoa and focused my intentionality. . . .

CHAPTER TEN

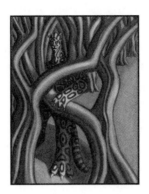

Fifth Journey:
The Nature of Reality

NAINOA WAS SITTING IN HIS ROOM, listening to the rain and reflecting on his meeting with the old recluse in the forest earlier that afternoon, when the attractive young initiate arrived with a message from the Kahuna Nui. He was invited to join the director at her cottage during the period before the evening meal. He thanked the woman, who departed, holding the broad leaf of a *taro* plant above her head to ward off the rain. He noted that she had left one for him just outside the door, and reached for his cloak on its hook on the wall.

As he slung the damp cloth around his bare shoulders, he watched the figure of the woman recede across the compound and thought longingly of Maraea. How he would like to be with her right now. His body responded to the thought, much to his amusement. It had been almost three lunar cycles since they had seen each other—too long when in the initial stages of courtship.

He glanced at the bottle that he had found among the tree roots, and his thoughts shifted back to the present. The artifact would forever serve as a reminder, a connection to the extraordinary conversation he'd had with the old man on the ledge by the waterfall. He wondered where Pali was now, and the answer appeared in his mind: *The old mystic was in his cave, seated in deep meditation, listening to the rain.* And where was this cave? In the cliffs, Pali had said, probably somewhere hidden deep in the bamboo grove. He sensed that he would find it someday.

He slipped on his sandals, took up the *taro* leaf, and headed for Kahu Sala's house through the rain. He would deposit the leaf at the kitchens later, where it would appear in tomorrow's steamed greens. He arrived at the house, striking the wooden slab with the mallet to announce his presence. He was ushered in immediately by the young woman who had summoned him.

As before, the Kahuna Nui was seated, looking out through the opened screens at the lagoon. She invited him to sit with a gesture, then for long moments, the two of them remained in silence, watching the raindrops pock the water's surface. The late afternoon sun suddenly broke through the clouds low in the west, and a double rainbow appeared, one that seemed to touch down right before them. The director smiled and shook her head with wonder, then turned to Nainoa and spoke.

"There are moments when one feels that the boundaries between the worlds become very thin . . . very thin, indeed." She gestured toward the double arc of color standing vertically before her house and called to her student to come and see it. The tall young woman came and stood beside them, raising her hand to her mouth as she gazed with wonder at the rainbow. Nainoa glanced up at her, his eyes taking her in from her strong feet to her mane of dark hair. Kahu Sala noted his glance and introduced him to the woman for the first time.

"Chief Nainoa, this is Chiefess Kaonokianalu. She is a distant kinswoman of High Chiefess Maraea, being the daughter of her sister's husband's cousin on his mother's side, I believe." The girl nodded to the director, then looked down into Nainoa's eyes and smiled.

"*A me ke aloha pumehana*, Ali'i Kaonokianalu," Nainoa rose to his feet and greeted her formally, but with warmth. "And when was the last time you saw my lady, Chiefess Maraea?"

The Kahuna Nui chortled as she perceived his appreciation of the girl's physical beauty. "Everyone calls her Nalu," she said, giving the girl permission to speak with a gesture.

"Salutations to you in return, Chief Nainoa," Nalu said in a soft voice. "High Chiefess Maraea has sent her warmest greetings to you. I saw her five days ago on my way to the Place of Refuge. She is well and is looking forward to your return to the capital. She has instructed me to give you a gift. Forgive me for not informing you of this sooner, but this is the first opportunity that I have had to speak with you."

"You did not tell me, Nalu, that you needed to speak with Chief Nainoa," observed the director matter-of-factly.

"You did not ask, Kahuna Nui," replied the girl, her eyes cast down.

Kahu Sala studied Nalu for a long moment, then said, "It is true that silence is customary during our daily routine here. We do not speak unless absolutely necessary, so your conduct was not in error. To the contrary . . ." She thought for another moment, then concluded, "Perhaps you can convey High Chiefess Maraea's gift to Chief Nainoa after the evening practice period before retiring for the night." The young woman bowed in assent, then the director dismissed her with a gesture.

"Lovely, isn't she?" she observed, once the girl was out of earshot. "High Chiefess Maraea is very fond of Nalu. They grew up together as children. She is only here for a short time. But to return to our original line of thought . . . the boundaries between the worlds. Let us discuss the nature of reality, Chief Nainoa. What have you learned about this intriguing subject?"

Nainoa reeled in the feelings that had been activated by the woman's presence and gathered his thoughts as he sat down once again. The amazing meeting he'd had with the old man in the forest surfaced first, so he gave the *kahuna* an account of what had happened that afternoon, including details of their discussion about the *aumakua* self. He then reiterated parts of his conversation with Chief Hakai dealing with the concept of the secret garden and described his ancestor's place of power in Hawai'i. He theorized that he himself had stepped through the mythic doorway between realities in finding the forest pool and suggested that he had found his own secret garden in the process.

The director said little until he finished, but there was little doubt that he had her full attention. "And how is it," she began, "that you will be able to find this place so easily once again? How is it that Chief Hakai can connect with his secret garden and your ancestor with his? The answer lies, of course, in understanding how the different levels of reality fit together, as well as the principles of how each works in relation to the others."

Her eyes returned to the lagoon before them. The rainbow was fading. "Take this level of everyday reality, for example. By what assumptions are we able to experience it, and how is it put together?"

"In my opinion," Nainoa began, "most people believe that this outer, physical world of things and objects, actions and events, is the only reality that is 'real.' I have come to understand that this is only the first of several levels of reality, experience, and awareness, but in this outer world, countless phenomena and processes are possible, and through our involvement with them, we are able to progress, to grow, and to change. This everyday world is, thus, a level of action, and as such, it possesses enormous, virtually unlimited potential.

"The way people experience this level," he went on, "seems to be determined by certain assumptions: the acceptance that everything is distinct and separate from everything else; the belief that effects are the result of causes; and by the perception that the patterned flow of life proceeds in a directional manner, from the beginning to the ending, from the past into the future, from one state of complexity and awareness into another. This outer world could be called the first level of reality."

He paused and looked at the director to see if she wished to add something. Kahu Sala simply smiled and waited for him to continue. Nainoa knew, with just an edge of uneasiness, that he was being evaluated.

"I have come to understand that when we think or create a thoughtform with the *uhane*, our inner director and middle self, or when we access memories or feel emotions through the *ku*, we have shifted into the second level of reality—awareness and experience— a level in which everything is in connection with everything else. The *kahuna* mystics believe that these connections are formed of *aka*, the primordial stuff out of which everything is made—matter and energy, thoughtforms and feelings, and even memories and spirits.

"When we have been to a place, we feel a sense of connection with it. We feel this because there is a fiber of *aka* that extends between our personal energetic *aka* body and the *aka* of that locality. That is how I will be able to find my way back to the pool in the forest," he smiled, "even in my dreaming-while-awake. In the same manner, when two persons meet, an *aka* fiber comes into existence between them. As they come to know each other well, the fiber thickens into a cord through which thoughts can be shared and feelings perceived. The closer the relationship, the thicker the cord, revealing *aka* to be the matrix through which all psychic phenomena operate.

"Most of us cannot see these connections or the personal *aka* body using our ordinary vision because they exist in the second level. Those with the gift of *ike papalua*, psychic awareness, can perceive though these connections, and those with *maka'ike*, true psychic sight, describe the *aka* body as a luminous field that surrounds and flows through our physical bodies. They can see it in this way because the *aka* carries our energy as *mauli*, as lifeforce. This, in turn, reveals that the second level of reality is also the level of energy.

"The *kahuna* mystics say that everything everywhere is connected to everything else though a great *aka* field that exists in the second level. In my visionary moments, I sometimes perceive a vast net or web that seems to extend outwards in all directions, and I have come to believe that this is the *aka* field. The mystics say that the web can be used to connect with people or places, or to send or receive information, revealing that the second level, like the first, is a level of action."

Nainoa thought for a moment, then added, "I have talked with many people of knowledge about the nature of my connection with my ancestor, and all seem to be in agreement. Such a phenomenon is possible because I am his descendant, and therefore, part of my *aka* body must be derived from his. Energy is the connection—energy that has its source within the *aumakua* of which we are both manifested embodiments.

"This is how he and I are able to find each other, how we can perceive each other's thoughts and emotions, and how we can shift backward and forward across time. Our *aumakua* exists in the spirit world, in the third level of reality, but its connection to us extends through the *aka* field in the second into my world here and into his world there. This curious experience has led me to believe that at the second and third levels of reality, past, present, and future are all at once, and time does not exist in the same way it does in the first.

"I have also thought a great deal about the death experience in relation to all this," Nainoa continued. "With the death of the physical body in the first level, our energy body must exist in a free state, and our essence, our soul/spirit complex carried by the energy, then returns through the second level to its *aumakua* source in the third. If this is true, and based on my own direct experiences, it certainly seems to be, the inescapable conclusion is that we are all immortals."

Nainoa's voice drifted into silence as he waited for some input from his mentor. Kahu Sala thought for a moment, then pursed her lips and asked, "What about dreams, Chief Nainoa? And where is your secret garden that you found this afternoon?"

Nainoa replied, "When we dream during sleep or when we

journey into the inner worlds while very much awake, our awareness shifts into the third level of reality in which everything is a
dream. This is also the level of the spirit world. The Upper Worlds
of Lanikeha are the dreaming of the gods and goddesses, the mystics and ancestral *aumakua* spirits. The Lower Worlds of Milu are
the dreaming of the animals and plants, the rocks and the air, the
water and the fire—the collective dreaming of nature. And so this
is where the nature spirits reside. In between these regions is Waena,
the dream world of humans. And that is where my secret garden
is found.

"My ancestor experiences these spirit worlds in much the
same way. He uses the concept of *ailona*, of 'symbol,' with relation
to this level of reality and awareness. For him, everything at the third
level is symbolic and is woven into an ever-expanding design or pattern in which everything is in relationship to everything else. It is
in this way that meaning is determined. In this light, my ancestor
believes the spirit worlds to be primarily a level of information."

Kahu Sala sat and digested this for long moments, her gaze turned
inward. Then her eyes brightened and she asked, "And what about
power, Chief Nainoa? You have said that *mana* is carried by the *aka*
that exists in level two, but is that level also the source of power?"

"No, Kahuna Nui," Nainoa answered respectfully. "The *kahuna*
mystics across time have always posited the existence of a dimension that lies beyond the spirit worlds, a state of pure consciousness and raw, unformed power in which everything, everywhere,
is part of a great, ever-expanding oneness. Although energy can be
carried by the *aka* field in the second level, the power itself is a manifestation of the great Source that exists in the fourth level of reality. The Source, known to the ancients as IAO, carries the universal
mind-spirit of which everything everywhere is a part—even I'o, the
all-generating void."

Nainoa shivered as he remembered what that incredible, dark
vastness was like. The American had been there, too, he knew, and
within his mind, a pulse of appreciation was felt, startling him. He
suddenly realized that his ancestor was in connection, and he

warmed to the thought.

"What is it?" the director asked. Nainoa smiled. A strong *aka* cord had formed between them during his time at the place of refuge, and she had been able to perceive the shift in his awareness through it, confirming everything he had said about the second level.

He politely deflected her by observing, "There are several things that old Pali talked about this afternoon that got my attention. One of these was the necessity of integrating the positive and negative aspects of the self and bringing them into balance with each other."

Kahu Sala smiled. "I'll bet your friend said that this is accomplished by discovering the positive and negative roots of one's own character." A glance at Nainoa confirmed her insight, and she added, "It is true. The understanding of how the self is put together and how one's different aspects function is absolutely essential if we are to experience authentic initiation.

"It is also most important when dealing with spirits," she went on. "The discovery of one's own true nature is necessary if one is to align oneself with the higher Guardian spirits. The essence of the connection between a human and a spirit depends on the consciousness of the human. Like attracts like, and discrimination is obviously important in determining what sort of spirit is contacted. Your connection with Pali, interestingly, reveals a great deal about the level of consciousness you have achieved, for this spirit seems to be a very highly evolved soul indeed."

"Pali also talked about the soul breath, the breathing-in and breathing-out of the soul forces," Nainoa put in.

"He knows about polarity, then," the director responded. "As we observe the world around us, we discern that all life is a coming together of positive and negative opposites, and in saying this, I am not just talking about right and wrong or good and bad, although these values are part of it. The positive polarity includes forces such as love, humility, patience, generosity, altruism, or kindness. These have their source above the Earthly plane of existence and work primarily through the spiritual and mental aspects of reality—and, of course, through ourselves. The negative polarity includes forces such as attraction, arrogance, impatience, anger, fear, greed, envy, or the craving for pleasure or prestige. These have their source within the Earthly plane and work through the elements of the physical-material world, including ourselves once again." She smiled.

"These two polarities, and all they represent, must be balanced. It is in this way that the negative is mastered and its great power transformed by the positive. In a like manner, the positive is grounded by relationship to the negative, and its enormous power then becomes available to us. When these two opposing forces are truly integrated, an inner light appears within us, flowing through our bodies and minds, coming together in the center, which is our heart, the *pu'uwai,* and our heart's knowing, the *nau'au.*

"This ceaseless ebb and flow between the Heavenly and the Earthly is the creative pulse of the Universe. The *kahuna* mystic learns to distinguish between them through their experience of life. If we try to deny or ignore our own negative impulses and tendencies, we achieve only ignorance. We cannot help others who are ill as a result of negativity if we have no direct experience of the negative forces ourselves. The *kahuna* must be fully experienced in all aspects of life in order to achieve true self-awareness and true self-mastery."

"Pali said much the same thing," Nainoa replied, repeating some of the old man's saltier comments for the director. Her laugh shook the room in response. "He must have been quite a handful for the monks in his monastery, and for the women in town as well." More laughter. Then her demeanor sobered once again as her face settled and she merged with the calm presence that was speaking from within her.

"When the *kahuna* achieves harmony within him- or herself, an outer balance follows, and it is this equanimity between the inner and the outer, the positive and the negative, that allows us to facilitate in the healing of others. While working with spirit medicine, the *kahuna* becomes the Earthly-negative pole, and the *aumakua* becomes the spiritual-positive pole. The two must work together, and it is in this manner that the *kahuna* becomes the point of connection between the one suffering and the unseen levels of reality.

"Once the inner light, the *kukui*, appears within our minds and bodies, our *aumakua* then constantly feeds and renews this light. Our heart becomes the center, the magical garden, where our personal power and the power of the great Universe converge. From that point on, the *kahuna* has unlimited contact with the great power, enabling him or her to live a life of service to others, guided by the highest principles and sustained by visionary contact with the spirits who wish to work with us.

"It is quite interesting," the *kahuna* went on, "when you consider all this in relation to the levels of reality that you have described. We live our lives on the physical plane of existence in level one, but we connect through the web in level two with the power that has its source in level four, and we do this with the assistance of the compassionate spirits who exist in level three, including our own personal spirit self, the *aumakua*.

"There is one further point of great importance," she continued. "The relationship between the positive and negative forces is not a stable one because the circumstances of life are constantly shifting, and within this unsteady dynamic, our own personal motivation becomes a most powerful agent of change. We have talked about your maternal gandfather, the great sorcerer whose name no one will speak. His case is a classic, and a lesson to us all."

Kahu Sala paused and looked at Nainoa with gravity. He met her steady gaze without flinching. He knew she was going to say something of import. He was not disappointed.

"The greater our personal advancement along the path of power, the more vulnerable we become to the flaws in our own character."

A long period of silence followed in which each considered the implications of this statement. Then, the rhythmic sound of the large slit drum resounded across the sacred grounds, announcing the end of the afternoon practice period and summoning the residents to the evening meal. Nainoa felt his *ku* respond to the sound. All this talk of mystic awareness and levels of reality had made him hungry. The Kahuna Nui smiled as her own stomach growled. Nothing more needed to be said. The teaching was complete.

"I've been informed that the cooks are preparing a substantial meal this evening." She glanced at the sky in the fading light. The afternoon was over, and the transition into early evening had occurred. The rain had virtually stopped, and the sky was clearing in the east, revealing the pale orb of the full moon just rising through the mists. The forest beyond the walls of the center was filled with riotous birdsong, as if in celebration of its appearance.

"Oxen have been sacrificed in the marketplace to celebrate the changing of the moon," she continued. "Akua Lono has been generous with us this harvest season, and so we will eat well." She smiled again, then her eyes became vacant as her attention shifted inward. "You must excuse me, Chief Nainoa. I must now attend to my spiritual duties that include the offering of the great prayer."

He rose and prostrated himself full length, touching his forehead to the floor out of respect for the teacher he felt so privileged to have met. As he turned to go, Kahu Sala smiled and added, "Perhaps you will have the opportunity to achieve the deep state this evening. I'm sure you and your ancestor have much to discuss."

CHAPTER ELEVEN

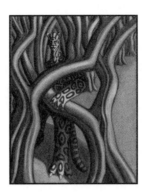

The Human Spirit

JILL TURNED IN HER DREAMING and snuggled into my arms, shifting my awareness and terminating this visionary journey as she pressed herself against me. The early winter light coming through our bedroom window revealed that it was time to rise and start the day, but for long moments, I just lay still, holding my lifemate in my arms and reveling in the great love I felt for her. I listened to the silence and realized that the rain had stopped.

Nainoa's mention of the word *IAO* as a symbol for the mysterious Source encouraged me to turn to my library later in the day, and there I found Laura Yardley's *The Heart of Huna*, which contains a chapter on the teachings of David Kaonohiokala Bray (1889–1968), one of the last of the publicly practicing, initiated *kahunas*. According to Bray's perspective, everything in the Universe is a manifestation of divine energy—energy that is neither self-existent nor self-created, but which originates from the mysterious Source, symbolized by the sacred name *IAO*.[1]

"I" is the symbol for the original creative act by which

everything everywhere was manifested—an event that only happened once. "A" refers to the actual transformation of divine energy into the multidimensional Universe of space and time, extensions of which we experience objectively on the physical plane of existence, and subjectively through our mental processes, emotions, psychic states of awareness, dreams, and spiritual experiences, including the after-death and between-lifetime Bardo states.

According to Bray, the "O" function of the sacred name allowed humanity to utilize this divine power to create reality. This was obviously a pivotal point in the evolution of the human lineage, a threshold that began with the first chipped stone tools that appeared in Africa 2.6 million years ago—a genesis that enabled the evolution of today's current mind-boggling technology. Interestingly, this cumulative process of technological innovation came with a catch, because it also allowed us to experience what Bray terms "un-reality"—illusion, misperception, misinterpretation, and misunderstanding; as well as negative thoughts, emotions, and actions—all of which have resulted in unhappiness, disharmony, and illness.

The *kahuna* mystics felt that humanity's dual nature came into being in response to this split, one aspect connected to the material world on the Earthly plane (the negative polarity), the other connected to the spiritual world and expanded states of awareness (the positive polarity). As Kahu Sala revealed to Nainoa, balance between the two is required. If we focus on spirit alone, we miss the involvement with the physical world around us through which we experience the beauty and power of nature. When we turn to materialism alone, we lose the experience of love and the potential for achieving mystic states of awareness. Both aspects are necessary to fully experience the unity of what it means to be human.

The *kahuna* mystics traditionally believed that humanity originated from out of another dimension, traveling across the Universe to this planet as individual seeds of light. They believed that we were accompanied by Guardians who possessed the knowledge of our destiny and the purpose for living. As the "O" function of the sacred name came into operation, Bray believes that much of humanity

148

abandoned the balanced teachings of the Guardians and sought power purely through matter and the physical world.

This failure of character is regarded by the *kahunas* as the source of humanity's suffering. However, Bray's teachings reveal that those who rediscover and return to the ancient teachings of the Guardians can still restore humanity to a state of balance and harmony. There is only one method of return—selfless service. This activity alone allows us to experience self-realization, joy in the beauty of nature, as well as the rediscovery of our divine nature through the experience of love for one another.

Bray also comments on the nature of spirits, categorizing them hierarchically into those that are of the highest energy and beyond our planetary evolution, those that are linked with the planet and are involved in the sphere of the natural world, and those that are now specifically concerned with the sphere of humanity. Bray subdivides this latter group into those concerned with particular periods of time, those involved with particular groups or family lineages, and those involved with spiritual initiatory orders and traditions. He also adds a cautionary note about those whose nature is demonic and whose motivation is deception.[2]

I could see now why Kahu Sala spoke of the negative and positive polarities and of the necessity for alignment with the appropriate members of this spiritual hierarchy. I mention this because many well-meaning spiritual teachers in the modern mystical movement often sidestep the whole issue of negativity, as well as evil, and simply proclaim that there are no evil spirits. While this may be true in the experience of some of us, there are others who have come into connection with some less-than-wholesome entities. Let me share an example from my own life experience.

Several years ago, I was approached by a student who had attended one of my college anthropology classes focusing on religion and magic in the lives of traditional peoples. This young woman knew of my interest in shamanism and proceeded to tell me a very strange story. For the best part of a year, she had been waking up terrified in her bed in the middle of the night, aware that there were three entities in the room with her. She couldn't see them, but she could hear what they were saying, and she could feel their hands upon her. And virtually every night, the moment they saw she was awake, they would hold her down and molest her in the most unsavory ways for extended periods of time.

As she told me her story, I shifted into a light trance state, and as my awareness expanded in response, I looked her over. I saw before me a young woman who had deep circles under her eyes and whose face was very pale and waxy. Her clothes were wrinkled and disheveled, and she looked exhausted. By the time her story was told, she was trembling, and there were tears streaming down her face. She was obviously terrified by what was happening to her. From the shamanic perspective, it was apparent to me that she lacked protection.

I am not a psychologist, but I was aware that there could have been any number of psychological explanations for this woman's distress. For starters, she could have been suffering from the onset of what Western medicine defines as mental illness. There could also have been molestation issues in her past, but it wouldn't have been ethical for me to ask, nor was I interested in probing into her personal life or in pathologizing her behavior. I could feel her fear with my *ku*, however, and it was obvious to me in those moments that she needed immediate relief. As a student of shamanism, I had a clear sense of how to proceed, but spiritual ethics required that she ask. When she didn't, I decided to prompt her.

I looked into her drawn face and asked her if she remembered the part of the class in which I had discussed the interesting relationship between traditional shamans and their spiritual allies. "That's why I came to you," she said. "I sensed that you had gone beyond scholarly research into direct, personal contact with your subject matter. You've spent a lot of your life with traditional people. That's what made your class so interesting." A glimmer of hope crept into her tired eyes. "Do you think you could help me?"

That's what I was waiting to hear. I smiled and rubbed my hands together. "Yes, I will help you. I know exactly how to take care of this problem." I could see in her posture and demeanor the immediate relief that she experienced in response to my words. I looked at my watch, then turned to her and asked, "Can you go home to your house in the next half hour?" She nodded. "Good. Two of the amazing things about the ancient shamanic method are first, that it works, and second, that it can be done long distance. We don't have to be in the same room together for me to help you."

I continued, "I want you to go home and go into your bedroom. It would be good to light a candle, close the door, and take the phone off the hook, then lie down on your bed. Try to set yourself on "receive mode" at precisely 1:30 P.M. That's your part of the ritual.

"My part is a little more complicated. I'm going to go home to my house, where I'll use my rattle to induce a trance similar to the one in which traditional shamans do their work. Then I'm going to put out the call to my most powerful spirit helper. We're going to put up a perimeter of protection around you, and when it's in place, your problems will be over. As of 1:35, they won't be able to touch you again."

The young woman looked more and more relieved as she listened to this statement of intent, and she smiled for the first time. Then her smile faded, and her fear returned. "What if it doesn't work? What if they come back?" she asked plaintively. She was really shaken and obviously needed something extra to reassure her. I decided to put out a call to my *aumakua* for additonal information.

The answer appeared in my mind immediately. It came in the form of a memory of something Sandra Ingerman had told me at Westerbeke Ranch years ago. If I recall the incident correctly, Sandra had apparently been talking with a Chumash medicine woman at some time in the past and had asked her a similar question. The Indian woman had smiled and described what she did when she felt that she was under psychic attack. She simply used the power of her creative imagination to build an image in her mind of a blue egg. Then she visualized herself getting inside the egg. When she was in the blue egg, nothing could touch her. She was protected.

151

I shook my head with wonder as I received this information. This was strong medicine because it suggested a way in which this frightened woman could act on her own behalf and protect herself whenever the need arose. As I shared the story of the blue egg with her, she seemed satisfied and then went home, promising that she would do as I had asked.

When I got to my house, Jill was at work and the children were at school, so at 1:25 sharp, I got out my Hopi gourd rattle, which has a nice, dry sound, and propped myself in a chair in front of a large oil painting that I had made of the leopard man while I was still living in Hawai'i. I remembered what Tehura had told me about being able to see through Gauguin's painting into the gallery of the Metropolitan Museum of Art and decided to try it in reverse. I looked into my spirit helper's eyes, then started to shake the rattle. When I felt my *ku* shift down into the shamanic state of consciousness, I used the painting as a window to go to my spirit ally. I simply looked into the leopard's green gaze and put forward my request.

I explained the nature of the problem and asked the spirit to extend his defense to this unprotected woman so that whoever was molesting her would be unable to find her or get to her in any way, shape, or form. I also asked that this protection be extended to me and to my wife and daughters, a most important part of the ritual, because the last thing I wanted was for these entities to find their way into my dreaming or that of my family through my connection to the girl. I finished by asking that the leopard man not hurt the offenders in any way, but to simply isolate and neutralize them. I mention this because I, like Nainoa, had learned a powerful lesson from the Paleko incident.

The altered state suddenly deepened, and the blood started to hiss in my ears. To my amazement, I saw those green eyes close, then open again, then close, conveying reassurance and good intentions. There was no doubt in my mind that I was in connection with my ally in those moments. Once again, I saw those eyes close and open, close and open. My request had been received. The perimeter of protection was in place. The ritual was complete.

I stopped rattling, and my consciousness shifted. The painting was once again a painting. It was 1:35 exactly. I put down the rattle and went to pick up my children at school.

Several days later, the woman rushed up to me at one of the colleges where I teach. She looked good. The circles were gone, and there was color in her skin and light in her eyes. Her clothes were pressed, and her hair looked great. She was even wearing makeup. "It worked, Dr. Wesselman, it worked!" she proclaimed effusively, and then went on to tell me that she'd had four uninterrupted nights' sleep in a row, the first in a year, and that the "boogeymen" had not returned since the ritual had been done.

This account had an interesting ending. I ran into the woman about a year later at a bookstore, and in the course of making light conversation, I asked her if she had ever had any further problems. She gave me a funny look, then smiled and said that she'd had no more molestation visits, but that something interesting had happened one night in her dreaming.

"I dreamed that I was walking down the street in a city," she began. "I don't remember what city it was, but I was window shopping. I could see what was in the store windows quite clearly, and I could also see the reflection of the street behind me." Suddenly her expression changed. I saw the fear return.

"At one point, I looked into the reflection, and there, across the street behind me, I saw three teenage boys. The minute I saw them, they saw me, and I knew, without a doubt, that they were the ones who had been messing with me. As the realization hit, I saw one of them say something to the others, and they started to cross the street. They were coming to get me . . ." Her voice drifted off, and her body went rigid.

"And what did you do then?" I asked her gently.

"I whirled around and looked right at them," she said, "and as I did, I noticed that right in front of me, there was a blue Volkswagen beetle parked at the curb. It was like a blue egg . . . ," she said with wonder creeping into her voice. I saw the fear depart.

"I grabbed the door handle and found it unlocked, so I jumped in and locked both doors in a flash," she said with glee. "In an instant, they were at the car, pounding on the windows, trying to open the doors, making obscene gestures, and shouting lewd things at me. But I couldn't hear them, and they couldn't get to me. I was protected. I was in the blue egg. I looked down and noticed then that the keys were in the ignition. I thought about it for a moment, then figured, 'What the hell, this is a dream,' so I climbed into the driver's seat and started the car. Then I simply put it in gear and drove away and left those loathsome thugs behind." She laughed cheerily. "I've never seen them again."

I was delighted with this outcome. Not only had the protection ritual worked, but she'd had a teaching dream in which she'd learned how to take care of herself. This was good medicine indeed, and at the next opportunity, I thanked my spotted ally, reporting in about the outcome.

This case could be analyzed from many different perspectives. In keeping with my own interests, let me draw once again on David Bray's wisdom and look at this incident from the *kahuna* point of view.[3] Two interpretations present themselves for consideration.

First, it is possible that the entities tormenting this young woman could have been created by her own distorted emotions and thoughts as a result of what Bray calls "chronic mental poisoning." As the woman focused on these negative thoughtforms repeatedly, in full awareness or not, they received *mana* from her, and they may have become so strong in response to her sustained attention that they appeared to her as separate beings attacking her in her dreaming. When such negative thoughtforms become habitual, the *kahunas* believe that they can assume *personae* of their own and can act as psychic vampires, drawing off the vitality of the sufferer. In this sense, they actually "feed" on the client's life force, but they have no reality in themselves and will cease to exist without the support of the energy supplied by the patient's fear and sustained attention.

To dispel such harmful thoughtforms, traditional *kahunas*

functioned much like psychologists do today, and led their patients into self-awareness by uncovering the roots of the thoughtforms, including how they function and why they are clung to, thus helping the patient let go of them. When the conscious inner director is self-aware and empowered, it allows the patient to choose another attitude of mind and emotion, enabling them to determine a new course of action in life. *Kahunas* who were trained in this field were known as *kahuna la'au kahea*.

A second interpretation is also possible. Sometimes, negative thoughtforms or "dark spirits" can be projected upon a person by another. Such thoughtforms, invested with the energy and negative emotions of their senders, can take on a phantomlike presence in the inner life of the one at whom they are directed. If the projected forms are actually dark spirits, they can be a formidable force to reckon with. Unfortunately, Western medicine knows very little about such things.

Traditional people know a great deal about this, however, and in dealing with such cases, the negative thoughtforms or hostile spirits must be prevented from gaining access to the sufferer and are usually sent back to their source, where they often end up consuming their sender. In old Hawai'i, specialists in the art of counter-sorcery were known as *kahuna pale*, which translates literally as "defense experts," or as *kahuna kupua*, the "masters of spirits," a term ascribed to shamans all over the world.

In this case, it's possible that the hostile spirits attacking the young woman were actually the projected thoughtforms of three teenage boys. She was only a year or two out of high school, and it may be that she was targeted by some fellow adolescents who had stumbled into the knowledge of how to spiritwalk without the guidance of a positively focused elder teacher. I utilized the shamanic method of drawing upon a spirit helper to defend the young woman, and although a Western psychologist or psychiatrist might find this explanation intellectually unsatisfying, it worked. It is worth noting that I refrained from intentionally sending the negative spirits back to their source(s), thus avoiding the trap of practicing negative witchcraft myself. But I was well aware that I could have. . . .

The next few months were filled with the practical concerns of raising children and teaching classes, and I had little time for shamanic journeywork, nor did I have any deep altered-state connections with Nainoa until later in the spring. As the time for the regathering of the shamanic three-year group approached, I began to feel my anticipation rise. I had come to regard this week-long training session both as an opportunity to acquire knowledge and experience, and as a time in which I could engage in some serious fieldwork in the inner worlds.

I hadn't been to my secret garden for a while, so expectations were high when the drumming sessions began in our meeting room at Westerbeke. My curiosity about the nature of the collective "field" of the Human Spirit was aroused, and I decided to see if I could make a journey of investigation in that direction from my secret garden.

When the opportunity presented itself, I was lying on my old Navajo rug with a bandanna tied around my eyes to darken my visual field. I listened to the driving, rhythmic sound of the drum and instructed my *ku* to open the inner doorway, flooding my body with the feelings of force. The transition was swift. I arrived on the *heiau* and looked around. All seemed in order. I walked to the edge of the platform and surveyed my estate in the dream world with affection, then went over to the dark stone altar and lay down upon it.

I have written about my first encounter with the phenomenon of spiritual dismemberment,[4] a level of initiation common among traditional groups that practice shamanism, especially the Siberian tribal peoples. In dismemberment, the neophyte shaman is usually attacked while in the visionary state by a powerful supernatural being, taken apart in various culturally determined ways, and boiled down to the bare bones. After a period of time, the initiate is put back together again and given a new spiritual body, but with all one's former flaws and "bad parts" left out. It's quite an experience, to say the least, and as Michael Harner and others have observed, dismemberment, like spirit possession, is poorly understood in the West.

I was unaware that dismemberment can occur in stages as I lay upon the long black slab of basalt and focused my intentions—to journey to the Human Spirit. Suddenly, I felt an enormous surge of the power sensations, and glancing upwards, I saw why. Towering over me was the tall, dark spirit that Nainoa calls Keaka—the one I had come to perceive as the guardian of the threshold. It was the first time I had seen it in almost ten years, since the time that Nainoa had had to wrestle with it in the city in the forest.[5]

As the power sensations continued to grow within me, I felt concern that I was going into one of my cataleptic altered states in which my body experiences total paralysis. With this thought, the enormous force that Keaka wields slammed into me, rendering my physical aspect as rigid as a stick of wood. There was no escape or backing out of whatever I had gotten myself into. The power swiftly compressed me with incredible force, and I felt myself becoming smaller and smaller, denser and denser. Unlike my many blissful experiences, this one was an ordeal—a truly frightening one—and my physical body in the workshop room was struggling for breath. My unease rapidly shifted toward panic. I briefly wondered if I could be dying.

As I stared up at the dark spirit's formidable form, my breathing labored, I saw that it was attended by the curious, reflective ball of light that I had seen in its presence once before. I had never figured out what this luminous orb was, but on this day, I got a demonstration of what it could do. A flash of brilliance suddenly shot into my eyes from the bright sphere hovering near Keaka's shoulder, blinding me with a blast of white light. It was at this moment that the force seemed to crush me like a grape on the slab of stone.

There was a distinct pop or snap (but curiously, no pain) as "I" exited at the base of my neck, up between my shoulder blades. It was as if I had lifted effortlessly into the air, as though my life force had been squirted upwards from my body's husk like an energetic grape seed, carrying my awareness with it. I could see in all directions at once. Below me on the slab was my form, lying there like an empty sock beside the dark spirit and the ball of light.

I suddenly understood that this was a dismemberment experience, albeit an unexpected one, and my fear abated. I had no desire to see the rest of it and recalled my intention to journey to the Human Spirit. Could dismemberment have been part of the given before I was granted access? Did I have to go through a death experience before I could approach the collective, spiritual field of humanity—the "home" to which my old friend had been taken by the griffin? There was no way of knowing the answers to these questions. I could only observe closely and pay attention to whatever happened next.

A sense of movement began, and I abruptly found myself ascending rapidly, rising along a luminous fiber through a long series of nested curves or arcs of light that converged toward a brilliant body of enormous size at the zenith of the sky. As I looked toward it, my vision seemed to darken, and its luminosity deepened into a rich golden-orange hue. Although I had the sense that I was rising with increasing speed, the golden light never seemed to get any closer, but remained ever distant. Within my self, I perceived a feeling of familiarity, accompanied by a definite sense of longing. But exactly what it was eluded me.

My attention shifted away from the beautiful misty-golden field. All around me were other fibers or lines of light, whizzing by. I was traveling through the grid, along the *aka* web Nainoa had described to his mentor. It was a little like flying over a major city like Los Angeles at night, but the lines of light, instead of being flat, extended outward in all directions, forever. This interpretation of what I saw comes forth in retrospect, because in those incredible moments, my ability to think—to convert perceptions into concepts—seemed to have been turned off. I could still perceive, however, and within my self, I could also discern memories and feelings. Among them, I vaguely recalled my intention for the journey.

Far above me and slightly to one side, I perceived a shape that was roughly circular. It looked both reflective and opaque at the same time, constantly shifting back and forth between one state and the other. It was a little like being underwater looking up at the moving surface of the ocean, but it was constrained into a definite shape, with edges. I noted that the fiber I was following was headed right for it. Perhaps it was a doorway of some sort.

When impact seemed inevitable, I seemed to squeeze through it. There was some resistance as this occurred, but I didn't have time to think about it, because I seemed to have emerged at the edge of what appeared to be a wide, luminous plain. The brightness of the light suggested that I was in the shamanic Upper Worlds.

As I began to move across the bright, misty region, it seemed to resolve itself into units—into uncountable numbers of lights, looking somewhat like tiny, glowing bubbles or globes. As I got closer, each took on the appearance of an elliptical milky orb within which a brilliant "X" or cross formed a denser, central core. My perspective abruptly shifted, and the plain appeared to me like a great matrix composed of endless numbers of these luminous bubbles, each enclosing a neon cross, all fitted together into a definite, composite whole, like an endless cluster of tiny grapes.

My mind registered an immediate sense of familiarity, and I knew with certainty that this wide place, or cloud, as I was coming to think of it, was and is the collective spiritual essence of all humankind, a composite field of which each of us is a *holon,* an expressed microcosm containing within it the totality of the macrocosm. As I progressed more deeply into the cloud, I was able to perceive that I, too, had assumed a luminous orblike appearance—a shimmering, flowing, oblong form in which my denser interior resolved itself into a moving, vertical bar of light. Curved streamers of energy seemed to be flowing into the top of the orb and out the bottom, creating a shimmering, swirling field somewhat like an elongated, luminous doughnut or torus. There was no frame of reference, so I had no way of determining how large I was.

My *ku,* my emotional consciousness, was very much intact, and I was aware of a great tranquility, one that verged into a profound and utter silence. As I focused on the stillness, I discerned some-thing within it—a beautiful, vibrational tone that was incredibly sub-tle. The moment I became aware of it, it began to flow within me. Or was I flowing within it?

There was no way of knowing which was true at this point, but I immediately recognized it as an indescribable sound I had occa-sionally heard in my mind's ear out in the Rift Valley—a sound of silence, if such a thing is possible. My consciousness began to fol-low the sound more and more closely, tracking it until I literally became one with the vibration. It was much like a whisper or sigh that surged or pulsed periodically, like the sea breaking on a beach.

As I listened, entranced, I became cognizant of an aware-ness—one that resolved itself into a huge collective mind within which my own consciousness seemed to be nested. It was as though I was a part of it, and because I was in connection, I under-stood something amazing in those incredible moments. This aware-ness was *dreaming*.

With this understanding, the feeling of connection deepened, and I could perceive my sense of self evaporating as my mind flowed toward and into the ocean of dream—the human dream. Imagery began to take form in my consciousness, shadowy shapes made of light, fractioned shards of pale pastels that swirled and changed. It was as though I was looking at reflections on the surface of a pool of water. It was incredibly, almost unbearably, beautiful. And I was merging with the the beauty. I *was* the beauty.

It was at this point that I became aware of a distinct throbbing sound. My dissolving attention refocused on it, wondering at it . . . and with this sound came a memory—a pulse of recollection. My spiritual dismemberment . . . the journeywork . . .the shamanic work-shop. I recognized the throbbing sound as the drum, and there was just enough of my self left to make a decision—the resolution to return. A sense of the personal began to regrow with this deter-mination, and I began to pay close attention to the drum. It was as if the sound was coming from a great distance below me.

A sense of disappointment began to grow within me. I knew what I had to do and felt an enormous reluctance to separate from the great luminous dreaming presence of which I was once again a part. I understood that this was indeed "home," and I felt no driving need to withdraw from the dream . . . but I realized that I had to. With great effort, I kept my attention focused on the drumming—and I felt my self slowly re-forming.

A feeling of density began to manifest once again, and with it, a sense of motion began. I felt myself begin to drop . . . to sink downward. A profound wistfulness pervaded me as I separated from the vast cloud, and the drumming got louder. The sense of descent increased, and right below me, I saw the mirrorlike surface of the interface. As I rocketed through, it shattered into shards of light, and around me once again I saw the glimmering nested arcs, sweeping by in a blur, as though I were in some sort of tube or tunnel made of light. I could feel my energy increasing with my deepening sense of self returning. Below me was a reddish orb—a sphere that darkened and changed, growing ever larger until it manifested itself into our vast ocean-covered planet swirling with dark clouds.

It seemed only a heartbeat before I elongated into a spectral bolt of lightning that tore through the fabric of the sky and buried itself like an arrow in my now-reconstructed form lying prostrate on a slab of black stone. My body in ordinary reality shuddered with an enormous jolt of energy as this reconnection occurred, and I took a deep, almost gasping breath. The paralysis lessened and began to withdraw.

At that moment, the beam of blindingly bright light from the brilliant orb hovering near the darkness of Keaka ceased, and the ball of light abruptly disappeared. I suspected that the entirety of my visionary journey to the spiritual source of humanity had somehow been achieved through this luminous sphere, but I still had no definite sense of what "it" was for sure. I closed my eyes as I lay on the altar, feeling my chest with my hands, taking deep breaths in ordinary reality. I had been put back together, and my sense of self was almost complete.

When I opened my eyes again, the dark, shadowlike form of Keaka was gone. I sat up. I was alone on the *heiau*. I felt light, airy, etheric, and my blood seemed to be sparkling. My body felt wonderful. I looked my self over. There was something different about me, but I couldn't tell exactly what it was.

I got up and went over to the edge of the temple platform, descended the steps, and walked around the pond. I felt incredibly energized as I climbed the steps of my house. The leopard man was there on the lanai in feline form, sitting with his eyes closed and paws tucked in as though in deep meditation. I sat down next to him, assumed correct posture, and listened to the drum as I reviewed what I had just experienced, beginning to put it together conceptually. When I heard the drumbeat change and sound the call-back, I rose, bowed to my spirit helper, and returned through the inner doorway, emerging within my form lying on the rug on the floor of our workshop room.

As I sat up, I realized that there was a ringing in my ears. It was as if I could still hear a ghostly whisper of the tone—"hhhaaaa-aaaahhh." This sound remained within my mind's ear for the rest of the day, well into the evening.

I felt no desire for sleep when the evening training session was complete, so I went and soaked in the communal outdoor hot tub, but said little to anyone. Toward midnight, a spectacular meteorite with a long fuschia-colored tail streaked across the sky, exploding with a flash of green fire. It was one of the largest I have ever seen, and I wondered if it could have been a sign, a portent.

I returned to my cabin shortly thereafter but couldn't sleep. Imagery of my journey to the human spirit kept coming into my mind, as if to reinforce everything I had seen. My conceptual understanding was increasing, and I was able to accept that those uncountable numbers of brilliant spheroids had been individual human *aumakuas*. I had paid a visit to Heaven.

I finally relaxed close to dawn and began to drop down into sleep.

It was not to be, however. The inner doorway opened suddenly, and I went into one of my deep altered states in which I once again achieved the mystical connection with Nainoa. Interestingly, my notes reveal that my thoughts were resting on the spirit stone immediately before the shift occurred.

CHAPTER TWELVE

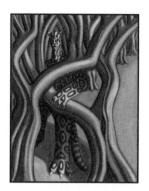

Sixth Journey: The Gift

NAINOA LEFT THE COMMUNAL MEN'S HOUSE where he had just eaten his evening meal in silence. As Kahu Sala had predicted, it had been substantial. The sky had cleared, and the moonlight created a sense of mystery as he ascended the stone steps of the main *heiau* platform and walked along the raised wooden lanai that ran around the open interior courtyard like a wide shelf. On one side rose the great hall where he would sit in meditation for the next period, practicing *lokahi* and establishing harmony within himself.

He paused before entering the building and looked at the cluster of standing stones placed in the raked sand of the courtyard's center. He felt a sense of attraction for the monoliths and studied them in silence for long moments. His thoughts turned to the spirit stone in the keeping of his mentor and kinsman, Chief Kaneohe, and as always, he felt a sense of connection. The fact that the stone was a day's travel away seemed to make no difference. There was an *aka* cord between him and the stone now, one that had grown thick in response to repeated contact—one that could be activated at any time and place simply through sustained attention.

It was at this moment that something made him look up, and he saw a huge falling star streak across the northern sky. He watched its fiery descent until it disappeared below the horizon. He wondered if it was a sign. Perhaps a person of great accomplishment had passed into the spirit world, or maybe someone of great potential was coming in from that same source.

He turned, placed his sandals on a rack built into the wall, and entered the hall. He bowed to the low altar in the center of the room and found his place, crossing his legs and settling onto his woven cushion. He glanced at the small, elongated stone standing upright in a tray of sand in the altar's center. There was a bowl of water and two small flower arrangements on each side. The burning wicks of a flat stone bowl filled with *kukui* oil provided light on the altar itself, with other lamps positioned around the large room's interior. Incense smoked in stone bowls, providing aromatic clouds in the dim light that sent a strong message to his *ku*: This was a sacred time, a *kapu* time. . . .

He looked around the hall. It was almost empty. A three-month practice period had just been completed, and there had been an exodus of students during the past two days. Many of the priests had departed as well, heading for meetings that were to be held in one of the land divisions to the north. He sighed and wondered when Kahu Sala would release him from the *kapu* she had placed upon him and send him back to Maraea. Their marriage would happen soon, and Chief Kaneohe had hinted that the Governor would probably appoint him to a position in the capital to keep both him and her beloved granddaughter close at hand.

He wondered what gift Maraea had sent to him with Nalu. The young woman was probably seated in the women's hall on the other side of the *heiau*. What a beauty she was. His curiosity about both her and the gift increased. What could it be? He glanced around the hall again and attempted to quiet his thinking mind, to become silent and still like the stone on the altar. Immediately, images of Maraea and Nalu appeared in his consciousness. So they had grown up together and were close friends. Nalu's rank could be quite high, in which case she would make a highly desirable wife for some worthy personage. Perhaps she was already married. He wondered what she was doing here at the center. Kahu Sala had said she was only to be here for a short time.

He groaned inwardly. His attempts at achieving the emptiness of mind were not meeting with success. Through an act of will, he cleared his mind of thoughts. No sooner had he done so when he felt the inner awareness that belied the possible presence of his ancestor. Then again, it could be his *aumakua*, or even both, he conceded. Chunks of his afternoon conversation with Pali surfaced for reconsideration once again. What an amazing turn his life was taking. His deepening understanding was now being complemented and enhanced by an ever-increasing internal awareness.

His thoughts shifted back and forth between the opposing polarities of his growing spiritual realization on the one hand, and the deep, emotional and physical bond he felt for Maraea on the other. Then there was Nalu and her gift. He continued to wrestle with his thoughts and feelings and finally breathed a sigh of relief when the student near the door rose and struck the wooden plaque hanging outside the hall, signaling the end of the session. He got up, bowed once again to the altar, then left the hall and retrieved his sandals from the rack.

The center's grounds were bathed in moonlight as he walked back to his room under the palms. The night air was soft, and the thick, rich scent of the flowering coffee trees flowed across the compound. The tree crickets shrilled from beyond the walls of the center, accompanied by the mighty chorusing of frogs and toads. Memories of his nights in the great forest moved through his mind.

As he approached the guest house where he was staying, he saw torches out on the water of the bay at some distance from the center. From the spread of the moving points of light, he was able to estimate the size of the canoe. He could just hear the chant of the paddlers and guessed that someone of importance was arriving late, heading for the port of the Pukui land division.

He entered his small room, noting that a student had lit the oil lamp in his absence and that fresh bedding had been provided, including a newly made cotton blanket with a simple, yet pleasing design woven into it. He smiled in appreciation and settled himself on his cushion at the end of the room to wait for Nalu, his anticipation rising.

It wasn't long before someone tapped on the door post and softly asked permission to enter. He granted it and rose to his feet as the young woman came into the room, her eyes cast down in deference. As she settled herself on the woven mat before him, he noted curiously that she bore no bundle or wrapped package.

"Chiefess Kaonokianalu, I feel gratitude at being in your presence," he began formally, as he sat down on his cushion once again. "I must also confess that the revelation of your recent meeting with High Chiefess Maraea and the knowledge that you bear a gift from her has completely disrupted my attempts at achieving *lokahi* in the hall this evening."

The girl smiled broadly at this admission. "My lady Maraea has told me of the strong heart spirit connection that exists between the two of you. I was among the large number of people at the capital who heard your account of your long journey into the interior of the continent, and I must admit that I feel both amazement at your accomplishments and great gratitude that you and my Lady Maraea are to be married. She has chosen very well, I think . . ." her eyes regarded him appraisingly. "And you are such a beautiful man."

Nainoa felt his blood begin to sparkle in response to her compliment. There was also something else. He could feel the presence of Maraea somehow. *It must be attached to the girl,* he thought. Perhaps it was because of their recent meeting. He was about to speak when a shadow passed across the door frame, and he looked up with astonishment as a tall, slender woman with long dark hair stepped into the room. His heart lurched. It was Maraea.

Sixth Journey: The Gift

"May I have your permission to enter, Chief Nainoa?" she said, taking in his complete lack of composure with a peal of merry laughter. Nainoa was momentarily speechless as he looked at the two women smiling broadly at him. Maraea's long frame was covered by a traveler's cloak that concealed her from her shoulders to her ankles. A thick lei of yellow flowers was wrapped around her head, matching another around her neck. Her white teeth flashed in her dark face. She was absolutely, breathtakingly lovely.

Nainoa gathered his scattered wits and rose to his feet. As her hand emerged from her cloak, he bowed and took it in his own, raising her fingertips to touch his forehead in deference to her higher rank. Her slim brown wrist was encircled by her bracelet, with the small carved ivory turtle in its center. His gaze swept up to meet her dark eyes. He could smell her scent mingled with that of the flowers.

"It does me great honor to present you with your gift, Chief Nainoa," said Nalu. "And it gives me great pleasure to be the source of such happiness that I feel flowing between the two of you. I shall forever remember this moment. I bid you good night." With a faint rustle of her clothing, the girl rose to her feet and departed, closing the door and leaving the two of them alone.

Maraea had not relinqished his hand, nor had her eyes released his. "It is a surprise of unsurpassed magnitude to find you here in my room, Chiefess Maraea . . ." Nainoa murmured somewhat breathlessly.

"Ali'noa . . ." she responded huskily, her eyes widening with the intensity of her feelings. "I remember an evening in the bathhouse when I asked you never to call me Chiefess when we are alone together." The blood began to hiss in his ears as he, too, recalled the moment. She moved closer to him and lifted the lei of yellow flowers from around her neck to place it around his own. Then she slowly took him into her arms and pressed her nose and forehead against his as her eyes looked deeply into his soul. With great care, he took her lovely face into his hands as they shared the breath and her mouth found his.

The kiss began with infinite gentleness, their lips barely touching, prolonging the moment as their breathing came more and more quickly. Then her full mouth softened and merged with his as the months of longing for each other flowed out of their hearts and into the room. She pressed herself against him, and the kiss deepened, her breath catching in her throat as she felt his response growing between them. Finally, she pulled back and looked at him searchingly. "It has been a long time," she whispered as her hands reached for the fastenings of his cloak and his hands found the fastenings to hers.

Within moments, they had divested each other of their clothing. The single light of the small oil lamp created a sense of mystery and intimacy as the sweet scent of the night-flowering coffee plant flowed through the room. His lips and hands slowly rediscovered the beauty of her long body as she kissed him continuously and rubbed herself against him feverishly, her fingers as bold as his own.

The moment came when they could wait no longer, and reaching down, she took him into her body with infinite, exquisite slowness. They remained motionless for a time, simply holding each other and savoring the long-awaited moment of their reunion as the intensity of their feelings grew . . . and grew. Then, Maraea's muscles began to ripple, and the ancient dance began.

The initial stage of their ritual culminated in a blazing, fiery release of incredible power, one that left them both shaken and trembling. Maraea burst into tears and cried like a little girl, repeating over and over, "I missed you so much . . . I missed you so much." Throughout, he held her in his arms, comforting her as she sobbed, and slowly . . . slowly, she calmed. He reached over and pinched out the light.

The moonlight was now shining down fully upon them through the window, causing the petals of the ruined *lei* scattered around them on the bed to glow as though the moon was blessing them and their lovemaking with fragments of itself. Nainoa responded to this magical display with wonder and pointed it out to Maraea. She reacted by gathering a handful of the moonbeams and pouring them over his naked torso with a giggle. She dried her tears then and snuggled against him, her face tucked into his neck, her long body wrapped around his. The transition of their reunion was accomplished.

"My mother and father are currently guests of the Pukui family at the port across the bay," she began. "We arrived several days ago. It was all I could do to restrain myself from coming over here to see you right away. Nalu helped me with the timing of everything. We even drew Kahu Sala into our conspiracy. She was very supportive and watched you carefully, determining when the time would be just right. I came over on the canoe this evening while your attention was being distracted in the hall," she concluded with another giggle.

"I saw it in the distance returning to the port . . ." Nainoa let the thought trail off.

Maraea was silent for a time, then she whispered, "Ali'noa . . . I have a strong feeling of premonition that we have just created a child together. A presence of great power came to me in the climax of our lovemaking. This arrival was unexpected, and it was part of what overwhelmed me. I have never encountered such a presence before, not in my dreaming nor in my everyday life. I believe that the spirit of a great ancestor has decided to return . . . that it has chosen me as its mother, and you, my lovely man, as its father. It is a great honor to be chosen in this way . . ." her words drifted off as Nainoa remembered the great star that had fallen from the heavens earlier that evening.

Maraea rose up on one elbow then and looked at him with her serious look. "My grandmother, the Governor, has sent for you. She has plans for you. She has decided to establish a new land division on the eastern side of the inland sea, one from which a road will be cut through the great forest toward the mountains so that horses may be captured and brought from the Ennu lands to the east. You are to be involved at all levels of this most important project. Your time here is now officially at a close."

Maraea sat up in the moonlight and ran her hands through her tangled mane, the moonlight streaming down her body and casting her curves and hollows into stark relief. The rich scent of her was intoxicating, and noting that her nipples were stiff, he reached out to take her lovely breasts into his hands. She sighed and moved against him sensuously, then wrapped her arms around his neck, drawing him into her embrace and planting a passionate, breathy kiss on his mouth. "I have plans for you as well," she murmured, and threw a long leg across him before pushing him backward and lying down full-length upon his body.

Nainoa held her in his arms and began to stroke her back lightly as she buried her face in his neck once again, her long hair covering them both. The fingers of one hand trailed languidly down to her bottom, exploring her softness and rediscovering her intriguing cleavage and the thick fur at the joining of her thighs. She remained very still as he continued to touch her there . . . but her breathing began to quicken . . . to quicken in response to his investigations. Finally, she could stand it no longer and snaked a hand down between their bodies to find him aroused and ready. She kissed him breathlessly, her fingers stroking him . . . stroking him as her tongue invaded his mouth. The second stage of their ceremony began. . . .

The night was almost over before their dance was done. In the darkness before the dawn, they slept in each other's arms, and deep within their souls, *lokahi* was achieved.

The sound of the door being discreetly opened woke them as Nalu slipped into the room. Her delighted smile embraced them both, then she sat down on the bed next to Maraea, informing them in a whisper that Kahu Sala would receive them as soon as they were ready. She helped Maraea rise and dress, then restored order to her thick hair with a long wooden comb. When they were ready, they slipped out to visit the women's *lua*, telling Nainoa that they would return for him shortly.

Nainoa rose and tied on his simple yellow *malo*, then combed out his long hair and arranged it in a thick knot at the base of his skull. There was a deep feeing of peace within him, engendered by the sense that everything was as it should be and that the world was good. He slung his yellow cloak around his shoulders and walked out on the lanai, breathing in the salty fog drifting off the lagoon. *The sky and the water were one at moments like this,* he thought. The palms were indistinct, standing like ghostly spirits in the opaque, flat landscape.

He visited the *lua*, then walked down to the water's edge and looked for the turtle, but he did not see it. The realization that he was going to leave this place was slowly sinking in. It had been his home for three lunar turnings. He knew every tree, every stone. He also understood that this place of refuge was inside him now, and he reflected on the days he had spent here, days of training and deepening insight that had been extraordinarily important. He knew with certainty that this period of his life would forever stand out as pivotal. Yet within himself, he felt doors closing, and he knew that the time had come to go.

He looked up as Maraea and Nalu appeared out of the mist, materializing as if the flat sheet of gray air had just given birth to them both. The women were wearing freshly made *leis* of yellow flowers, and cloaks that came down to their ankles. As they walked up to him, Maraea embraced him, kissing him warmly. "My heart spirit greets you with my warmest *aloha*, Ali'noa," she whispered, placing a *lei* around his own neck. He just held her, his eyes taking her in as her beauty created light within his soul. There were pearls of dew sparkling in her long hair, and her teeth flashed as she grinned in response to his sustained attention.

Nainoa turned and looked at Nalu, who was standing alone to one side, beaming at them, her eyes filled with tears. He reached out and drew her into their embrace, pressing his nose and forehead to hers, and looking deeply into her eyes. "Thank you for your gift, Chiefess Kaonokianalu. I will never forget it." Then he looked into the eyes of his wife to be. "I will cherish the gift forever."

They turned and walked across the compound, traversing the gardens and heading for the director's small house. Nainoa struck the wooden plaque upon their arrival, and the Kahuna Nui herself came to welcome them in. Nalu left them then, withdrawing to the kitchens to bring them refreshments. The director and her guests sat down together, looking out through the opened screens at the sky, the palms, and the lagoon. The early morning fog created a sense of isolation, as though this place of refuge existed outside of time and space, an island of tranquility and safety in the great, etheric ocean of the *aka* field.

"It gives me enormous pleasure to sit here this morning with the two of you," the *kahuna* opened with a warm smile. "There is also some sadness because your time here is now at an end, Chief Nainoa, and I shall miss our daily discussions of the great mystery. I shall miss them dearly. You have few peers, as you will discover."

She was silent for a period, then she raised her hands and said, "I now officially release you, Chief Nainoa Kaneohe, from the *kapu* I placed upon you when you arrived here. As I mentioned yesterday, I feel privileged to have been of service to you in this period of purification and training. I also feel great confidence in you as you leave this sacred place of power and go back out into the world. I know that you will serve our people well because you have always expressed a deep sense of humility combined with a strong perception of your responsibilities within the social order.

"Your sharpened skills of perception and sustained concentration, as well as your deepened self-realization and connection with your *aumakua* level of self must now extend themselves outward into the world of humanity, participating in all its myriad activities and enriching all levels of our society. For this is always the goal of the accomplished *kahuna* mystic, to acquire understanding of the true nature of reality, illuminated and enhanced by the realization of the true nature of the self, and then to transform this knowledge into wisdom through appropriate action for the benefit of all.

"With this woman's love, understanding, and support," she glanced at Chiefess Maraea, "you will become a powerful ruler and spiritual leader." She smiled broadly "Despite the high levels of status and power that you will achieve, I know that you will always be a true servant to your people.

"Accordingly, it gives me great pleasure to give you my permission to wear the yellow cloak of the Order of Kahuna associated with the Pu'uhonua o Pukui, the Place of Refuge in the Pukui land division." She glanced at several large tapa-wrapped bundles in the corner of the room. "Only those of highest spiritual merit are granted permission to wear the yellow cloak in the outside world. Although I have released you from the restrictions placed upon you here, you are now a *kapu* man, Chief Nainoa, a sacred individual of high achievement to whom even the highest chiefs will show deference.

"From time to time," she finished, "even the most powerful *kahuna* must withdraw from the outside world and its concerns in order to refresh their spiritual connections and purify themselves so that their *mana* can continue to flow in a life-enhancing manner for the benefit of all. You will always be welcome here."

Kahu Sala then turned to Maraea and said, "It has also been my privilege to serve as a fellow conspirator in your joyous reunion with this wonderful man." She chortled knowingly, then her eyes grew misty as she looked at them both. "I have a strong sense that the two of you are destined to be the progenitors of a new lineage of *kahuna* mystics, a family that will extend across time and distance, one that will have a powerful effect on the future of all humanity. Let me share something interesting with you both.

"Last night, in my dreaming, I was visited by the spirit of one of my ancestors, one who was once a personage of great merit and high spiritual achievement in this level of reality. Amazingly, and to my great wonder, this spirit informed me that it is also a member of *your* ancestry, Chiefess Maraea, and of *yours*, Chief Nainoa. This great ancestor, distantly related to us all, has apparently decided to return."

Her words drifted off as she saw the expression on Maraea's face. The two women looked at each other in silence for long moments, then the director smiled warmly and murmured, "I see that you already know, Chiefess Maraea, and how could you not? I knew when

I first met you as a child that you had the gift." The older woman reached out to clasp the hands of the younger, and tears of joy ran freely down their faces as the future locked into place, and a new facet of the great pattern came into being.

The Kahuna Nui raised her hands then and spoke the ancient words of blessing and affirmation.

> *"I call on the spirits of our ancestors,*
>> *from the sun's rising to the sun's setting,*
>> *from the zenith to the horizon,*
>> *on our right and on our left,*
>> *before us and behind us.*
> *I call upon the spirits of this place*
>> *and on all the benevolent, timeless powers*
>> *that have always existed in relationship with humanity.*
> *Convey your blessings on this woman and on this man.*
> *May you support their endeavors,*
>> *in all the levels of reality, awareness, and experience.*
> *Provide them with the gifts of your power and protection.*
> *Give them strong health and great abundance.*
> *And may these gifts be extended to their children*
>> *and to all those who assist them on their path through life.*
> *Any limiting restrictions are lifted.*
> *My prayer has flown."*

In the silence that followed, Kahu Sala suddenly shook her head and chuckled. "The *aumakua* works in wondrous ways. Although it was not my original intention to do so, in offering you the great blessing, your union is now sanctified. This means . . ." she threw up her hands in a gesture of wonder, "that you are now officially married."

As Nainoa and Maraea looked at each other in amazement at this unexpected turn of events, the Kahuna Nui added, "Of course, I'm sure your grandmother, the Governor, will provide another, more elaborate ceremony upon your return to the capital."

At this moment, the early morning sun broke through the fog, and a rainbow appeared before them, standing vertically as it had the day before. The director shook her head in amazement at this apparition and murmured, "The rainbow is nature's bridge to the great company of compassionate spirits who serve humanity. The rainbow encourages us to practice patience and right action, and to honor the ancient teachings of the Guardians."

Nalu could be seen approaching through the gardens with two students, each bearing a large tray heaped with refreshments. Nainoa's attention was drawn to the surface of the lagoon, where he saw the light gleam off the eye of the turtle who was observing him stoically. He glanced at the ivory turtle on Maraea's wrist, and a sense of wonder overcame him—an emotion that deepened into astonishment as a word in Old English suddenly appeared within his mind.

"Congratulations . . . "

CHAPTER THIRTEEN

The Gateway to Transcendent Experience

IT WAS CLOSE TO DAWN when I emerged from this wonderful connection in my bed at Westerbeke. I felt like the blessing of the Kahuna Nui had somehow been extended across time to me and my family as well, and tears flowed as I was simply overcome by emotion. I was also very much aware that I couldn't share what I had just experienced with anyone else, at least not yet. Fortunately, it was the last day of the week-long session, and as I went through the motions, my *ku's* response was to retreat into silence and stillness.

This state of suspended animation stayed with me for the rest of the day as I drove home to my family in Sacramento. I needed to go sit in the woods for a week and meditate on all I had learned and digest all that I was taking in. It was not to be, of course. I had to make the shift back into my everyday roles of being father to my children, husband to my wife, teacher to my students, payer of bills, cooker of meals, and doer of all the many tasks that my daily life at the end of the 20th century required.

It must have been difficult for Jill and the children to have me come home, completely detached and uncommunicative after being away for a week. Fortunately, the magic that touch creates worked its wondrous effects, and as my wise and beautiful wife drew me into her embrace at the end of that long day, we celebrated our feelings for each other, and the transition of our reunion was accomplished.

As I drifted into sleep for the first time in 48 hours, my last conscious awareness was pervaded by wonder and amazement, for the close resemblance between Jill and Maraea at the soul level was quite obvious to me now. I sensed, from the place of deep, intuitive knowing, that she and I had found each other once again within the vast, etheric fabric of time and space, an insight that has fully liberated me from any remaining fear of death.

Several weeks later, at the end of May, the Universe responded to one of my ongoing needs and dropped something totally unexpected into my lap—the scientific validation of my altered-state experiences.

I received a large envelope in the mail from the School of Public Health at the University of Illinois at Chicago. I opened it curiously and found several reprints of some scientific papers with a cover letter. I looked for the name of the sender and read: Norman S. Don, Ph.D., Department of Psychiatry and Co-director, The Brain Function Laboratory. As I perused his letter quickly, my excitement mounted.

Dr. Don had read my first book, *Spiritwalker*, and he expressed professional interest in my descriptions of my altered states. His letter discussed several scientific papers that had addressed the abilities of certain individuals known to be able to achieve states of profound alteration of consciousness during meditation and yoga.[1] But the crux of his letter lay in the revelation that only one paper in the scientific literature had ever presented psychophysiological data from a yogic practitioner during the ecstasy experience—that of Das and Gastaut, an electroencephalogram (EEG) study, done in the late 1950s and published in French, in which the brain waves of seven members of a spiritual community in India were measured in 20 separate recording sessions while practicing Kriya Yoga.[2]

The study, which Don sent me, presents data only from the guru, as he was the only one able to enter the state of *samadhi* (ecstatic trance), during which EEG recordings of his brain waves revealed that he was physiologically hyper-aroused. Allow me to provide a little background information so that the reader unfamiliar with the fine points of human neurophysiology will be able to understand the significance of their findings.

In so-called ordinary levels of consciousness, alpha brain waves are produced by individuals who are awake and aware, but who are not involved in any particular mental activities. Alpha waves are typically thought of as resting states in which the brain fires nerve impulses at between 8 and 13 cycles per second (Hertz). Beta brain waves are produced when the person is fully conscious and thinking, or concentrating on something, and under these circumstances, the brain fires impulses at between 13 and 20 Hertz (HZ), typically generating 10–15 microvolts of amplitude.

The states of deep calm and mental clarity achieved by experienced yoga practitioners, meditators, and Zen masters have also been measured, and under these circumstances, the brain usually slows down to between 3 and 7 HZ, the subject typically generating what are called theta waves. Interestingly, it is known that these very slow brain-wave states are also experienced during epileptic seizures, and Professor Henri Gastaut, one of the authors of the paper Don sent me, was, in fact, the world's foremost investigator of temporal lobe epilepsy at the time he conducted his research project in India.

His study of the guru's brain waves recorded in two different sessions revealed something quite unexpected. When the guru went into the ecstatic trance, his brain did not go into the theta state, but, in fact, went in the opposite direction, rising from 15–20 HZ (typical beta waves) to 30 and 40 HZ respectively, generating between 30–50 microvolts of amplitude. And while in this radical hyper-aroused altered state, EMG records of the guru's quadriceps muscle showed no increase in tonic activity, revealing that he was deeply relaxed, an interesting correlate to the paralysis that I experience during my own ecstatic trance states.

Dr. Don went on in his letter to explain that this single case study had not been seriously challenged in the 40 odd years since its publication, possibly because of the impeccable scientific credentials of Henri Gastaut. And so it remains a landmark paper in the psychophysiological literature in its examination of an advanced subject in the state of yogic ecstasy, or samadhi, considered to be the direct, conscious experience of the godhead.[3] "The question" came at the end of Don's letter: Had I, by any chance, been able to bring my own ecstatic trance states under some degree of conscious control, and if so, could I induce them voluntarily?

I sat back in my chair and smiled. Ever since the publication of *Spiritwalker* in the summer of 1995, I had hoped against hope that someone in the scientific community would read my account, someone who was seriously interested in investigating deep trance states, someone with a laboratory full of equipment for measuring things like brain waves. I saw that Don had included his pager number at the bottom of the letter. I reached for the phone.

This was the beginning of a most interesting series of conversations. It also marked the inception of a new level of understanding of my deep altered-state connections with Nainoa, as well as what I was experiencing in my goal-oriented shamanic journeywork. I also learned that Dr. Don and Dr. Gilda Moura, a Brazilian colleague, were currently conducting an ongoing program of neurocognitive research into brain function and altered states of consciousness. Over the past six years, they had recorded the EEGs and produced topographic brain maps of over 100 subjects in Brazil—shamans, trance-mediums, and traditional healers—all while in various types of religious trance.[4]

I told Don that in my personal psychosymbology, I had come to conceptualize the existence of a doorway within my mind,

within my subconscious *ku,* to be exact, one that opened periodically, allowing my conscious awareness to perceive nonlocally
beyond the boundaries of my physical body. I also informed him
that I could now open this inner doorway at will, an event that always
flooded my physical body with sensations of force or power, producing varying degrees of ecstasy, somatic paralysis, muscular
vibration or shaking, as well as visionary experience.

I concluded by offering the opinion that my deep altered-state
connections with Nainoa were experientially the same as my
lighter trance states achieved during my shamanic journeys—
that they were the same phenomenon simply experienced at different levels of intensity. Dr. Don was most excited by all of this and
invited me to come to Chicago to run some tests.

To make a long story short, I was unable to go to Chicago because
of my teaching schedule, so Don came to Sacramento, bringing his
portable field equipment with him. He set up a laboratory in his hotel
room, and the recording session took place on August 18, 1996. For
those interested in the method, let me throw in here that Don used
a Lexicor Medical Technology, Inc., Neurosearch-24 system, con-
sisting of 19 AC-coupled amplifiers for EEG recording (time constant approximately 0.3 sec), plus five additional channels and related
software for data editing and analysis.

For the first hour and a half, he applied electrodes to my
scalp, using an electrode cap and conducting gel made by Electro-
Cap International, Inc. The elastic skull cap had tin electrodes prepo-
sitioned over the 19 standard scalp sites of the International
"10-20" system. A forehead ground was utilized, and reference electrodes were applied to my right and left earlobes and linked. In everyday terminology, this was hard science.

My EEG baselines were collected first while I was seated,
relaxed, and in an upright position with my eyes closed. It is
worth noting that these baseline recordings were typical of normal,
resting EEGs, with no sign of abnormal brain function, such as epilep-
tiform patterns or slowing in the EEG. When he had what he
needed, Don asked me to open that inner doorway of mine. Just

for fun, I had him give me a countdown, and when he said "zero," I opened the doorway, and WHAM! The power sensations flooded into me with full force.

I held the state for about 15 seconds, my body vibrating with the soaring ecstasy, then I closed the door and turned to Don. "Did you get it?" He had been watching the computer screen behind me, and his first words were "Wow! You can really do it, can't you?"

"I said I could do it," I responded with just a hint of impatience. *Why would I lie about this and waste his time and mine,* I thought.

"Can you do it again?" he asked with excitement, ignoring my pique. "The guru in India could only do it twice."

To make another long story short, I voluntarily induced the ecstatic trance state within myself 11 separate times over the next hour, during which I experienced the sensations of power and perceived the typical phosphenic visual hallucinations of flashes or patterns of light. In one episode, I made conscious connection with the stone through the *aka* cord that connects us. The EEG recordings made during these intentionally induced altered states reveal that my brain waves consistently reached 40 HZ with amplitudes of 50–60 microvolts, the result of a single, high-energy process, maximally affecting the frontal and prefrontal regions of my brain.

Both Don and I were very excited by this confirmation of my ability, and when he came over to my house for lunch at the close of our session, he looked at Jill and said, "Your husband is a very unusual man. The ability to voluntarily enter the extreme hyper-aroused state of ecstasy appears to be very rare."

In the discussion that followed, Don revealed that a great deal of interest has recently been focused in the neuroscience literature on these 40 HZ brain waves, sometimes called the gamma rhythm, because of their apparent relationship to the mechanism by which the brain binds its broadly distributed functioning processes together into integrated conscious experiences.

Don also told us that he and Moura had been able to locate only 13 other subjects who can achieve these high frequency hyperarousal states at will. During the recording sessions that took place in a variety of field settings throughout Brazil between 1990 and 1996, all 13 subjects, like me, were able to voluntarily enter and leave hyper-aroused trance states in which they achieved high frequency 40 HZ brain waves, with 40–50 microvolts of amplitude. The highest amplitude waves were found over the prefrontal recording sites, again like my own, although the effect was generalized over the entire scalp.

All the Brazilians, like me, also reported sensations of paralysis during their altered states, as well as the related feeling that they were linked to a higher consciousness, or connected with a non-human being (a spirit), or even God. Unlike me, however, all 13 have had the alien abduction experience and report that their ability to enter trance developed only after their reported contact with non-human beings.

As far as I know, I have never had any contact with what the popular and scientific presses have termed "extraterrestrials," or "aliens." Gilda Moura called me from Brazil shortly after Don's departure from Sacramento. She questioned me closely for over an hour to see if I had ever had such contact, but the closest we got was a very early memory that she extracted from my *ku* using hypnosis.[5]

In this memory, it was the middle of the day, and I had just been put into my crib for my afternoon nap by my mother. I was still in diapers, and I was unable to stand or sit up, although I could turn over and thrash my arms and legs, so my guess is that I was less than six months of age, probably closer to three. As I say this, I am very much aware that contemporary mainstream science affirms with confidence that memories from such an early stage of development are not possible, but then, current scientific mythology would also include most of what I have reported in my books as impossible as well.

In this recovered memory, the ceiling and walls of the room were white. I was not the least bit tired, nor was I interested in taking a nap, so I thrashed my little arms and legs like a steam engine, vocalizing away until I suddenly became aware of a sound. It was a high-pitched whine or ringing sound, with a curious vibrational quality to it, not unlike that of a Tibetan bowl when "stroked" with a wooden beater, or that of cicadas shrilling away from the trees in the heat of summer. However, I was born in the month of August, so this event must have occurred between November and February when no cicadas were active.

The sound was quite audible to me, and I clearly recall looking around for its source, but I could see only the walls and the ceiling, and, of course, the railings of my crib. The sound increased in intensity, getting higher and higher, and as it did, the room seemed to get brighter and brighter. The sound continued to rise until it passed beyond the range of my hearing. It was at this same moment that the room became so bright that I experienced a total visual "white-out." I can remember nothing after that.

Moura was quite excited by my recovery of this memory, but whether or not it qualifies as an "alien encounter" is doubtful to me. The whole question of aliens and extraterrestrials is beyond my direct experience, so I cannot comment on it, although as I say this, I must admit that I have always wondered whether these so-called aliens could, in fact, be spirits. I have read several published accounts of experiencers that have struck me as similar to my own, and this has led me to question whether these abductions might, in fact, be spiritual experiences.

Interestingly, the *kahuna* David Bray stated in his teachings that spiritual guardians from outside our solar system visit us from time to time, presumably to see how we're doing with our practice. He proclaimed that these visitors are our friends, and that we have no business challenging or fearing them.[6] This leads one to wonder if these so-called aliens could, in fact, be such spiritual guardians, but then, the clearly dreadful encounters endured by many experiencers may suggest that some of them may fall into the category Bray designated as "demonic."

As an anthropologist, I am aware that each of us learns how to interpret reality through the cultural lens that we acquire as children from our parents, our teachers, and our friends during the early stages of our socialization. Could it be possible that the consensual fear-based interpretation of the whole alien phenomenon held by Western culture at large may have been strongly influenced, or even created, by Hollywood and the film industry? Would an indigenous Indian from the Amazon basin with little or no exposure to Western culture interpret such contact in a different manner?

It is worth noting that both Moura and Don speculated about a most intriguing possibility. Could it be that those of us who can voluntarily enter radical hyper-arousal trance states are evolutionary prototypes for a new species of human? This is a provocative thought, revealing the levels of consciousness and experience that might be available to us all during the next stage of human evolution. Of course, it is also possible that those of us who can vision in this way may be archetypes from a time when virtually everyone was able to do it.

The archeological record of the last 40,000 years of human prehistory, for example, preserves a rich record of rock art that reveals the definite influence of the shaman.[7] Until relatively recently, the shaman was a universal figure found in virtually all of the world's cultures, and it is known that among the traditional !Kung San bushmen in southern Africa, for example, up to 50 percent of the men and 30 percent of the women could shamanize, achieving the deep, mystic trance state in order to find the game animals, influence the weather, or accomplish healing work for each other when the need arose.[8]

This raises an interesting question: Could it be that we in the West are in the process of losing the ability through lack of use due to centuries of misunderstanding and suppression by our religious, political, and medical hierarchies? As many have observed, if you don't use it, you lose it. Yet many investigators of shamanism, including Michael Harner, have suggested that the majority of us possess the ability to achieve the shamanic trance state, whether or not we are aware of it. If this is so, it gives rise to another, intriguing possibility.

The 13 subjects in Don and Moura's study all claim that they were unable to achieve the hyper-aroused state until their purported contact with nonhuman extraterrestrials. In my own case, I was unable to enter this state until my initial contact with the formidable, shadowlike spirit that Nainoa calls Keaka.[9] Is it possible that the experiencing of a "mind-blowing" altered state of consciousness, elicited in response to (or directly caused by) contact with a powerful nonhuman entity, causes chemical and structural changes in the brain of the experiencer?[10]

This is a heretical question for a scientist to consider, yet traditional people maintain that the spirits function as teachers for the neophyte shaman, especially during the initial stages of the relationship. Is it possible that such contact and experience can indeed function in a "teaching capacity," inducing a form of neural programming, or reprogramming, that then allows the experiencer's subconscious to access the state voluntarily?

To be more specific: Is it possible that a powerful altered state of consciousness could actually alter the experiencer's DNA, activating a preexisting biomolecular program within the neurons of the central nervous system, *or even creating one*, which can then be switched on and off by the experiencer once he or she has learned how?[11] If this proves to be so, and there exists scientific evidence to support the supposition, it would confirm the shaman's claim that the ability to enter specific altered states is a learned skill that improves with practice.[12]

Many have hypothesized that 40-HZ brain waves are caused by cortical circuits that are intimately linked with the region of the midbrain called the thalamus, and that these hyper-aroused states occur especially during processing tasks that require the binding of processed sensory information with attention, memory, and motor responses. If this is so, it may reveal, as Don and Moura have suggested, that these 40-HZ brain waves may be related to the generation of consciousness at the physiological level.

The 13 subjects in Don and Moura's study, the guru in Das and Gastaut's report, and the visionary narratives detailed in my books, have all demonstrated that these high-amplitude brain waves are involved with superconsciousness states, both physiologically and experientially. Despite differing cultural ways of interpreting or even understanding such evidence, it is clear that for those who can achieve them, these hyper-aroused states appear to be a gateway to transcendent experience.[13]

As our lunch came to an end that day in Sacramento, Don sat back in his chair and delivered the punchline—one that had a direct bearing on my altered-state experiences. He said that it is very likely that individuals, including myself, in the hyper-aroused trance-state characterized by those broad-band 40-HZ brain rhythms, are in a prime condition to receive information unconstrained by space, time, and ordinary causality.

In support of this, he cited a well-known paper by R. Fischer, published in *Science* in 1971,[14] on the cartography of meditative and ecstatic trance states. In his mapping of the perception-meditation-hallucination continuum, Fischer proposed that the constraints on normal, waking consciousness are *bridged* during extreme hyper-aroused states, and that a higher order of self or personality then prevails, one which seems to transcend both space and time.

As I considered the extraordinary events to which I had been privy to over the past ten years, I reflected that I couldn't have put it better myself.

My summer months in 1996 were filled with speaking engagements and workshops, from Montreal and New York in the east; to Montana, Los Angeles, and San Diego in the west. Occasionally, some confident soul who had read *Spiritwalker* would confront me, asking me how I reconciled my intellectual practice of doing hard science with my mystical practice of studying and teaching shamanism. This is very easy for me to do, but not always so easy to explain in ways that others find intellectually satisfying.

As a scientist, I utilize my mental-intellectual mind-aspect—what Nainoa would call the *uhane* or the *lono* mind; what Freud would have called my ego; or Jung, the conscious mind—through which I approach truth as something objective. And there is no doubt that this inner director and decision maker is essential in studying fossils that possess a form and a dimension that can be measured, quantified, and reproduced. In this manner, I can learn the secrets that they possess.

As a student of mysticism, I utilize my deeper subconscious mind, my *ku*, and my spiritual superconscious aspect, my *aumakua*, approaching truth through my emotional-intuitive capacities, through which I can access the subjective levels of reality, awareness, and experience. These can be dimensionless and formless, *and* they can be just as real as the objective physical level of reality that we all take very much for granted on a day-to-day basis.

When combining these two lines of investigation, I might describe myself as an evolutionary explorer—as one who managed, by chance, to cross an unknown inner threshold, in the process triggering some mechanism built into my biological makeup, evoking a biophysical-energetic program that was seemingly asleep. And when this program was activated, I discovered, much to my astonishment, that it was oriented toward the expansion of consciousness. It was in this way that I, like countless others before me, became a player of the Master Game.

I suspect that this ability was discovered tens of thousands of years ago by our Stone Age ancestors. The wisdom of the traditional peoples suggests that this biophysical capacity is a learned skill, available to everyone. But before one can do it, one must accept the fact that such an experience is possible. If you don't believe it is possible, then that's your first obstacle.

I have also come to understand that as we play the great game and the transcendent self increases and grows within us, it unfolds like a flower or a butterfly, much as I saw it in my vision, and when free of the confines of the physical body, it may assume an energetic shape much like a doughnut, or what science calls a *torus*. This process of growth cannot be forced, in my opinion, nor do I believe that it can be hastened by engaging in various spiritual practices with great expenditures of energy and dedication. I suspect that the key to spiritual growth and awareness is not fervor and commitment, but the removal of obstacles.

I heard an elder Navajo medicine man and shaman say something once that I have never forgotten: "In order to walk in beauty with all things, we must connect with all things. We must take them seriously, with reverence," he said. "In this way, we participate with all things and become one with them. It's from our direct experiences with life that we encounter the timeless and learn its hidden secrets."

I suspect that this insight reveals where and when we find our secret garden. This is our paradise, our heaven, and as accomplished shamans and mystics across time have always maintained, there must be no strain, no striving, no haste. The keys that open the inner doorway are the ability to achieve harmony and balance between the three selves on the one hand, and the practice of reverence and appreciation on the other.

My next contact with Nainoa occurred late in the summer. I was home with my family, consciously practicing appreciation, functioning as an active participant-observer with my wife and children, valuing my connection with them and their connection with me. I understood quite clearly that my evolving spiritual *aumakua* aspect is profoundly moved by the practice of appreciation—that it was and is being enriched by my ongoing ability to experience and value the beauty in everything and everyone around me.

And since this transcendent self is the aspect through which my conscious awareness can move through time and space, I reasoned that if I rewarded it sufficiently, it might respond, so to speak, by rewarding me. So I continued in my daily practice of reverence and appreciation, and nowhere was this experienced more joyfully than in the love relationship I shared with Jill.

It was in response to one such celebration of each other at dawn that I was able to become the bridge once again and connect my consciousness with my transcendent self, releasing my awareness into the vast, mysterious regions of the mystic ocean, in search of the island that I have come to know as Nainoa.

CHAPTER FOURTEEN

Seventh Journey: The Visitors

NAINOA HAD JUST TAKEN A MEAL at the Men's House and was sitting on the broad lanai of his new residence at the capital. It was late in the afternoon, and the low sun was casting swaths of yellow light across the land and water through the broken clouds to the west. It had not rained that day, and the smoky haze generated by cooking fires hung over the sprawling town, creating a dreamlike quality to the landscape. Sea birds wheeled in the air above, heading back to their own places of rest before the fall of night.

Nainoa detected the familiar presence the moment it arrived within his mind. He settled himself on his carved wooden stool, waiting for the thoughtline to begin. Then he smiled and initiated it himself, bringing up memories of all that had happened since his return from the Place of Refuge. He looked around at his new abode. This had been Maraea's great surprise for him on their arrival at the capital almost a month ago. The compound was located on a newly cleared and terraced hillside above that of Maraea's family. She had planned the layout of the buildings herself, utilizing most of her parents' staff and a large number of commoners to finish as much of the work as possible before his return.

Nainoa let his eyes roam along the compound's perimeter delineated by freshly planted bamboo, banana trees, *ti* plants, and various flowering bushes, including coffee. Stone walkways linked the buildings to each other, and stone-lined gutters had been set into the ground to carry off the rainwater. Needless to say, the Governor's blessing and support had ensured the swift completion of the project's initial phases.

Dominating the cluster of houses was the large peak-roofed reception hall, still under construction, in which all public activities and meetings would take place. At the compound's lower level were the servants' quarters—the men's on the left and the women's on the right. Above them were the just-completed kitchens and dining halls, composed of several large, thatched buildings in which men and women took their meals separately, according to ancient custom—again, the men's to the left and the women's to the right. The two *hale pe'a* for the menstruating women were located on the compound's far right side, one for the chiefs and the other for the servants, their privacy ensured by planted bamboo that would eventually grow into a grove. Above and to each side of the reception hall were the bathhouses and the *luas*, men's to the left, women's to the right, and there were two guest houses, as well as a large storage house under construction near the entrance to the compound.

At the top of the compound were his and Maraea's private residences, hers to the right, his to the left, joined by a short, covered walkway. The single room in each *hale* had a raised sleeping platform along one side and a stone-lined fire pit recessed into the floor to provide warmth during the cool nights of the rainy season. Their houses were bordered by broad lanais, with sweeping views of the town below. There was also a small cottage next to Maraea's house in which Nalu, her heart-sister, had recently taken up residence. Nainoa smiled. The two women were inseparable, and he sensed that Nalu would enter the formal dynamic of their family as a junior wife at some time in the future.

He turned and glanced down the length of the lanai toward the forest above and saw the edge of their private bathhouse. The thatch-roofed structure rested on a newly made stone terrace nestled into the trees at the compound's upper limit, and had finely woven screens that could be raised or lowered, allowing them privacy as well as views into the forest. The water for the wooden plank-lined plunge had its source in the same spring that fed the entire compound. It was heated in a small oven house off to one side and was channeled to the large tub through fitted and caulked sections of timber bamboo. Maraea was very taken with their bathhouse, as their relationship had gotten off to a most propitious beginning in a similar setting.

Nainoa's gaze took in the totality of his new home, and within himself, he felt a sense of profound gratitude and appreciation. This was a far cry from his humble beginnings as a servant's son. His nose widened as he breathed in deeply, taking in the smells of the newly cut wood and fresh thatch of the roof, mixed with the aromatic scent of incense burned daily to sanctify the dwelling and discourage insects.

A light wind appeared from the west, and Nainoa pulled his yellow cloak around his shoulders, his thoughts shifting as his eyes swept down to Maraea's family compound on the edge of the lagoon below. He could make out the roof of the long-house where their double-hulled canoe was now situated. It would be good for her to live close to her family, and for him as well, for he had established a close bond with Maraea's father, Chief Wilipaki. They had liked each other from the start, and their time together at the Place of Refuge had provided the two of them with a rich beginning on which to build a deep, ongoing relationship.

His thoughts returned to his last day at the retreat center. The Kahuna Nui had released him from the restrictions, as well as the daily schedule followed by the residents at the center, so he had taken Maraea and Nalu for a walk in the forest. He was curious to see if his "secret garden" was really there or whether he had dreamed the whole thing into existence.

He had located the magical place once again, and the three of them had spent part of the day there, swimming in the long pool and frolicking under the waterfall. Old Pali had not appeared, but he had sensed the watchfulness of someone or something—an awareness that intensified in response to the two lovely women sitting nude on the ledge above the pool as they combed and dried their long hair in the sun.

The surface of the water had been strewn with yellow flowers from the crown of a tree high above, and the women had made *leis*, utilizing a ball of fine palm fiber Nalu carried in her sling bag for that purpose. When the shadows began to grow long and they had finally dressed and made ready to depart, Nainoa had asked Nalu to make one more *lei* for the spirits of the place. He had then hung it on a branch above the ledge for the old recluse with a whispered prayer of farewell.

Chief Wilipaki had arrived at the center with his long, double-hulled canoe in the mid-afternoon and was waiting for them when they emerged from the forest. His possessions had already been packed and loaded, and the Kahuna Nui and many of the residents at the center had come to see them off. Kahu Sala had embraced him and pressed her forehead and nose to his, looking deeply into his soul as they shared the breath.

"Until we meet again," she said, "please take with you my very warmest *aloha* . . . and this small token to remind you of your time here." She had placed an object wrapped in *ti* leaves in his hands, and upon opening it, he discovered the sun-bleached skull of a turtle, polished and decorated with shell and stone beads from the market. She had smiled, nodding toward the lagoon. "It contains the *mana* of this place as well as that of Honumakua."

The master gardener Chief Hakai had then clasped Nainoa's shoulders fiercely and given him his own digging stick, instructing him to do some garden work every day in the months and years to come. Nainoa had received their gifts with gratitude, then he had turned and helped the two women onto the craft waiting in the shallows, swinging on-board himself as the ancient Hawaiian song of farewell rose into the air. The paddlers had taken the great canoe out toward the bay, and there had hardly been a dry eye to be found as all responded to the poignancy of the moment. As the wind caught the sails and the canoe had surged in response, Nainoa thought he saw old Pali grinning at him from the edge of the crowd on the beach, the *lei* of yellow flowers wrapped around his bony chest. But then, it could have been someone else.

They had spent the night as the guests of the Pukui family at the port across the bay and had returned to the capital the next day. Sharp-eyed children had been posted to watch for their sails, and the Governor herself had been waiting to greet them as the paddlers brought the long canoe up to the dock in front of Maraea's parents' compound.

Many family members had come for the evening to share in the sumptuous feast of welcome. The Governor had stayed, temporarily lifting the *kapu* against men and women eating together and listening with delight as her granddaughter gave the gathering a detailed account of how she and Nalu had conspired with Kahu Sala to disrupt the evening meditation practice of the new *kahuna* in the family. Ruth Kahalopuna's eyes had rested thoughtfully upon Nainoa for much of the evening as he answered questions and shared anecdotes about his days at the Place of Refuge, skillfully valuing his teachers and his training without discussing details of his actual practice.

"And what did you find most valuable of all during your time there, Chief Nainoa?" she had asked him at one point. Silence had fallen, and all eyes had turned as he paused as though in deep thought.

"Nalu's gift."

The Governor had burst into a peal of merry laughter and beamed at him approvingly. Maraea had blushed, something no one could remember seeing her do, and the general hilarity that followed had escalated into applause. All had then called upon Maraea to dance, and she had risen gracefully to her feet, her mane of hair flying and her eyes and teeth flashing as she performed an energetic, impromptu *hula* that expressed her unmistakable feelings for her husband-to-be. As the drummers increased the tempo on their slit drums, and the eroticism of her dance grew more exaggerated, Nainoa had thrown off his yellow cloak and joined her, provoking a new wave of approval mixed with mirth. At the dance's end, the Governor had impulsively risen to her feet and embraced them both, breaking protocol, to everyone's amazement.

When the evening finally came to a close, Ruth Kahalopuna had taken the hand of her granddaughter and invited all present to attend the formal ceremony of her marriage to Kahu Nainoa Kaneohe ten days hence at the Governor's mansion. And so it had happened.

Imagery of the event ran through his mind. The Governor's chief ceremonialist had led the ritual in which sacred *awa* had been prepared and offered, sanctifying their union and creating a *kapu* around them and their marriage. After Nainoa and Maraea had honored their ancestors by chanting their genealogies, they had exchanged vows and proclaimed their love for each other as they placed *leis* of woven white ginger flowers about each other's necks. Large numbers of oxen, pigs, sheep, and plant-foods had been ritually sacrificed for the occasion, and there had been thunder and lightning on the fog-enshrouded hills around the capital—all sure signs that the spirits were pleased with both the "sacrifices" and with their marriage.

Then a feast worthy of the occasion was enjoyed by the guests, including anyone and everyone who was related by blood or marriage to either Nainoa or Maraea. Chief Kaneohe and more than 50 members of his immediate family had come on four double-hulled canoes, a contingency that included a large number of servants among whom Nainoa had grown up as a child. The exact number of people in the Governor's extended family was not known, but the inner circle of the celebratory throng had numbered close to 1,000. Maraea was well loved by the populace of the capital, and most of the commoners of the Kahalopuna land division had come to pay their respects as well.

The celebration had gone on for three days, during which time the Governor had ceremonially redistributed much of the surpluses accumulated during the previous harvest season. Everyone—chiefs and commoners alike—had gone back to their homes loaded with food, cloth, tools, baskets, and personal ornaments. When the grand affair was finally done and the long canoes bearing their distinguished guests and servants and all their possessions had departed at last, no one could recall anything like this celebration since the Governor's marriage almost 50 years before. The lavish event had stood in stark contrast to Nainoa's 90 days of silence and introspection at the Place of Refuge.

Nainoa's thoughts shifted back to his training. His conversations with Kahu Sala had been incredibly detailed, rich with *kaona*, hidden meaning and metaphor, and had included many principles of knowledge of which he had been previously unaware. The levels of the self and the nature of reality had only been the beginning, but this knowledge formed the foundation for understanding how the *kahuna* mystic could serve their people as a bridge between the spiritual dimensions and the everyday world.

There had been long discussions about the nature of *ike*, the spiritual power that gave the *kahuna* the ability to heal others through prayer. He had also been instructed about the great power called *mana*, and how everything in existence received a certain amount of this energy from the higher guardian spirits. This had led to the understanding that everything in nature, including human beings, are both manifestations of and repositories for this *mana*. He had learned ancient *kahuna* methods for drawing on this power to assist in accomplishing various things, like creating thoughtforms in order to manifest effects into the everyday world. But to be truly successful at these endeavors, the *kahuna* first had to establish connection with the spiritual levels of reality and the spirits that resided within them.

"The *kahuna* develops an awareness of and a relationship with the spirits that are found within everything, everywhere," Kahu Sala had said, "but most especially with their own personal *aumakua* aspect, for it is through this spirit-self that the power is most easily accessed. My mother used to say that the Universe is like a great ocean filed with *mana*, and the *kahuna* like a small pond that is constantly being replenished—the *mana* falling into the pond like rain, coming through the *aumakua*."

"Does this mean that the *aumakua* is like a cloud floating in the air?" he had asked her, to which she had laughed and said, "Exactly. Our spirit self is much like a cloud floating above and around us, but we usually can't see it because it is energetic and exists in the spirtual levels of reality."

But of all the many things they had discussed, it was the nature of the inner worlds and the spirits one could meet there that had fascinated him the most. Kahu Sala often talked about the guardian spirits that had come into association with the evolving human lineage in the remote past, emerging from the spirit world to take on the task of assisting humanity in the achievement of its destiny. She had discussed how all manifested life forms had such guardians, and how these powers often came into relationship with particular humans for whom they felt a special affection— Nainoa's friendship with the spirit of the spotted tiger being a case in point.

"In addition to those spirits who function as guardians and servants for the many life forms, there are those concerned with particular individuals," she had said, "as well as those concerned with special family lineages or with certain *kahuna* orders. It is also well known that such a spirit will sometimes take up residence within an object, a carved image, or one that is naturally formed, like the ones we use as meditational images in our *heiaus*—or the stone of your mentor and kinsman, Chief Kaneohe."

Long discussions had followed, focused on the nature of how such spirits could affect the individual with whom they were in relationship. She had then gone on to talk about the hierarchy to which all life forms, as well as all spirits belong, and how the *kahuna* had to be able to connect with the appropriate members of this hierarchy in order to function effectively as a bridge between the spiritual and material planes.

"Among the most fascinating are those incredibly powerful entities concerned with the activities of nature. There are also those higher powers who operate largely beyond the scope of the evolution of our planet. When an exceptional individual has proven themselves worthy, one or more of these great ones may come into connection with them, providing the *kahuna* with the direct experience of universal power and offering them teachings concerned with the nature of the all-that-is. One is never quite the same after such contact." The memory of the awesome *dorajuadiok* flickered briefly in his mind.

Nainoa paused in his thoughtline as his reverie was interrupted by the chattering of monkeys. He looked up into the forest that rose steeply above the compound. The uncleared land above the house was unsuitable for terraced agriculture and too steep for additional habitation. He had explored the area early one morning and had found an irregular, but mostly level rocky ledge up the wooded hillside, one that could be enlarged, terraced, and made suitable for a small *heiau*. He had decided that this would be his dreaming place among the trees, his personal place of refuge tucked into the wooded, rocky escarpment. He sensed that the spirit stone would reside there someday, when it passed into his keeping with Chief Kaneohe's transition into spirit.

Nainoa suddenly felt a strong urge to go up to the ledge. He glanced at the sky. There was still time before nightfall. He remembered the mind nested within his own and smiled again. Perhaps his ancestor would like to have a look at this place. He rose, took his sandals from the rack along the wall of his house, and slipped them on, then descended from the lanai, reaching the edge of the compound near the bathhouse in a few short strides. He looked up for the monkeys, but he didn't see them. They had moved into the forest, and he could hear them quarreling higher up the hillside.

Nainoa opened the low gate and passed into the dominion of

the trees. He closed his eyes for long moments and stood still, feeling the thick presence of the forest around him. Ever since his long walk, it always felt good to be in connection with the peculiar, dreamlike consciousness of the trees. Then he opened his eyes and sought the familiar, finding a clump of flowering bromeliads clinging to a branch high above. A birdcall sounded from higher up the hill.

There was no real path as yet, so he made his way up to the ledge by utilizing the thick roots of a banyan tree that snaked down the hillside like a ladder. A light mist began to drift through the trees as he stood up on the narrow rock platform and began to study his surroundings. A hibiscus bush growing out of the rock wall attracted his attention. It was dotted with bright red flowers. He couldn't remember seeing it during his former visit, but perhaps it hadn't been flowering at that time. He detected movement higher up the hillside and saw a large duck observing him with a flat stare. He wondered briefly what it was doing up here. Perhaps it had a nest among the stones and mosses.

Nainoa turned his attention to the proportions of the ledge and began to dream his *heiau* into existence. The rocky shelf would have to be enlarged over here and leveled over there. He looked closely at the stone, studying it for cracks into which wedges could be driven. He noted absently that much of the brown rock protruding from the hillside was pocked with many small holes, much like the black stones that had been brought by his voyager ancestors from the home island of Hawai'i. It seemed to be the same kind of rock, although a different color.

With this observation, he suddenly felt a presence appear in proximity to him. The feeling was unmistakable, and chickenskin formed on his arms and legs. It was quite different from the presence connected with his mind. The blood started to hiss in his ears. Something or someone powerful was watching him, of that he was sure, and it felt enormous. Perhaps a spirit lived here on this ledge, or within these stones. He looked around carefully but saw nothing unusual. He waited, but nothing untoward occurred for long moments. Then the fog seemed to thicken into a swirling density at the far end of the ledge. He watched the mist curiously. The form, if it could be called that, was easily twice his height. It seemed to have a pinkish tint, and there was a curious smell—like the steam rising from fresh-cooked eggs.

He had a sense of time passing and suddenly looked away from the smoky form, breaking the contact. The light was beginning to fade. He glanced back at the end of the rocky shelf, but the shape was gone, as though it had never existed. He thought about what had just happened, and on impulse, he picked a red hibiscus from the bush and left it on the rocky shelf with a whispered prayer as an offering to whatever spirit had come. He glanced upwards. The duck was still there, watching him impassively, its gray and brown feathers merging into the drifting fog.

Nainoa climbed back down the slope toward his house, and as he passed through the gate, the light seemed to come up once again. The air was clear, and he could see down toward the town. He turned and looked back into the trees. The fog seemed to be restricted to the forest. The feeling of being watched was still there.

As he climbed the steps of his lanai, he happened to look down and saw an outcropping of the same pocked rock emerging from the ground next to his house. The stone platform of the building was actually resting on it. *An altar,* he thought. *I will build an altar up there in the trees so I can leave offerings for this spirit. Perhaps I will find out who or what it is and so come into relationship with it.*

Nainoa's awareness shifted with the arrival of Maraea and Nalu. They had just returned from taking a meal at the Women's House and were wearing similar dresses with matching *leis* of yellow flowers around their necks and woven into their long hair. His pulse quickened. "My heart sings in response to the presence of two such lovely women . . ."

He was rewarded by a warm embrace from both, followed by a kiss from his wife. Maraea was most definitely pregnant with their first child, but this seemed to have had no apparent effect on the ardor that arose between them. Nalu laughed with delight as she picked up their feelings for each other. As Maraea drew back with a breathy sigh, her sparkling eyes suddenly narrowed into seriousness. "We have a visitor," she said quietly. "There is something or someone hovering around you, dear husband, something very powerful . . . something big. It definitely seems to be female as well."

Without missing a beat, she took the flowers from around her neck and bowed, placing them on a low table at the edge of the lanai with a whispered prayer of welcome to their invisible guest. Then she straightened and raised her eyes to the forest. Nainoa rubbed the chickenskin on his forearms as his hair stood up and the feeling of presence surged. Then the moment passed, and whatever had approached them was suddenly gone. Both felt the transition and glanced at each other. Maraea turned to Nalu and took note of her rigid posture. "Do not fear," she said, embracing her. "Our visitor has departed. Let us retire to the bathhouse in preparation for sleep." Then she smiled. "Please join us, Ali'noa, so that you can tell us what you have perceived."

And so it occurred—the three of them withdrawing to the pool of heated water in the growing darkness. Nainoa lit the oil lamps on small shelves set into the walls on both sides of the tub, then settled into the water with the two women and told them about the presence on the ledge. Nalu continued to watch him with gravity, her blue eyes expressing concern. Maraea's dark eyes radiated knowledge and understanding.

"A duck . . . ?" she inquired with a rise of her strong eyebrows. "Yes," he said, "a large one. It had black feet and curious furrows in the feathers of its neck. It was mostly gray with a dark crown. I've never seen one quite like it before. Perhaps it was a goose."

An unbidden image suddenly flitted through his mind—a barren, dark rocky landscape with an immense, rounded black mountain rising into the sky in the distance. And there, among some low shrubs nearby, he saw a group of large ducks standing, just like the one he had seen on the ledge. They were looking right at him. Maraea was watching his eyes and asked, "What is it?"

"I have just had a curious thought," he said. "Actually, it was more like a memory, but definitely not one of mine . . ." His words drifted off as he realized that the American was still in connection, and the man had just projected an image into his mind. He glanced at the two women with him. Maraea, mindful of the effect of the heat on her growing baby, had emerged from the water and was stretched out on the wooden platform that ran along one side of the tub. As his eyes took in the length of her naked loveliness through the steam, he wondered how she would react if she knew that a man who had lived 5,000 years in the past was observing her through his eyes.

Maraea was still watching him, a half-smile on her face. Abruptly, her eyes widened, and he knew that she knew—that she had perceived the American's awareness through the *aka* fibers that connected them. Nainoa waited for her reaction, intrigued. After a long moment, she sat up, cocked her head at Nalu, and smiled broadly.

"I am going to retire now, and I am going to take this beautiful man with me. Enjoy the bathhouse as long as you wish and come find me before the morning meal." She extended her hand to the girl who rose from the water, took it, and touched Maraea's fingers to her forehead. Maraea embraced her then and pressed her forehead and nose to Nalu's, sharing the breath and looking deeply into her eyes before kissing her warmly.

Nainoa emerged from the steamy water and wrapped his wife in a wide cotton blanket before tying one around himself. He took her arm and boldly steered her toward his house, padding barefoot with her down the lanai. She smiled and allowed this. Ordinarily, it was she who invited him to her bed. Servants had prepared the raised sleeping platform along one wall, arranging woven blankets and pillows on the many layers of finely woven mats. Incense smoked in a stone bowl to one side of the recessed fire pit in the floor in which a low fire glowed, providing warmth. The light from the oil lamps filled the room with a soft radiance.

Nainoa glanced at the wooden altar along the wall near one side of the bed. Various personal objects rested upon it, including the bottle he had found the day he met old Pali, and the turtle skull given to him by the Kahuna Nui. His chief's necklace, presented to him by Chief Kaneohe, was kept in a woven container, and Chief Hakai's digging stick stood to one side. The necklace of beads put together by Kenojelak hung from a hook on the wall. It included the small carved talismans made for him by the Ennu men of her band, with the ivory fetish carved by William right in the center.

As Nainoa's eyes roved across these objects, his thoughts rested briefly upon those who had given them to him. As he brought the image of each person up into his mind, he experienced the love that he felt for them and sent pulses of his *aloha* through the *aka* cords of connection, adding an extra surge of power and affection for Kenojelak, his Ennu wife so far away.

As always at moments like this, he wondered briefly what Maraea would think of Kenojelak. Would Maraea like her, or even love her, as she did Nalu? He considered the possible shape of the future unfolding before him and knew that he would see Kenojelak again, perhaps many times in the years to come. But would he ever bring his two heart-wives together? He pursed his lips as Kenojelak did when she was in thought, then caught himself and smiled. The shape of the future was still forming, but he knew that she would always be a part of his life—always.

The moment passed, and Nainoa returned to the present, using a long pole to lower the plaited palm fiber screens that covered the high windows at each end of the room near the roof peak. He glanced at Maraea, who was reclining nude on the bed, her slender arms thrown over her head, accentuating her height.

He felt his blood rise in response to her beauty. He placed some more wood on the fire, then strode to the bed, lowering himself beside her and taking her gently into his arms. She giggled as he rubbed his face in the thick fur of her underarms, inhaling the dizzying scent of her hair and skin. Then he brushed his lips across her nipples before raising his mouth to hers. She took him into her arms and kissed him warmly, then drew back and looked deeply into his eyes.

"Although we are now alone, dear husband, I still sense the presence of another . . . an awareness distinct from the one I felt outside on the lanai." She left the thought hanging as she continued to watch his eyes closely. He was about to speak when she smiled and said, "It's your ancestor, isn't it? The one you call the American? His mind is in connection with yours, and he's here, isn't he?" Nainoa stared at her, amazed at the accuracy of her intuitive perception. Very slowly, he nodded.

"I have come to accept the strange experience of these periodic mergings as part of my life without fully understanding the why of it," he began. "I have come to understand that the American and I are both physically manifested incarnations of the same *aumakua* source self. What I have not told you before is that I suspect that you are the descendant-self of the American's wife, and that through us, the two of them have found each other once again across the millennia that separate their time and place from ours."

He watched her as she withdrew into herself to consider the implications of his words. And when she looked at him again, there was something, some quality in her gaze, that he had never seen before. "Tell me about her, Ali'noa. I sense that you have come to know her very well indeed. What was she like?" Nainoa's gaze swept down the long, slender body of his lover, and his eyes softened as his mind moved into the remembering. And when he spoke, the words that surfaced were only partially his.

"Her name was Jill. She was a very beautiful woman, tall and dark-eyed like you; with thick, black hair; slender hands; and long, willowy limbs, but her skin tone was very pale. She was a wonderful mother to her children, as well as a powerful medicinemaker and healer for her people. She possessed *maka'ike*, true psychic sight, like yourself.

"But the real resemblance between the two of you . . ." He paused again, searching for terms, his gaze unfocused as his mind moved down shadowy trails, half-glimpsed. It was at this moment that the presence within him suddenly stepped forward, and the whisper of words that emerged from his lips came out in Old English.

"She had a bright spirit, and her mind expressed a quick, incisive intelligence, like your own. You are much like her, and she like you, in so many ways. She was funny and wise, and I had a deep heart connection with her. Although I had many close women friends, she was the love of my life."

Nainoa paused, amazed, then saw that Maraea's eyes brimmed with tears. She was versed in the classics, like himself, and she had understood the words spoken in that ancient language. Deep emotions surged within him, and moved beyond words, he simply took her face between his hands and gently placed his lips upon hers. Her breath caught as his mouth began to kiss her in a new and different way. Both drew back, startled. Then a mischevious smile appeared on her face.

"What was she like as his lover? How did she kiss him? How did she like to be touched?" Her smile widened as she watched his eyes. "I think you know, dear husband . . ."

Nainoa felt a flash of humor as the blood started to hiss in his ears. "There are no words to express these things accurately," he responded in a mock serious tone. "However, there are ways of exploring such matters, ways of experiencing . . ." Maraea's breath quickened as he began to kiss her again. She wrapped her long legs around him and let her fingers trail lightly down his back, continuing onwards until his own breath caught in response to her caress. Her eyes became luminous as their evening ritual began.

Much later, Nainoa lay in the darkness, holding Maraea in his arms, feeling her breathing deepen as she shifted into dream, his body still vibrating with the power of passion's aftermath. His thoughts turned idly toward the two visitors who had approached him this day, the American and the presence on the ledge. He wondered dreamily if they could be connected. Perhaps this new spirit, like the spotted tiger man, had been one of his ancestor's allies.

With that thought, the fading ecstasy of their lovemaking suddenly surged again, and the sensations of power abruptly appeared within him. Nainoa shuddered and gently disengaged from Maraea, who sighed and settled deeply into sleep. As the feelings swept into him with full force, the familiar flurry of sparkling lights appeared and began to coalesce into the bright fibers of the *aka* field.

Nainoa briefly thought about his ancestor with a pulse of excitement, and then the sense of movement began . . . movement outward. It was very fast now. His last thoughts, curiously, were of the fleeting image perceived earlier in the evening, the cluster of large ducks and the huge black mountain soaring into the sky. Then his vision darkened, and all thoughts and feelings ceased as he entered the place of transition.

CHAPTER FIFTEEN

Hawaiian Encounters

AND WHERE HAD NAINOA GONE at the end of that connection? My awareness had detached as he passed through the zone of silence, so I wasn't sure, but I had suspicions. Confirmation came when my family and I returned to Hawai'i for Christmas several months later.

We spent the first few days on the Kona side of the Big Island, revisiting known places and reconnecting with old friends. We checked on our farm, swam in the warm waters off familiar beaches, snorkled with the sea turtles, and had sunset picnics under the palms down at the Pu'uhonua, the Place of Refuge at Honaunau. As Jill and I watched our daughters reacquaint themselves with the place where they had been raised as small children, I sensed a familiar presence, just there at the edge of awareness. There was very little doubt in my mind as to who it was.

During the years we had lived on the island, we had fallen into the custom of taking flowers from our garden to the volcano goddess Pele on an ongoing basis. It had seemed like good insurance at the time, residing as we did on the western flank of Mauna Loa, the world's largest, continually active volcano. I believe now that this act of offering was the beginning of my relationship with the mountain spirit, one that had extended beyond the confines of the island after I had left, and which now seemed to have included Nainoa, for I suspected that the presence on the ledge of volcanic stone above his house had been she.

It was close to midnight when I drove alone into the crater called Kilauea at the 4,000-foot level, a side vent on Mauna Loa's eastern shoulder. We had driven around the island earlier in the day so that I could do a book signing in Hilo, and had then gone out to a sumptuous dinner in Volcano Village with friends. It had been a long day, and I was very tired, but I felt the need to reconnect with Pele as soon as possible. Seven years had passed since my last visit to this mountain, but as always, I had come with gifts.

I glanced down at the large Liberty House shopping bag on the car seat next to me. It was filled with offerings from the various shamans and medicinemakers I had come to know. I had wrapped each "power bundle" in a *ti* leaf from plants growing on my land, honoring the manner in which the Hawaiians leave gifts for the formidable spirit who makes this stark, lunar landscape her home. On top of the leafy pile was my own *pu'olo* (wrapped offering). I had brought my rattle, a candle, and some incense as well.

I drove slowly, watching the sides of the road and wishing that I had not drunk quite so much wine with dinner. I saw no one. The crater seemed completely deserted. I briefly thought back to my Eastern establishment upbringing in New York City, then shook my head with a wry smile. Nothing in my background had set me up for this strange errand in the middle of the night on an island in the center of the Pacific Ocean. I considered my years of academic teaching and research and shook my head again. Dealings with spirits had definitely not been part of my training as an anthropologist.

As my attention refastened on the road, something odd happened. The moonless night seemed to darken visibly, swallowing the headlights only yards in front of the car. I slowed the vehicle to a crawl and observed this phenomenon curiously. I had never experienced the likes of it before. Had I made some transition or passed through some doorway? I stuck my head out of the car window and looked around. Aside from the dark curtain that seemed to surround me, everything looked normal. I continued on, slowly heading for a place I remembered from past visits.

I stopped at the spot I was looking for, switched off the engine and the headlights, and got out of the car. The vast bowl of the sky was brilliant with tropical stars, the Pleiades directly overhead. The silence was total. I could barely see the dim smudge of lights delineating the hotel many miles away on the crater's rim where Jill and our daughters were now asleep. The dark mass of Mauna Loa soared into the starry sky to the west, its rounded summit clear of clouds. As always, the sheer immensity of the black mountain filled me with awe.

At this moment, as if on cue, I felt something and snapped fully awake. My inner director accessed my *ku* for information and received the confirmation for which I had been waiting. Nainoa had finally come, joining me in this place of power as I had suspected (and hoped) that he would. My feelings of excitement surged as I formed words of warm welcome in my mind. I was in my ordinary state of consciousness, however, and perceived only silence within.

I presented my inner guest with a mental review of where I was and what I was doing, then switched on my flashlight and surveyed my surroundings. The crater's surface was strewn with volcanic rocks and riddled with fissures out of which steam was issuing. I continued to listen carefully. Nothing. Perhaps Nainoa was amazed to find himself here on the home island once again.

I hooked the shopping bag of offerings over my shoulder, stuck my rattle in my belt, then walked out onto the crater floor, scanning the rubble-covered substrate carefully to avoid stumbling or stepping into one of the many cracks whose black mouths were stained yellowish-white with sulphur. The luminous circle made by the flashlight seemed minuscule. This place was designed on a truly monumental scale fit for a goddess.

As I proceeded across the lava flats, I was suddenly enveloped in a warm cloud of mist pungent with sulphur. It was just what I needed to clear my head of the wine fumes, and as if in response, my mind abruptly began to disgorge a series of recent memories. I smiled to myself, very much aware of what was happening. Among them was an amazing encounter that had happened only two days before.

I had been invited to speak before a group at the New Millennium Institute in a newly built Frank Lloyd Wright house on the northern part of the island. Moments before my presentation, the door had opened and several Hawaiians had entered, led by a tall, burly man with a long, bushy beard and a thick, white ponytail hanging halfway down his back. He had walked up to me, his broad face beaming with *aloha* as he embraced me and placed a fragrant *lei* around my neck. My hosts, Susanne and Sanderson Sims, introduced him, and I got chickenskin all over me. Until this moment, I had known about this man only from hearsay.

The Hawaiian standing before me was the council elder of the spiritual warrior society known as Na Ao Koa o Pu'u Kohola Heiau.[1] He was also a *kahuna* visionary and wisdomkeeper known all over Polynesia. As he introduced me, in turn, to his companions, I realized that the Hawaiians had finally come to look me over. I had been expecting this ever since the publication of *Spiritwalker*. As an anthropologist, I was well aware of the unease felt by indigenous people when outsiders trespass into their spiritual traditions. I had done precisely that with the Hawaiians in writing my book, and I breathed a short prayer to my spirit helpers as I launched into my evening's talk, a discussion of the core beliefs and values held by those involved in the spiritual reawakening currently going on in the West.

At the end of my presentation, I looked over at the Hawaiian elder and asked him politely if he had anything he would like to add. The big man smiled and thought about it for a moment. Then he slowly got up, leaning on his *akua ko'o*, his carved spirit stick, and observed me for several moments in silence. The audience leaned forward.

"A friend of mine alerted me about your book," he began in a strong voice, "and so I read it. Then, I read it again just to make sure I got it right. Shortly after, I went down to the ocean and put your book down on the sand. Then I called in the spirits of my ancestors, and we had a long talk about you." The *kahuna* paused dramatically. He looked serious. The roomful of people was dead silent.

"The ancestors asked me what your name is and I told them, 'His name is Wesselman.'" Long pause . . . then he smiled. "The ancestors told me that I was not pronouncing your name right. They said that your name is Vessel-man—that you are a vessel . . . like a canoe." The *kahuna* paused again, as if to see the effect of his words.

"The ancestors told me that you are one of the light-carriers of *aloha*."

I was stunned. I had steeled myself, half expecting that he would condemn me, instructing me to stop writing about Hawaiian spirituality. Instead, I had been blessed—and honored beyond expectation.

"We Hawaiians do not write," he continued, as if reading my thoughts. "We talk, and we share what we find within our hearts. But it is the tradition to write in your culture. I have talked this over with the ancestors, and I have been instructed to say before these people here that everything you have written in your book is true. I have also been told to say to you: 'We Hawaiians support you! Keep spreading the word!'"

The *kahuna* beamed at me. The release of tension in the room was palpable. I looked around at the cluster of unfamiliar faces before me and saw smiles blooming everywhere like the flowers of the *lei* around my neck. I glanced at Jill and saw tears tracing the contours of her high cheekbones. The Hawaiian felt the emotional discharge within the room and laughed, then walked over and embraced me in another bear hug. Then he looked directly into my eyes and said, "We should have a meeting before you leave the island."

The flow of memory ceased as I glanced around in the darkness at the floor of the crater. The meeting would take place here, tomorrow, on this sacred mountain. I let my awareness expand into and through my surroundings. The clouds of sulphurous steam seemed to be increasing. This would be a good place to meet with a *kahuna*.

I stopped walking and listened once again for any communication from within. Still nothing. I thought about Nainoa's recent training period with Kahu Sala and surmised that he was just as amazed as I was that I had been brought into connection with this Hawaiian spiritual elder—and Nainoa had just had a good look at him through my memories of that event.

On impulse, I began to sing a song that had come to me on this mountain years before. As I started to walk once more, my song shifted into a sort of chantlike refrain—an entirely new one that included Hawaiian words announcing who I was and what my intentions were for entering this sacred place in the middle of the night. This struck me as being most appropriate protocol on the one hand, and on the other, I was very much aware that the intention to do this had not originated from myself.

I breathed a sigh of thanks to my descendant for his teaching and support, and continued to chant as I walked, accompanied by a slight breeze from the ocean to the east. I looked around, drinking in what I could see of my surroundings, but the farther I went, the more the volcano's breath filled the night air around me with odiferous steam, obscuring both the place and the overhanging stars.

In the center of the crater is a vast pit a half mile across and about 500 feet deep called Halema'uma'u. This is a place out of myth and legend, and within its precipitous depths is a frozen lake of stone from which clouds of steam vent from fissures. I had been here in the late 1960s when the lake was boiling with molten lava, but on this night, the crater was dormant. I approached the chasm, stopping just short of the edge. This monumental opening in the Earth is Pele's traditional home.

I shined my light around with some concern. I was not in the carefully roped and fenced area set aside for tourists, and I was well aware that the fractured ground all around me was unstable. I tried to see the floor of the pit, but my flashlight beam was completely inadequate. There was just the edge of the awesome cliff with its walls dropping vertically into the blackness of the void. I wondered if Pele was down there watching my puny light and wondering who this tiny human was, singing in English and Hawaiian. I hoped she remembered me.

I switched the light off and stood still in the darkness, singing my song and feeling the shape of the reality that was opening around me. I looked up, but the fog rising out of the ground was now total, and the sky was completely invisible. I wondered briefly if I would be able to find my way back to the car.

Something shifted at this point, and the air around me suddenly felt nervous. I was acutely aware of how vulnerable I was that close to the edge, and I switched on the light again, respectfully backing off a bit and almost stepping into a fissure as I did so. I looked down into the long crack and saw a wide ledge, about a foot below the crater surface—a place that suddenly struck me as an appropriate spot to make our offerings. I shined the light down the crevasse but could not see the bottom. Warm air smelling like boiled eggs puffed out of it gently. It was a direct entrance into Pele's domain.

I sat down, propped the flashlight between two blocks of lava, and began to take the offerings out of my bag. I got the thick candle lit and set it on the ledge's center, well back from the warm gusts of air. I took out a robust sage smudge, got it smoldering, and wedged it in a crack. Then I carefully passed each leaf-wrapped offering through the smoke, arranging them around the candle on the ledge and saying the name of each maker out loud, visualizing my friends as I offered their power bundles with my *aloha* attached to theirs. Interestingly, one offering jumped from my fingers on its own and dropped from sight into the depths of the mountain. I took this as a sign that Pele was aware of my presence and that the individual whose offering had been taken in this way was especially blessed.

When all was in place, I switched off the flashlight and made my prayer, offering our bundles and expressing my deepest respect. I acknowledged my ancestors and my descendants, then I blessed Pele and her mountain in the Hawaiian language, chanting the ancient words in what I hoped was the correct way. I finished by asking for power and protection for my family and myself, for my friends and for their families, and for our mutual endeavors as medicinemakers in service to our people.

When I was done, I took up my rattle, a rawhide one with a rather loud voice useful in large spaces, and began to shake it in the monotonous steady rhythm I use for shamanic journeying. As the night filled with its familiar sound, I adjusted my posture, settling into the position I use in Zen meditation. Then I closed my eyes and continued rattling, using my wrist in an effortless, repetitive rhythm.

Before long, the dreamy state of light trance descended upon me, a familiar experience now, and I let it deepen . . . deepen. When it reached a certain level, the sound of the rattle receded into the distance, and the words I had been waiting for appeared within my mind.

"Warm greetings, esteemed ancestor . . ."

An extraordinary dialogue followed, one in which I was able to ask Nainoa specific questions about his training as a *kahuna*, as well as questions relating to his life and time. I have made mention, for example, of the long ocean voyage that brought his ancestors from the Hawaiian Islands to the coast of America in long double-hulled voyaging canoes. In response to my curiosity about this event, Nainoa began to repeat parts of a long chant he had committed to memory during his training at the place of refuge—a "songline" that released a veritable avalanche of data.

As I continued to sit there in the dark, rattling away to maintain the trance state, it was possible to discern the details of this epic journey on a day-by-day basis. The chanted narrative described not only events of note, but included the names of all the crew members of the 108 canoes, producing a list in excess of 7,000 names that, in turn, included long ancestral genealogies for each person of rank.

One can easily see that the transcription of such information can only reach as far as my mind can manage it, an overwhelming task for a Western urbanite who knows little about my own genealogy and next to nothing about sailing canoes or maritime travel. This prompts me to observe that the scope of the knowledge that I continue to acquire through Nainoa is limited not by lack of detail or depth of information, but rather by the shape of my own culturally determined mind and worldview, and by my inability to fully understand and remember such vast quantities of raw data.

On this night in the volcano, Nainoa was also able to ask me questions about my life and time frame. He was especially interested in details of my training in the shamanic tradition, as well as any information I might have about early Hawaiian and Polynesian history. Deep feelings of friendship flowed between us as we shared wisdom and experience, and at one point, he used a Hawaiian term, something close to *kahu'kikola*, in referring to the two of us. Because of the nature of the connection between our minds, I was able to discern the term's *kaona*, its hidden meaning. The expression had temporal and historical implications that implied that Nainoa and I were in the process of becoming "keepers of time."

Throughout our long talk, I watched carefully with my mind's eye, alert for anyone else who might arrive, but aside from Nainoa's thoughts and feelings within my conscious awareness, the inner imagery was elusive, probably an effect of all the wine I had drunk. I continued rattling for perhaps 45 minutes, then paused, somewhat disappointed that Pele had not made an appearance.

The sudden stillness of the night after the prolonged sound of the rattle was quite dramatic. I felt suspension in Nainoa's thoughts as well, as though he, too, was waiting for the arrival of our expected guest. I was about to resume rattling when the silence was shattered by an absolutely immense, thundering roar. The ground around me trembled with the force of it, and my awareness shifted in response to the soul-shaking sound. I could no longer hear Nainoa's thoughts.

My inner scientist emerged immediately, took note of what had occurred, and concluded that part of the crater's rim had broken away and crashed to the floor of the pit below. I switched on the flashlight and looked around, but I was unable to see more than ten feet in the mist. I couldn't tell if the collapse had been close or if it had happened on the other side of the chasm. I was within yards of the edge, however, and I wondered uneasily if my section would be next.

The awesome sound reactivated my sense of vulnerability in this place of raw power, and I almost began to castigate myself for coming out here in the middle of the night. Then, another emotion arose, and I realized that I would just have to trust that my section of the rim would hold and that I would be okay. Whether this feeling came from myself or whether it originated from Nainoa is hard to say.

In that moment of recovery, I picked up my rawhide rattle once again and absently began to shake it in a circular pattern. This produced a pleasing and continuous rushing sound not unlike the noise I often hear in my deep altered states. I began to feel more self-assured. I recalled the ritual I had just done for Pele and the offerings I had brought for her. I felt confident that my intentions had been pure and that the huge spirit who lived here would not swallow me, at least not tonight.

Another thought appeared. Could that monumental roar from the pit have been her response to the comparatively minuscule roar of my rattle? It would be presumptuous to claim this and yet, in those moments, it did not seem impossible.

As I continued to rattle away, the trance state slowly descended once more, and imagery finally began to move through my mind—ghostly presences that stayed for a few moments and then left, as though they were stepping through some doorway to watch me curiously before returning whence they had come. Were they the ancestral spirits of the Hawaiians who had once functioned as sacred custodians of this place? There was no way of knowing, but as I felt them come and go, I could sense Nainoa's watchfulness nestled within my mind, waiting, like me, for "the big one" to come.

Eventually, I felt completion and stopped rattling. The silence of the night returned. The candle, still flickering in the steamy darkness, was almost out. I stood up and stretched out my cramped legs and stiff back. I switched on the flashlight and peered around once more. I was still alone. Pele had not come. I felt very altered, however, and as I glanced at my watch, I discovered that several hours had passed. The night was on the wane, so I offered four deep Buddhist bows to the mountain, then bid the place farewell, picked up my empty shopping bag, stuck the rattle in my belt, and started back across the crater floor.

I hadn't gone more that 20 yards, when goosebumps formed on my arms, and my hair stood on end. The air felt nervous once again. I could still sense Nainoa's watchfulness and could tell that he felt it, too. I was absolutely sure of it. I switched off the light and waited, letting my eyes adjust to the darkness once more. I looked back toward the locality I had just left . . . and I saw something.

There seemed to be a lighter place in the steamy darkness, a large, luminous spot that moved and swirled with the clouds of moisture. Could it be the light from the candle reflecting up off the steam above it? With this thought, the shape disappeared. I continued to stare in that direction in the total blackness, and it reappeared, then almost as quickly, winked out again . . . and then on again.

This time it remained, presenting me with a radiant, smoky form floating in the darkness near where I had left the offerings. It was much too big to be reflected candlelight. It seemed to be at least 15 to 20 feet high, with a dense central core. The image continued to intensify, becoming more brilliant, with a subdued reddish or rosy hint of color. There was no question in my mind as to who it was. I bowed once again, going all the way down and pressing my forehead to the crater floor, offering her my deepest respect, my reverence, and my *aloha*.

Within my mind, Nainoa's familiar voice whispered. *"It resembles the spirit who appeared on the ledge above my house. It is she-of-the-mountain, is it not?"*

"Yes, esteemed descendant," I replied, looking up once more. "It is Pelehonuamea—Pele of the Sacred Earth. I was told by a *kahuna* several years ago that she often comes into relationship with spiritwalkers who are *kaula*, who are seers across time and have the power of prophecy. We have been blessed beyond measure by her presence. You must build the *heiau* on the stone ledge above your house, and you must include an altar for her. And when you make your offerings to her, please include my own *aloha* with yours. Perhaps she will remember me . . ."

I fastened my attention on the volcano spirit, remaining on my knees, and offered an account of my activities since the last time she had visited me at the ranch in northern California. I then formally introduced her to the man within my mind, describing him and explaining the nature of the relationship between us. I finished by asking for her blessing, requesting that she continue to visit with us often—me in my place and time, and Nainoa in his.

There was a long moment of silence during which I could feel the attention of the great *akua* focused upon us. Then my awareness shifted, and my vision came up, and I saw a set of eyes looking straight into mine, point blank. This had happened before, but it was still somewhat unnerving, to say the least. I heard her ancient Hawaiian greeting flow through my mind's ear with a breathy vibrational tone. "*Vayyy-leee-naahhhh . . . kaaa-maaakaaanaayyy . . . meeeleeemeeeleeeee . . .*" It was repeated once more: "*Welina kamakane milimili*—greetings with affection, beloved man-child."

These words were followed by a Hawaiian phrase, one that I did not understand at first, but since my mind was in connection with Nainoa's, I was able to comprehend the meaning of it through his *knowing*. The mountain spirit, whose elements are fire and volcanic stone, clearly said to us both, "I shall be with you always, children of the Earth."

This message and the awareness of what it meant moved me profoundly, and I became completely still as tears coursed freely down my face. Within my soul, I could feel Nainoa's own emotional response, and suddenly, I felt him step forward. To my amazement, I heard his voice issue from my lips as he broke into a chant, an ancient Hawaiian song of honoring, of valuing, and of blessing. For long moments, he offered the fabric of his song to her, woven with the fibers of his love, and then he, too, fell silent, moved beyond words by the presence of the deity.

How long I remained on my knees, staring at the luminous form I do not know, but a moment came when the warm breeze suddenly reappeared from the ocean, and the mist cleared. The shape evaporated, leaving me alone with Nainoa in the darkness. The waning moon was rising in the east, bathing our bleak surroundings in a ghostly glow and revealing the vast shape of the crater with the immense mound of Mauna Loa looming above us to the west. I slowly stood up and took in the totality of this strange landscape, reestablishing a sense of the here-and-now. As I did so, I heard a last whispered observation within my mind.

"What a magnificent mountain! And what an amazing encounter! We have truly been blessed, esteemed ancestor!" There was a long pause and then the words: *"The stars look strange in your time. They are different somehow . . ."* This snapped me out of my dreamy state, and I spent long moments observing the heavens intently, my eyes moving from one quadrant of the sky to another, studying the patterns.

I was now in my ordinary state of consciousness, and no further messages came from within, so I began the long walk back to the car. I drove back to the hotel without incident and let myself quietly into our room. As I slipped into bed beside my sleeping wife, it seemed as if I had stepped back through some doorway, and I immediately dropped into sleep like a stone.

The following day, Jill and I met on the mountain with the Hawaiian elder and his wife, who took us to a place known to them. When we arrived at our destination, the *kahuna* led me one way, while his wife took Jill in another. After a short walk along the crater's rim, he gestured toward a spot and told me that a *heiau* had once stood there. Then he pointed to a large stone with a *ti*-wrapped object on its summit, indicating that he had made his own offering earlier in the day when he had asked permission to bring me here.

Then the *kahuna's* eyes went vacant, and he began to chant in Hawaiian, his glance and gestures taking in the immense vistas of the cauldera spread out below us. As I listened, I was dimly conscious of another awareness watching this revered elder out of my eyes, listening to his words. My excitement rose. Nainoa was still in connection.

The *kahuna* chanted for a long time, then briefly shifted into English for my benefit, revealing that he was asking the spirits of his ancestors to come and have a look at my soul. He then called upon Pele to witness the meeting that was about to occur. The air around us felt nervous once again, like the enormous charge of static electricity one sometimes feels just before a lightning strike.

The Hawaiian finished his prayer by lifting any *kapu*, any restrictions, to our upcoming talk. Then we rejoined the women, who had done their own ritual at the women's place of power, and drove to a small picnic shelter put up by the park service for tourists. No one was there but us. As we sat down on the benches at one of the two tables, the *kahuna* grinned and said, "The office is now open. How may I be of service to you?"

We conversed about many things during that day, getting to know each other, "talking story" about our lives, and sharing sacred knowledge. Feelings of warmth, friendship, and trust grew between us, and throughout that long afternoon, the Hawaiian elder exuded power and gentleness, wisdom and humility—all enriched with his heartfelt *aloha*.

When such information is freely shared from the heart, carried on the breath from one person to another, it possesses a vitality and a power that can never be captured by the written word. But there was another mind nestled within my own that watched every gesture and listened to every word that was said, a mind highly trained since boyhood in the art of perfect recall. For him, this meeting was pure gold.

As the shadows grew long and the time of departure approached, the *kahuna* looked at me curiously and said, "I am aware that your descendant Nainoa is tapping in to your mind to recover lost knowledge of the past. He is, isn't he?" I nodded, startled. The statement suggested that the Hawaiian had perceived Nainoa's awareness watching him out of my eyes, and I knew that an important part of the puzzle was falling into place. The older man laughed and observed offhandedly that there was much that could be shared that would be of value to Nainoa and his people.

He then honored us by giving us a gift wrapped in *ti* leaves, a large green bundle tied in the traditional way. For long moments, Jill and I eyed the leafy gift with anticipation, savoring the moment. Then we opened it excitedly and found within a beautiful bowl made of *kamani* wood.

"This is your bowl of light," the *kahuna* said with a warm smile. "When we are born, each of us comes in from the great beyond with a bowl of light. This light nourishes us as we pass through life, but as we grow in experience and wisdom, things happen. Sometimes we lie, sometimes we steal, and sometimes we injure others with our words or thoughts or deeds. When we engage in such negative behavior, it is as though we put a stone in our bowl, and with each occurrence, some of our light goes out. Slowly, through time, our light gradually diminishes as we continue putting stones into our bowl, and the time may come when our light is almost gone.

"We finally wake up one day and discover what we are doing." The elder paused dramatically, his expressive dark eyes bright with enthusiasm. "At that moment, we become aware that our bowl of light is filled with shit!" He exploded into boisterous laughter, his big white teeth gleaming in his brown face, his long, gray beard quivering with mirth. "Then," he chuckled, "you simply turn the bowl over and you dump it out!" Another long laugh, shared by all of us.

"We start over then," he concluded, his laughter subsiding and his gaze becoming serious. "But from that time forward, things are different. From then on, we begin to live our lives with awareness, braided with the cords of *aloha*. It is then that we become spiritual warriors."

Reassuring words. They prompted a memory of something

William had once said to Nainoa: "To be a medicinemaker, you must have strongly developed ethics and you must have heart—a well-developed heart. You can acquire great power in life, but if you have poorly developed ethics and an underdeveloped heart, you cannot be a medicinemaker."

Whether this memory arose from within my own subconscious or from the mind that had been esconced within my own since the previous night, I could not tell. The separation between Nainoa and myself was becoming increasingly thin, and at times such as this, he and I seemed to be approaching a truly singular state of being.

When the long afternoon finally came to an end and the *kahuna* and his wife prepared to leave, he did something that up until this moment I had only experienced through Nainoa. He walked up to me and gently pressed his forehead and nose to my own, and briefly looked straight into my soul before dropping his eyes as we shared the breath. Then he smiled and kissed me on the cheek, and said, "We Hawaiians call this expression of greeting the *honi*."

His wife smiled and *honied* me in turn, then both *honied* Jill before getting into their truck with a cheery salute. As they drove away, the *kahuna* leaned out the window and called, "*A hui hou* . . . until the next time."

The *kahuna's* bowl travels with me now, holding the candle in the center of my medicine circles at my workshops and presentations. And each day, I put my face into the bowl and I breathe deeply, replenishing my supply of light.

As a result of this series of encounters in Hawai'i, my ability to draw Nainoa's conscious awareness into connection with my own has grown stronger, and when the opportunity presents itself, I sometimes reach out for him, inviting him to join me on my journeys of exploration across inner space.

One such event occurred after we returned to California in the early spring of 1997. It was catalyzed by a wonderful romantic interlude, and as Jill drifted into sleep, her fingers entwined with my own, I lay awake beside her, listening to the night rain on the roof. I decided to attempt a journey, and when the sensations of power appeared within me, I quickly focused my intentionality, consciously thinking: *I wish to learn more about the mysterious Source from which all being, including the manifested Universe, has sprung. . . .*

As the feelings of power surged, I added that I wanted Nainoa to join me. Perhaps he and I could finally discuss the "*dorajuadiok* material" face-to-face. The trance state deepened, and when the phosphenes appeared, the field of golden dots and lines was swirling like the wind in the stormy night outside.

As my teeth began to chatter with the exquisite feelings of force, I decided to invite Nainoa to join me in my secret garden, and we would take it from there. The question was, could I do it? As the invisible fist seized me and I gasped for breath, I decided to call for assistance and reached out for my spirit helpers. What occurred next exceeded my expectations by degrees of magnitude.

CHAPTER SIXTEEN

Eighth Journey:
The Voyage to the Source

I<small>T WAS NIGHT, AND IT WAS RAINING HEAVILY,</small> but Nainoa was only dimly
aware of the watersound beyond the thatched roof and woven
walls of his house. Maraea embraced him with urgency, her hair
and the taste of love in his mouth as their bodies moved in the timeless dance. Her breathing quickened and her body began to tremble as she moved toward climax. He responded swiftly, touching her
in a way she found irresistible. Then the dynamic shifted as her fingers suddenly found and cradled him. It was too much. . . .

He laughed breathlessly, knowing that he had lost the game. She
knew it, too, and her mouth smiled against his in triumph as he shuddered into orgasm, his body becoming rigid as the waves of pleasure swept him over the edge and into the abyss. Maraea caught him
as he fell, crooning to him as he shook uncontrollably. Then she seized
the moment, thrashing her hips against him feverishly and gasping
aloud as she found her own release and joined him in the deep ecstasy.

As they slowly relaxed, he became aware once again of the sound of the night rain. Maraea's voice came to him as if from a great distance. "You are indeed a treasure, Ali'noa . . . I am so fortunate to have found you. I love being with you." She brushed her lips across his mouth, then pressed her face to his and looked directly into his eyes. "And I love being your lover," she whispered fiercely.

"*O'au pu manu maka ona'ona* . . . me, too, soft-eyed bird-woman," he breathed in response, quoting a line from an ancient chant. As they disengaged and moved into positions of comfort next to each other, Maraea continued to hold him in her arms, his face pillowed against her breast, her fingers woven into his long hair. Nainoa felt himself drifting toward the dream worlds, his nose still filled with her intoxicating scent.

It was at this moment that his dissolving consciousness picked something up—something that came from within. It seemed like a summons or request of some sort. As he reemerged from sleep, the abyss loomed once again, its vastness beckoning to him, drawing him inward . . . inward. Any vestiges of sleepiness vanished as the sensations of power rushed into him, and the moving pattern of lights appeared in the darkness.

The brilliant spots became lines, connecting with each other and taking on the form of the great *aka* web. He was still dimly aware of the sound of the rain and of Maraea holding him when one of the fibers seemed to thicken, curving upward into a crescent like the new moon. He felt himself being drawn inexorably toward it, the power feelings increasing . . . increasing. His body tensed as he gasped once, twice, with the effort of breathing. He felt Maraea's fingers stroking his scalp, and he relaxed, his mind quickening as transition was achieved. Imagery began to appear behind his tightly closed eyelids, but curiously, the watersound remained.

His vision came up then, and he found himself looking down a trail through a tropical landscape filled with riotous, verdant foliage. There were tall trees of all types, huge multitrunked banyans and buttress-rooted cotton trees with lianas and vines twisted around their fantastic shapes. There were coconut palms, breadfruit trees, and magnificent dark-leafed mangos, as well as several that were unfamiliar. The ground beneath them was filled with uncountable numbers of multicolored *ti* plants and flowering ginger. He looked around in wonder. This was, without doubt, one of the most beautiful places he had ever seen. But where was he?

The sound of water drew his attention to his right. The trail seemed to parallel a small stream that descended the slope of the hillside. Looking up, he discovered a waterfall tumbling down a rocky cliff face. His eyes followed the rim of the cliff to his right until he saw the dark wall of a huge mountain looming in the distance above the canopy of the trees. Intuitively, he knew it was Mauna Loa. He had been drawn back to the island of Hawai'i once again, but where was he, and why?

He studied his surroundings carefully, his gaze coming to rest on the waterfall. *That was it,* he decided. The sound of the water had brought him here, matching as it did, the sound of the rain outside his house. With the thought, the scene before him dimmed, and he felt the arms of his beloved around him once again, her fingertips caressing his scalp. He smelled her scent and briefly felt conflicted. Should he wake and talk with her? His curiosity returned. Why had he been brought to this place?

The waterfall reappeared in his visual field, assuming density as well as reality as he felt its spray make cool points of contact on his upturned face and arms. He looked out into the trees again, studying the patterns of the leaves, and he saw a familiar visage observing him intently—a spotted face with an intense set of pale green eyes. It was his spirit ally, the spotted tiger man, who, at this moment, appeared decidedly feline. The great cat stared at him for long moments, then emerged from the cover of the foliage. With a backwards glance at Nainoa, he set off down the trail, flowing silently between the trees like the wraith that he was. Without thought or intention to do so, Nainoa followed.

As they reached the foot of the hillside, they passed a large wall of black boulders, then the forest thinned, the stream widening into a small pond, beyond which he could see a crescent of beach fringed with palms and red-leafed *kamani* trees. There was a long, double-hulled canoe under the trees, its sails furled and its two masts lowered. The beach encircled a wide bay, beyond which the immense, blue vastness of the ocean stretched to the horizon, its distant surface pocked with whitecaps.

Nainoa looked to his right and saw a house just beyond the pond's edge, set back among the trees. It had a multileveled thatch roof and a wide lanai wrapped around it, with steps descending to the ground. Glancing to his left, he saw the dark stone wall of a *heiau*, a big one. He could just see the top of a tall *lele* altar on its surface. The place seemed familiar, and after a moment's reflection, he knew where he was. This was the secret garden of his ancestor. He glanced back at the house and noticed for the first time that there was a man sitting in a chair on the lanai. The spotted tiger turned and headed in that direction. He followed, his pulse quickening.

As he reached the wooden steps, he glanced to one side and saw a dark object standing on a small stone platform. It was Kapohaku'ki'ihele, the spirit stone. There could be no mistake. Wrapped around its pointed apex was a *lei* of orange flowers, and on the small altar before it rested a red hibiscus blossom. He knelt and placed his hands on it, greeting the spirit in the stone with affection. He was rewarded with a pulse of *mana* that penetrated his hands and forearms. Then he stood and climbed the steps, the blood hissing in his ears.

The American rose to meet him. He was sporting a short, trimmed beard that was turning gray, and he was simply dressed in long white pants with a *lei* of red and yellow flowers resting around his neck. Next to him on the lanai stood a woman Nainoa had never seen before. She appeared to be Polynesian. On a low table near them was a single, beautifully crafted wooden bowl. There seemed to be a ball of light glowing within it. Nainoa smiled, remembering the day on the mountain when the *kahuna* had presented the bowl to his ancestor. The American bowed, a smile of welcome on his face. Nainoa bowed in return, bringing his hands together and whispering words in Old English.

"Warm greetings, esteemed ancestor . . . we meet face-to-face at last."

"*A me ke aloha pumehana, mo'opuna makamae,*" the American replied in Old Hawaiian, smiling broadly. "My heartfelt greetings to you, too, highly valued descendant." Then he shifted into English. "Our long-anticipated meeting has finally happened, facilitated for both of us by fortuitous circumstances that seem to have happened virtually simultaneously in your life and in mine—events that allowed us to access the shamanic state of consciousness at the same time."

Nothing more needed to be said. Both knew and understood. The warmth both felt at being in the presence of the other flowed out of their hearts. Nainoa glanced again at the woman to the American's left, and recovering his composure, he bowed, greeting her formally in the Old Hawaiian language. The woman smiled and replied, using an archaic form of the ancient tongue. A length of brightly colored cloth was wrapped around her lower body. A *lei* of ferns encircled her head with another *lei* of orange flowers resting on her chest.

The American spoke. "May I present Tehura, who once lived on the island of Tahiti in the southern ocean, and who now honors me by serving as the *kahu* of my house and garden." He smiled. "I have discovered that she is a woman of wisdom who possesses great healing power."

The American then turned to her and said, "May I present Kahu Nainoa Kaneohe, the one of whom I have spoken so often." Tehura smiled again, and reaching up, she drew him gently down and pressed her face to his in the *honi*, glancing into his soul as they shared the breath. She kissed him lightly on both cheeks before placing her *lei* around his neck. Her mouth felt warm and unbelievably soft.

"As you know," the American continued, "this place is my secret garden in the Middle Worlds of dream. This is where I come to restore myself and gain access to the inner levels of reality and experience. I know that you have briefly seen this place through my memories of it. I have invited you here today so that we may deepen our connection and travel together into the far reaches of the spirit world. Now that you have actually been here, this place will forever be accessible to you. It is a place of great power and healing, and you are welcome here at any time, whenever you have need."

As Nainoa digested this information, he suddenly felt dizzy from the heady emotions coursing through him. He looked from one to the other. Both were smiling at him, their eyes luminous. With a gesture, Tehura invited him to sit in the chair. As he did, she placed her hands gently on his shoulders, easing his body into a posture in which he felt completely relaxed. She then gently swept her fingers lightly across his eyelids, closing them.

For long moments, he just sat and listened to the birdcalls coming from the trees. Then the Tahitian woman placed one of her strong brown hands upon his chest, and the other on his back, as though she could hold his heart between her palms. Her hands abruptly warmed and started to vibrate. He waited, his eyes closed, as her hands continued to tremble. The birdcalls seemed to recede into the distance. After a moment, he felt Tehura raise the palm that was on his chest without breaking contact. She leaned forward, her long hair brushing across his shoulders, and began to blow into the hollow created between her hand and his skin. It felt as though her breath was actually penetrating his body, creating a warmth that spread rapidly within him, whereupon something totally unexpected happened.

Long-forgotten memories from his earliest childhood appeared within his mind, moving like ghosts down shadowy paths of the past. The faces of a woman and a man emerged, and he knew without a doubt that they were his birth mother and his birth father, the parents he had never known. Deep feelings of grief and loss suddenly suffused him, and he felt overwhelmed. As though in response, the faces smiled, and his heart began to warm. It felt as if they were filling him with light like the bowl sitting on the table—as though parts of himself, long gone, had suddenly returned. Tears sprung unannounced from his eyes, and his strong frame was abruptly wrenched with racking sobs.

Throughout, Tehura held him, her hands fostering the light that was growing within his heart, and after a period, his grief began to subside. The faces within his mind smiled once more, then dissolved, as her strong hands moved to his shoulders and massaged them briskly. A sense of peace, of tranquility, pervaded him, and within this silence, the American's soft voice broke in.

"You have just experienced parts of your soul returning to you, and you are now whole once again, as you were when you came in from the great beyond at your birth. I sense that these missing soul-parts left during your early childhood, carrying with them the deep grief that you experienced with the deaths of your mother and father. Unknowingly, you have searched for these lost aspects of yourself for much of your life, a search that has assisted you in discovering who you are. Now, complete once more, many things become possible for you."

Abruptly, Nainoa felt his blood rise like the golden light in the wooden bowl, and what remained of his grief was transformed into joy. Something extraordinary happened in the next moment. The American helped him to his feet and embraced him, pressing his forehead and nose to his in the *honi*. As the man's dark eyes gazed into his, Nainoa felt himself suddenly merge with his ancestor. It was as though the man had absorbed him into himself, and they were now one. He could clearly perceive the man's thoughts and feel his emotions—and yet they were also separate somehow, a paradox. The American smiled, and his words appeared within Nainoa's mind, yet his lips did not move.

"Esteemed descendant," came the mental message, *"how would you like to go with me on a voyage of exploration? I am inherently curious, and have always wondered about the nature of the mysterious Source. Let us go up onto the* heiau. *I have a place there that I use for liftoff."*

"Liftoff?" Nainoa thought back.

"A place of departure . . ."

The two men turned then and descended the steps from the lanai, walking around the pond and heading toward the dark stone platform of the *heiau*. Nainoa saw the canoe under the trees and asked, "Is it yours?"

"Only in a manner of speaking," the American replied, using spoken words once more. "I sometimes use it to visit a particular locality of power out there," he gestured, pointing out to sea. "There is a place beyond the horizon to which shamans and med-icinemakers go to have meetings and accomplish various things. Mys-tics of all times have always had a sense of this place, and so it is called different names in different traditions—names like Shamb-hala and Shangri-La, Belovodia and Avalon. The Hawaiians called it Pali Uli, the place of the green cliffs, but like the man who first told me about it, I prefer its Samoan name."

Nainoa looked at the older man standing beside him. The Amer-ican grinned, his eyes dark chips in his pale face. "Bali Ha'i . . ." and spontaneously broke into a song that Nainoa had never heard before, a song about a mysterious island in the dream world where the sky meets the sea. "Eventually, most of us who work in this tra-dition discover this place, and much to our astonishment, we find that it is real."

Nainoa studied the canoe with a practiced eye, appreciating its design and the woven tightness of its furled sails. "And where is the crew for the canoe, if I may ask?"

The American grinned again and gestured toward the south. "There is a Pu'uhonua, a Place of Refuge, down the coast. There is a large population of spirits who reside there, many of whom voy-aged in canoes in the past. It might be of interest to you that in my time and place, the Order of the Canoe is now being re-formed among the Polynesian peoples. The spirits, who dwell outside of time, seem absolutely delighted at this turn of events."

Nainoa smiled and looked to his left. The American followed his glance and observed offhandedly, "That pond, as you may know, is one of my entryways into the Lower Worlds of Milu. There is a powerful spirit who lives in the fresh water. You will recall that your first wife and heart companion, Kenojelak, has come into connection with this entity and calls her the Riverwoman. The waterspirit appears to me from time to time when I am called upon to facilitate in the healing of someone who is suffering from an illness. She almost always manifests to me as a blue woman, a very tall one with dark skin and a veil covering her eyes."

The American paused and picked a blue-and-white flower from a large vine growing up a tree, then placed it on the surface of the water with a brief prayer. He turned back toward the ocean and observed casually, "The Hawaiians regard Kanaloa, the spirit of the deep ocean, as masculine, or as *mahu*—androgynous. Perhaps the fresh waterspirit is its feminine counterpart." The American turned slightly and glanced at the spotted cat who was watching them from the shade next to the house, then he pointed upwards toward the *heiau* and whispered "Let us go . . ."

The older man led Nainoa up the stone steps and across the wide surface of the temple platform, passing the *hale mana* and approaching the flat, black stone that served as the altar. With a gesture, he indicated that the two of them were to recline on the stone, side-by-side. The smooth slab of basalt was wide enough for two, and as they settled into a prone position, they were touching at the shoulder and hip.

"The time has come to reconsider what we learned from the dorajuadiok out in Africa," the American communicated, using the mental channel once again. *"I have been able to recall much of it by now, but I have wanted to discuss it with you for some time. Since we are both here, perhaps we could reexperience it together. Let us see if we can access that spirit. This heiau is a place of great power, and we should be able to use its mana as an attractor field to pull in our fish. Let us focus our thoughts and intentions upon the* dorajuadiok. *Try to relax as we put out the call. If we are successful and the spirit comes, we will see if we can also discover something about the mysterious Source of all being, a nice, modest goal."*

In accordance with these intentions, Nainoa closed his eyes and focused. There was a momentary pause, and then he felt like he had been struck between the eyes with a hammerstone. Startled, he looked up, and there, on the stone platform near them, he saw the towering, dark obelisk of the mighty spirit. He felt amazement that it had arrived so quickly. The constraining pressure surrounding him was absolutely enormous, completely immobilizing him with the force generated by its presence. He felt a flicker of fear.

"Do not fear . . . trust," came the American's thought. *"This entity is of the highest energy, and I suspect that it is one of those that exists beyond our planetary evolution, yet is somehow linked with it. Perhaps it is primarily concerned with the nonhuman activities of nature, but ever since William brought us into contact with it at the Spirit Hills, I have come to wonder if it may also be involved with the well-being of humanity, for we, too, are part of nature. Focus your intentions on journeying to the mysterious Source, and let us see what happens."*

Nainoa shut his eyes tightly as the sense of pressure increased, almost cutting off his breath. Just when it seemed as if he was going to suffocate, a surging release was felt, and a sense of rising began— of rising upward. His vision came up then, and he seemed to be rushing through a luminous tunnel in the clouds toward a spot of light high in the copper-colored sky above. Within his mind, he heard the American say, "Yesssss . . ."

Nainoa was aware that he could still perceive the American's thoughts and feelings. *"We have merged and are traveling together as a singularity,"* came the American's thought in answer to his unasked question. *"I believe this is possible because we share an* aumakua. *Maybe in this moment, we are actually one with this ancestral oversoul. Yet because we are separate selves, we each produce our own thoughts, feelings, and reactions."*

Nainoa thought about this as he watched the circle of light in the sky. He was approaching it with great speed. On final approach, he braced himself for the impact. Then he seemed to push right through it, and the light came up dramatically. He appeared to have arrived at the edge of something much like a luminous cloud. He felt a sense of familiarity, combined with an immediate perception that the cloud possessed awareness—that it, whatever *it* was, could see them. There was silence within his mind, producing momentary concern. Was the American still with him?

"I'm here," came the thought-response. *"What do you think this place might be, Nainoa? Try to remember."*

As Nainoa merged more deeply into the cloud's periphery, his speed seemed to slow, and he found himself observing a vast, wide plain that looked misty, the opaque light expressing an off-white color tinted a pale orange. He began to hear a curious sound—a high-pitched ringing tone that pulsed. Once again, the strong sense of familiarity combined with an overriding peacefulness manifested itself. He perceived movement, a subtle motion of some sort, and he began to observe the rosy-orange light carefully. The concept of "energy" appeared in the American's thinking, and Nainoa understood that the whole field was energetic in nature. It was not static. It was in movement, and seemed to be composed of uncountable numbers of small lights. It was alive.

In that moment, understanding arrived, and Nainoa remembered that this luminous cloud was *Ka Po'e Aumakua,* the essence of all humanity from which he had been born, and the repository to which he would return at his death.

"It is indeed," came the thought within his mind. *"And there is more . . ."* Nainoa looked around carefully, studying the scene before him. Within each moving bubble of light was a denser, central core, producing a bright symbol much like a cross. But there was something else—it felt subtle, intuitive, like they were in the presence of something that could communicate.

With this awareness, his visual field seemed to shift, and a vast, transparent crystalline matrix became visible. It was all around them, suffused with a violet light, stretching into the luminous distance. There seemed to be discreet units or structures of some sort, and Nainoa was briefly reminded of the cities he had seen through his descendant's eyes and thoughts. He moved closer to one of the units, extending himself toward it, and much to his surprise, a voice seemed to whisper in his ears, accompanied by a flow of imagery. He listened and watched intently. It seemed to be part of a story. He moved close to another, and the same thing happened. The content made little sense to him, but as he looked around slowly, understanding came. This matrix was a library, a huge informational center. *"And it contains the accumulated wisdom of the entire human species. . . ."* the American's thought cut in.

Nainoa was stunned by the implications of this insight, then deeply reassured. Everything that had ever happened, including all known history, was somehow stored here in this spiritual home base. *"And everything to come as well. . . ."* came the thought.

"But how can that be?" Nainoa queried his host.

"This is part of what the dorajuadiok *revealed to us out in Africa,"* the American continued. *"We were shown that the great pattern of existence is like a fabric that is being woven continuously on an immense loom that stretches across time and distance. We humans are one species among countless others who are the weavers of this fabric—a living, cosmic tapestry made of matter, energy, and consciousness.*

"As we travel across time," he went on, *"we are presented with choices, and as we choose, the shape of our experience, our personal part of the fabric, shifts in response. The concept of woven cloth is most appropriate when you think of it. Our vertical fibers are the connections between our personal past and our potential future. Our horizontal strands are the events we experience as our life proceeds from the time of our birth to the moment of our death. And the same could be said for every living thing everywhere in the Universe.*

"We weave the fabric of our life, which changes constantly as we live it, revealing that nothing can be truly set in stone. Our lives are part of the greater human cloth—in turn, part of a still larger planetary tapestry—all levels of which are aspects of the great solar mind-field. Considered at the level of the Universe, we are only one among the uncountable creators of the great fabric of the aka field. Everything, everywhere, is in relationship. It is in this way that the great pattern changes and grows as it proceeds toward the future. This insight also presents us with a truly wondrous revelation . . ."

"The great pattern is both determined by consciousness and the source of all consciousness," Nainoa finished the thought. There followed a long period of stillness as each considered the ramifications of this insight. The American finally broke the silence. *"What is woven into the pattern creates new outcomes, meaning that there are literally endless numbers of possible futures."*

Both surveyed the crystalline light shapes all around them. *"Everything that happened in the past, to the unlimited potential of what will come into being,"* the American thought, *"is stored in the vast, informational matrix of the pattern. This light-filled stuff stretching all around us in this cloud is our particular part of it. This 'human spirit' is alive, constantly shifting in response to what is occurring in our world. And each of those spheres of light you can see everywhere is an individual human spirit, each an* aumakua, *traveling through time, growing and increasing and becoming more . . ."* The thoughtline paused, then the American concluded, *"The responsibility is quite awesome, when you think of it."*

A feeling of great reassurance was experienced by both. There was also a sense of surrender, and their awareness of being separate, distinct selves began to slip. Both understood that they were merging with the misty, light-filled cloud, and with this contact came a deep sense of rest, and of ease. It was much like going into deep meditation.

The tone of sound was always there, a vibration that carried them along like a river. It was not music structured in any cultural sense. Rather it was a beautiful, breathy "song" that was completely unstructured—and yet there was something within it, a curious throbbing rhythm much like the breathing of some huge organism. A question appeared in Nainoa's mind: "Does this composite human spirit have its own will forces, or is its will expressed only through ourselves as individuals on the physical plane of action?"

An answer arrived immediately, a pulse of thought-meaning revealing that both situations exist as possible outcomes. In addition to each person's individual will forces, the collective spirit does indeed possess will, but a will expressed as a general impulse—the impulse to grow, to increase, and become more.

The American cut into his thoughts. *"Let us proceed onward. There is more to see and experience. Although I live in a time when people are preoccupied with traveling in 'outer space,' countless shamans and kahuna mystics throughout history have discovered that there are no limits to traveling in 'inner space.' And one doesn't need a starship to do so."*

"A starship?"

"A machine for traveling across the enormous distances between the stars. People of my time are trying to create such machines, but they exist only in our mythology because the technology needed to build them has proved to be elusive."

"Technology?"

"The body of knowledge available to a civilization for use in fashioning implements, tools, or practices. As you know, my society possesses a highly developed technology that has allowed us to create the marvels you have witnessed on several occasions."

Nainoa's struggle to understand the terms used by his ancestor was almost simultaneously illustrated by a flow of imagery that had its source in the American's mind. He watched, fascinated, until the thoughtline came to an end. Their conscious awareness then began to expand outward once again, and he became aware of a great, dark, circular orb of immense proportions, from whose margins the omnipresent orange-golden light seemed to radiate.

"What is it?" Nainoa asked.

"It is our star, the sun, the source of the life force here in our part of the Universe," came the American's response.

"Why is it dark?" queried the Hawaiian.

The answer arrived immediately. *"I believe it appears dark because of the reversal effect. In ordinary reality, it is blindingly bright, but when I cross the barrier into the spiritual dimensions, everything appears to me in color negative. Why this is so, I do not know.*

"You will recall some of the wisdom we received from the

dorajuadiok *out in the spirit hills,"* the American continued. *"It was there that we learned that stars possess consciousness—the collective conscious awareness of everything within their solar system. In this same way, our awareness is part of our star's awareness. Let us see if we can approach it, but carefully. I have never been this close to it before."*

They headed right for the dark disc, ascending swiftly until it blotted out everything else. Abruptly, their frame of reference shifted and what had seemed "up" now appeared to be "down." It was as though they were flying above the surface of a dark planetary body, one whose surface seemed to shimmer and swirl like boiling water, moving restlessly like a black ocean. In the distance, they saw a black, whirling column of immense proportions erupt from its surface. Feelings of indescribable ecstasy soared through them.

On final approach, there was no all-consuming fire, no million-degree heat to incinerate them and convert them into elemental wisps of carbon. The enormous gravity of the great stellar being was most real, however, and they were drawn closer and closer until impact seemed inevitable.

Then something totally unexpected occurred. They "flew" through the surface of the sun, finding themselves immersed within surroundings that seemed to be composed of moving streams of contrasting lightness and darkness—an etheric, golden pattern flowing in ordered directions. There was also a sound, a ponderous vibrational tone not unlike the tolling of some monumental bell or gong. They simply rested there, within the sun's shadow ocean, marveling at the star's living, golden presence.

Nainoa suddenly received one of the American's boyhood memories, a chunk of information he had apparently acquired while exploring huge rooms filled with strange objects in a building of immense proportions. As Nainoa's curiosity arose, a thought from the American's mind came in response.

"Egypt . . . these things are housed in a museum in the city of my birth. The memory you picked up concerned a long-dead king called Amenhotep the 4th. This man changed his name to

Ahkenaten when he initiated a new religion centered on the wor-
ship of the sun. This Pharaoh, as the Egyptians called their kings,
was considered a heretic by the people of his time, yet he was a
great mystic who understood the star for what it is—a creator being.
He had its symbol depicted on the temple walls as the aten, *the*
sun disk. The literal translation of the Pharaoh's name Ahk-en-
aten *meant 'Shadow of the Sun.'"*

Nainoa noted how close the Egyptian word *ahk* was to the Hawaiian word *aka,* which also means "shadow." He wondered if both the
Egyptians and the Polynesians could have stemmed from the same
source population in the remote past.

The American commented, *"It is blazingly apparent that*
Ahkenaten understood that we are all shadows of the sun, an
insight reflected in the words attributed to Jesus of Nazareth—'I
am the light.'"

Somewhere the spirit of Ahkenaten smiled, and another luminous presence grew brighter. As these thoughts of the long-gone
Egyptian mystic and the spiritual teacher from Judea floated in their
merged yet separate minds, the *dorajuadiok* suddenly appeared
briefly in their visual field as a brillant, shimmering bar of light. A
rolling clap of thunder was heard, and their merged awareness shifted
in response, as though they had passed through some doorway and
entered yet another level in which all sense of separateness was lack-
ing. Now there was only the One, and they were a part of this Oneness, as was their star, as was the *dorajuadiok*—as was everything,
everywhere.

The great lacy *aka* net of the pattern could be seen stretching
into infinity across time and space in every direction, forever. The
fibers closest to them could be dimly seen as distinct lines, but these
rapidly merged into the misty distance filled with luminous light.
There was a subtle color, a yellowish tone to the infinite vastness.
Their awareness shifted again, and the light now seemed to be made
up of countless dots, creating a moving golden field that was both
warm and light, both cool and dark.

The movement within this great, glowing immensity seemed to

express a subtle vibrational quality, suggesting that this golden light was unmistakably alive. It seemed to be both calm and agitated, both stationary and in motion. The intensity of it was enormous, almost unbearable. As their merged minds searched for a concept to describe it, a word arrived virtually simultaneously in both Hawaiian and in English.

"Nani . . . beauty."

Like the infinitely smaller cloud of the human spirit, this greater radiance, composed of moving dots or particles of living gold, was growing, its aliveness and mind-spirit determined by all that it contains. There was no question that the power in association with the field was capable of everything, its potential unlimited. And pervading the "all" was a sense of tranquility, an absolute peace. The merged awarenesses of the American and the Hawaiian floated awestruck in this endless radiance, and a thought appeared, a memory of something that they learned out in Africa when they had been given a glimpse of it through the *dorajuadiok*—that this golden light was, is, and will always be, the mysterious Source of all being—the eternal IAO, the all-knowing One.

Another thought came through, one that distinctly originated in the American's mind. *"I did not allow myself to merge completely with this beauty when we experienced it before, as I felt concern that I might not return. This time, however . . ."* His thought dissolved, then re-formed.

"I have you with me once again as an ally, esteemed descendant. If you maintain some sense of personal integrity, you should be able to pull me out again, since we share the same spirit aspect. You know me well, so you should be able to remember me." There was another long pause in the thoughtline, then his last message came through. *"I am now going to merge completely. If you have trouble finding me, call on the most powerful spirit you can think of for assistance. Wish me luck . . ."*

Abruptly, all awareness of his ancestor's presence vanished entirely, like a candle flame that had been blown out. Nainoa waited, floating in the golden cloud for what seemed like an eternity, but no sense of the man or his mind could be perceived. The American was gone.

Nainoa began to feel great concern, and with it, his perception of his personal density began to increase. The responsibility of recovering his ancestor's soul was a formidable one. Feelings of panic crept in around the edges of his mind. What if he couldn't find him? The man's physical body, deprived of its enlivening soul, would die. Could this be how his ancestor had ended his life?

He pulled himself together and began to think hard, his sense of personal integrity steadily increasing as he did so. How could he pluck the man's soul back out of this great sea of all-being? Would it be like pulling a fish out of water? He realized that he had absolutely no idea of how to accomplish this. How did one locate a single fish in an ocean of this size—a sea without shores? He remembered the man's last words . . . *"Enlist the help of the most powerful spirit . . . ,"* and he forced his surging emotions to calm down. He abruptly recalled his last view from the altar on the *heiau.*

The *dorajuadiok . . .*

Nainoa felt a surge of renewed confidence, and the fear began to depart. That awesome being was, without doubt, the most powerful entity he had ever encountered. At a deep level, he also understood that he would have to stablize his inner turmoil before he could deal with it. To be a *kahuna kupua,* the master of spirits, he had to be calm and focused . . . calm and focused. Nainoa recalled an exercise from his training at the Place of Refuge and began to practice *lokahi,* settling his mind and emotions and reaching for his inner balance. An eternity may have passed, he was not sure, but when he felt ready, he formed the image of the towering, dark form of the *dorajuadiok* within his mind's eye and put out the call, drawing on the power of the great golden field and requesting assistance . . . asking for its help in recovering his ancestor's soul.

He held the thought . . . held the thought . . . and there was no mistaking the moment of the spirit's arrival. As before, he was simply stunned by the power of its presence. The formerly dark obelisk was now a blindingly bright bar of light that seemed to stretch upward and downward into the infinite distance, as though it was truly unconstrained and was now connected to both sides of the great Universe at once. Perhaps its source lay at the universal center or heart— if, in fact, there was one. Perhaps it was the universal heart.

All this passed through Nainoa's mind in a flash as he felt the enormous attraction generated by the spirit's monumental energy field. He knew immediately that he could not resist it. *Master of spirits?* he thought ruefully. Nothing in creation could possibly resist that force. He was being drawn inexorably toward it. He was going to merge with it . . . and he knew with certainty that when that happened, "he" would simply cease to exist. It had happened before.

He marshaled his will forces once more. He had to make one last desperate attempt. His ancestor . . . he needed the assistance of the *dorajuadiok* in recovering his ancestor's soul. He visualized the two of them lying side-by-side on the altar of black stone on the *heiau*. Then there was no more thought—no more anything. As the moment of contact occurred, there was a brilliant flash of light, and a sound like tearing cloth. . . .

For an eternity, there was only the light—only that luminous radiance of moving golden dots permeated by a tranquility that surpasses description—and then Nainoa's sense of self began to re-form by degrees, increasing slowly in ever-widening circles. He became conscious of a sound at first. It was a low, rhythmic, rumbling hiss— coming and going, coming and going—like the breaking of waves on a beach. He felt something under his back, and then . . . he saw light against his closed eyelids. His sense of being in his body was returning.

He knew that he had somehow survived his encounter with the *dorajuadiok*. It just came to him as he lay absolutely still, breathing slowly, concentrating on each breath. His mind felt bruised, and his thoughts moved in slow motion, like swimming under water. He remembered then, and felt an overwhelming sense of urgency. The American . . .

Nainoa forced his eyes open. He was lying on his back on the slab of black stone on the *heiau* once again. He raised his head. The American was there beside him. His own mind had somehow been returned to his body . . . to his dreambody on the temple platform in his ancestor's spirit garden. He propped himself up on an elbow with effort and looked around. Yes . . . he was there. Then he refastened his attention on the man next to him. He was breathing. He was alive.

Nainoa sat up carefully, and then he reached over and touched the man gently. The American's eyes slowly opened, gazing blankly into the sky. He looked decidely strange. Nainoa leaned over him, looking directly into his eyes. Nothing. Nainoa saw no person, no soul within. The American's eyes appeared completely empty, unseeing, like those of a blind man.

He remembered how he had felt the man's consciousness disappear into the golden cloud and how he had tried to enlist the help of the *dorajuadiok*. He looked again into the man's blank gaze and feared that he had failed. He recalled William telling him once that you had to be very careful in dealing with *dorajuadioks* because they were sometimes known to steal souls. Was that what had happened? Had he lost his ancestor?

Nainoa stared around wildly. They were alone on the surface of the *heiau*. The *dorajuadiok* was gone. He looked again into the man's eyes, searching, a sense of desperation beginning to grow within him. What was he to do? It was at that moment that a voice appeared within his mind.

"I'm here."

Astonishment! Nainoa cautiously formed a question within his thoughts, and an answer came immediately.

"I'm here . . . within you." It sounded like the American's voice. There was a long period of silence, then more words took form . . . slowly. *"You will recall . . . that we are both manifestations . . . of the same transcendent spiritual aspect. You were able to retrieve my soul . . . using your intentionality . . . and the power of our aumakua as an attractor field. With the assistance of the* dorajuadiok, *you were able to find my soul . . . and bring me back from*

ke akua kumulipo . . . *from IAO . . . from the great Source of all being.*"

There was another long period of silence. He watched the American's body. It was alive but somehow lifeless. It was as though the man beside him was in a coma. The voice within his mind spoke again.

"I am now merged with you, much like I am during my visits to your time and place while I am in deep trance. In this state, I could conceivably live for the rest of your life within you, returning with you and remaining within your body, communicating with you through your mind, assisting you in trying to re-create at least some of the technology of my time. We could have quite a partnership . . . unless you threw me out, of course." A dry chuckle rattled through his thoughts, accompanied by a flash of wry humor. *"I now understand spirit possession from a completely different perspective."* Then the direction of the thoughtline abruptly shifted.

"But much as I would like to remain with you, esteemed descendant, I cannot. I must return to my own time and place. There is my wife and my children, and there is my lifework. I have many tasks to accomplish before my time comes to a close. There is an agenda, what your people once called papa hana. *Therefore, I must return to my own dreambody."*

"How can I assist you in this?" Nainoa asked anxiously. "What must be done? How can I transfer your soul?"

"Hmmm, I have a sense of how to proceed, but let's ask for some help. It is always useful to call on spiritual assistance, as you have discovered. Where is the leopard man?"

"The leopard man?"

"Ahh . . . you call him the spotted tiger man. I call him leopard, as this is the name we have given to the large spotted cats that live in Africa and Asia. I have an interesting story to share with you, but it will wait. Let's put out the call for him to come."

Nainoa looked up as a sense of need, of yearning, pervaded his consciousness. He waited as the sense grew stronger. He formed the image of his spirit helper in his mind, and after a short period, a figure appeared on the edge of the *heiau*, followed by a second. It was Tehura, and the spotted tiger was with her. They walked quickly across the flat platform. Tehura's dark eyes expressed her unspoken concern.

"My ancestor and I have engaged in an extraordinary voyage of discovery and exploration," Nainoa said quickly. "He has returned with me, but his soul is now within me, within my body . . . or my dreambody, as he would say." Nainoa looked down at the pale, motionless figure beside him. "I need your help. We must return his soul to him—and quickly."

Tehura immediately cradled the American's head gently between her hands and closed her eyes. The spotted cat shapeshifted, assuming a bipedal stance, and placed his clawed hands on the American's feet. Then, from within Nainoa's mind, came a word-concept combined with a directive. "The *honi* . . . use your *ha*, your breath, to transfer my soul."

Without hesitation, Nainoa leaned over and pressed his face to the American's, looking deeply into that vacant gaze as he formed the intention and breathed into the man's face. He repeated the procedure, blowing his breath into the man's nose and mouth, imaging the shift. There was only a slight delay, and then he felt the release.

Nainoa drew back and looked anxiously at the man below him. The dark eyes closed . . . then opened and looked directly into his own. The mouth came to life and smiled. The American was back. He made a weak gesture with one hand, then he closed his eyes once more . . . and he slept.

Nainoa and Tehura kept watch over the sleeping man as the afternoon advanced. The spotted tiger man curled up next to the stone altar and went to sleep. Nainoa wondered if they were together, traveling across some place of adventure in the inner worlds of dream.

Abruptly, the big cat awoke, stretching its long body gracefully and yawning widely. As the man's eyes opened and he slowly sat up on the black stone slab, Nainoa was flooded with relief. His ancestor had merged directly with the Source of all being; he had looked into the face of the godhead, and he had survived.

The American observed the ocean below the *heiau* for long moments, and then he said, "I have recovered my personal power and sense of well-being with the assistance of our spotted friend." He glanced at the cat-man, who squinted his eyes and grimaced in response. It was an almost-smile that didn't quite succeed. "My unending gratitude goes to to you, too, Nainoa, for your role in the retrieval of my soul." He thought for a moment, then added, "I feel confident in saying that my wife and children will also be most grateful when our great adventure becomes known to them."

He glanced at Tehura, then smiled and said, "Let's go down to the beach." They helped him to rise, then the three humans and the spotted cat shaped like a man descended from the place of power and sat down on the sand below the stone platform. A gentle breeze from the ocean rattled the palm fronds overhead. The American continued to stare at the waves for some time, then slowly, he began to speak.

"In those moments of complete immersion with the Source, I experienced total soul separation from my physical body. There was only the golden light and its great, all-encompassing awareness. In those moments, I was the light, and my awareness was its awareness. I knew what it knows and felt everything that it feels." His gaze unfocused into the sheet of light reflected off the ocean's rolling surface, and his voice drifted off.

After a time, he gestured toward the seemingly endless body of water, as though searching for some tangible symbol to represent the light and thought-feeling of which he had been a part. "The power and the wisdom to which I have had access went far beyond anything that could be called human. And from this perspective, I believe that the statement 'The Universe is filled with love' is an erroneous one.

"The word *love* refers to a human emotion, and there was nothing human in what I felt. Nothing. A more correct way to express this thought might be to say that there are two predominant states expressed by the Universe—the state of being in balance, in harmony, and in connection; and the state of being out of balance, in disharmony, and dissociated. The first might be interpreted as a positive or life-enhancing state, or as 'love' in a human sense. The other might be experienced as its polar opposite, as negative or life-denying, or as destructive when interpereted through the lens of the human mind.

"All of our myriad human emotions and feelings might thus be said to be expressions of one state or the other. Both are necessary, it seems, comprising as they do the breathing-in and the breathing-out of the Universe . . . its soul-breath, one might say." He smiled. "The positive and negative poles of the immense universal data bank seem to be expressed in a singular shape, however. Perhaps the term *unity* comes closest, expressing the quality of the One that includes the manifested All.

"And the amazing thing is, that it is right here, all around us, all the time. The great golden field is not in some other remote dimension. It's everywhere. There's no need to go anywhere to contact it, because everything, everywhere, is made up of these luminous golden dots."

The American squinted his eyes and looked around. "I can see them right now, with my eyes open or closed . . . and I suspect that I will be able to see them all the time from now on. Perhaps this is what is meant when mystics talk about the veil being lifted."

He thought for long moments, then concluded, "To say that this experience and the insights it provided were overwhelming would be an understatement of vast proportions. The spoken or written word can never fully describe the magnificent yet terrible experience of that vastness and what it contains. The ultimate truth of this natural state can only be known by each of us through direct experience. The only way for others to see it is for them to become mystic witnesses themselves and *be* it. To say that I felt rapture doesn't come close to the awe I feel even now in saying these words. I was merged with the Divine . . . I *was* the Divine."

The American's eyes closed, and he fell silent. Tehura gently took him by the shoulders and helped him to lie down on the warm sand. She placed her hands over his eyes and held them there for long moments, as though to encourage him to go back to sleep. She bent down and whispered something in his ear at some length. The American smiled, then his face relaxed, and his body became motionless.

Then, Nainoa felt her cool hands on his own shoulders, and he followed suit, lying down next to his ancestor on the beach, relaxing deeply as Tehura's fingertips gently touched his face and closed his eyes. Her voice seemed to be drifting on the watersound of the ocean.

"Today you have rediscovered that you are a star being, Kahu Nainoa. You and your ancestor have traveled into the great beyond. You have been gods, and you will be gods again. But now, it is time for you to return to your lovely wife, and for this man beside you to return to his. Listen to the sound of the water, and the great spirit Tangaroa that resides within it will carry you back to your time and place. The *atua* of the ocean *est la provenance et la nourriture de la vie*, the begetter and maintainer of life, and you are one of its children. Tangaroa is the essence; it exists within everyone and everything. Until we meet again, great *voyageur*, I bid you *adieu*."

Nainoa listened to the rhythm of the waves as Tehura's fingertips moved into his hair, gently massaging his scalp. Gradually, her touch became still, and he felt himself slipping into sleep. The watersound diminished . . . diminished . . . then stabilized into a single tone—the sound of rain.

He became aware, once again, of Maraea's warm body wrapped around his and her fingers in his hair. He smelled her wonderful scent and listened to the night rain on the roof, and he knew that he had returned. As he slipped deeper toward sleep, he felt profound gratitude and a deep, pervading feeling of bliss. His lovely wife kissed his face once more, and he only half-heard her whispered prayer of protection as he drifted into the ocean of dream. His last awareness was of a set of pale green eyes on a spotted tawny field of color looking into his own. Then the eyes closed . . . and he slept.

CHAPTER SEVENTEEN

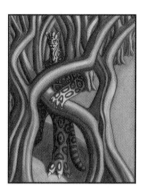

Medicinemaker

I ALSO BECAME AWARE OF THE SOUND of the early morning rain as I returned through the visionary gateway from this incredible voyage. Jill was still holding me in her arms, her fingertips gently massaging my forearms. I managed to crack open an eye and glance at the bedside clock. I had penetrated the great mystery to an entirely new depth, experiencing the endless, arching span of eternity in one long, enduring moment. I knew that neither I, nor my descendant, would ever be quite the same.

I glanced up at my beautiful wife. She was gazing at me with love flowing out of her eyes. I said nothing, but she smiled knowingly and continued to hold me closely. I closed my eyes again, totally wonderstruck by all I had perceived. The deep mystic bliss was still flowing through me like a river of energy. Or was it I that was floating in that etheric current? At this moment, my sense of singularity was still vague, and my deeper self, my *ku*, was still partly connected to the One—to IAO. I listened to the sound of the water pouring down outside, and it was as if there was no separation between myself and the rain.

I remembered Tehura's words about the ocean spirit Tangaroa (*Kanaloa* in Hawaiian), the great progenitor and sustainer of life, as well as the essence within everyone and everything. My thoughts refocused on the blue waterspirit that I sometimes encounter in vision, and I suddenly felt the rain reach out and touch me, activating some connection. There was an immediate sense of transition, and my breath caught as I began to sink out of my body in slow motion.

It was as though I were slowly dropping down through the bed, down through the floor of the house and into the earth. I continued to sink downward through the layers of geologic sediment until I appeared to arrive within a vibrant field or layer of color—the color pink. My thinking mind was functioning with incisive clarity, revealing that I had spontaneously slipped back into the shamanic state. My consciousness abruptly expanded, and I then perceived something of great beauty.

I was surrounded on all sides by the pinkness. There was no sense of myself as separate from it, although my will forces and my ability to act seemed to be intact. My curiosity was aroused, and I raised a finger, a dreamfinger if you will, to touch the pink field. An opening appeared where I touched it, and golden light began to stream out—a luminous shaft of radiance composed of millions of tiny golden dots or particles.

Amazed at this discovery, I used my finger to make the opening larger. The brilliant light increased as I unzipped the pink field much like opening a tent. Then I simply floated through this aperture and found myself in a place unlike any I have ever seen, either in ordinary reality or in the spirit worlds.

On first glance, it resembled a desert oasis, but one where everything was made of gold. There were golden palm trees with clusters of golden dates, and small golden birds chirping among the glittering fronds that rattled in the golden breeze. There were golden rocks and golden sand, golden shrubs and grasses. Even the mountainous sand dunes surrounding the grove of palms and extending into the hazy distance seemed to be made of gold. There was a pond in the center of the oasis, its water appearing as if made of liquid gold. And always, if I looked closely, I could perceive those dots, subtly moving, warm and dark and gold.[1]

As is usual for me while in the shamanic state, I was still dimly aware of my physical surroundings. I could still feel Jill holding me, and I could still hear the rain. I recalled the spiritual touch that had initiated this unexpected journey and reached out to pluck a golden flower from a shiny bush, gently placing it as an offering on the reflective mirror of the water.

Unexpectedly, a high, clear voice came out of the pool and began to sing. It was a tone poem that rose and fell, rose and fell, much like an operatic aria. The range of the voice was far beyond that of any human, however, and as I stood there, enchanted, there was no doubt in my mind as to who it was. I became aware of a sweet fragrance floating in the air. It seemed to have appeared with the song. Perhaps this unearthy melody had produced it, if such a thing is possible.

I looked around at the golden oasis and understood that I had been brought to yet another place of power and healing in the dream worlds. Enormous gratitude welled up within me, and I searched my memories for something I might offer in return. A poem appeared in my mind, a short one titled "Prayer to a Mountain Spring," written by Lew Welch.[2]

> *"Gentle Goddess,*
> *Who never asks for anything at all,*
> *and gives us everything we have,*
> *thank you for this sweet water,*
> *and your fragrance . . .*

I presented this prayer to the beautiful voice in the water, adding my own final line:

> *. . . and your song."*

When I emerged from the shamanic state, I could still hear the beautiful voice singing in my mind's ear. In fact, the song stayed with me for three days, a haunting, repetitive tune that never ceased as long as the rainy weather continued. When the skies finally cleared and the sun came out, it stopped.

I seemed to have crossed some threshold in response to the voyage to the Source of all being. To claim outright that I have looked into the face of God and had a direct, personal experience with that sacred state of universal consciousness would be pretentious in the extreme, and yet the statement would not be inaccurate. And how has this experience affected me? In every way possible. For instance, having mentioned to Nainoa that the waterspirit sometimes assists me in facilitating healing, please permit me to make some general observations about spirit medicine and then offer several examples of the kind of work I am sometimes requested to do on behalf of others.

First, let me acknowledge that my training with the Foundation for Shamanic Studies has allowed me to develop and refine natural faculties that otherwise could have remained dormant for life. One of these is the ability to access energy and use it to help allieviate pain and suffering.

Second, I make no claim of possessing extraordinary healing powers myself. All true facilitators of healing know that nobody actually heals anyone else. Rather, those who are suffering heal themselves with a powerful assist from the shaman/medicinemaker and from the helping spirits who are in relationship with them. Exceptions exist, but they are rare.

Third, let me observe that the role of the shaman is to become the link between the sufferer and the unseen realities. Most shamanic practitioners work with one or more spirits who provide the power as well as the guidance on how to use it in a healing capacity. By making their own body the bridge, the shaman serves as a conduit for this power, directing energy from the spirit helpers to the proper place in the sufferer's body. Of course, sometimes the spirits themselves convey the power directly to the one in need.

The examples that follow occurred on a single day in early August 1997. I was in River Falls, Wisconsin, attending a week-long conference sponsored by a multi-denominational group called the International Institute of Integral Human Sciences, at which I presented a keynote talk and two concurrent four-day workshops in core shamanism.

My workshops draw on my cross-cultural knowledge as an anthropologist, as well as my training in shamanic work, and provide an opportunity for individuals to experience the ancient methods of achieving mystic states of awareness. These goal-oriented sessions are designed to bring participants into connection with their inner sources of wisdom and power—the spirit helpers and spirit teachers that the traditional peoples tell us are intimately connected with our life goals. At the culmination of these gatherings, we often do healing work as a group for someone in the circle who is in need, giving participants the opportunity to draw on their new spiritual allies to help allieviate pain and suffering.

On this occasion, virtually everyone was in touch with their spirits by the end of the workshop, and the "battery" was fully charged, so to speak. Ordinarily, I do not discuss the details of the healing rituals in which I participate because of issues of confidentiality and because the actual procedure will vary according to what is appropriate for each person. A broad description of what happened on this occasion can be shared, however, because one of the participants has already published her own account of the extraordinary events that took place on that day.

In the morning session, a petite, elderly woman approached me and volunteered to be on the receiving end of the healing ritual. She told me that she that was suffering from severe myofascial restriction, the result of a whiplash injury sustained during a car accident several years before. Her neck and upper back felt like she was wearing armor, and she could barely turn her head at all. She informed me that her chiropractor had told her that she was never going to recover—a good example of medical pessimism coming from a socially sanctioned health-care provider. I also learned to my surprise that she was a nun in the Catholic faith.

In the ritual that followed, I had Sister Anne, as I will call her, lie down on my old Navajo rug in the center of the circle. I made sure she was comfortably propped up with pillows, then instructed the 50 participants to shake their rattles in a fairly rapid, steady beat. While doing so, each was to invite their spirit helpers to come into the room and stand behind them, requesting that these allies infuse them with power to help in the healing of the sister. When each person felt themselves to be power-filled, they were to gather the energy at their heart level, from which they could then direct it in a compassionate, healing capacity to Sister Anne. In this way, the circle could be visualized as a wheel with everyone sitting around the rim and the healing energy forming the spokes of connection to Sister Anne at the hub. My role was somewhat more involved.

When the ritual began, I knelt on the floor next to the nun and lit a candle as well as a stick of piñon incense with which I dowsed myself with smoke. I then closed my eyes and listened to the rhythmic sound of the rattles. After a short interval, I took a deep breath and opened my inner doorway, flooding my body with the sensations of force and inducing the expanded state. As the power shook me, I invited my helping spirits to approach. The shamanic state deepened as I felt them arrive, one at a time. I noted particularly the tall, shimmering blue woman I have come to think of as the waterspirit.

At times like this, the transcendent *aumakua* self often takes a hand in things, providing an intuitive suggestion, and on that day, almost as an afterthought, I extended the invitation to include any other spirits who wished to work with the sister in a healing capacity. Immediately, I felt a new presence come into the room. It was standing behind me, but I could perceive it quite clearly without turning around. It appeared to me as a tall human being with long hair and a beard, enfolded in a flowing white field in which I couldn't perceive his hands and feet. This spirit had an immensely powerful presence that was at the same time curiously gentle, and I assumed that he had come to work with Sister Anne. I mentally explained what was happening and invited him to provide power and support, as well as whatever healing she needed. I then proceeded with the ritual while everyone continued to rattle.

The next stage involved trying to "see" the sister's energy body. When I am in the shamanic state of consciousness, I can sometimes perceive the sufferer's energetic aspect, especially if one of my invisible allies is merged with me, endowing me with their power and abilities.[3] Under these circumstances, the energy extending around and within a person's body usually looks to me like a flowing field of light, appearing bright and glittering when in its normal, undistorted state.[4] At such moments, I try to locate any dark areas that could indicate intrusions or distortions producing blocks to the flow. Sometimes I perceive abnormally bright areas that might indicate the presence of old injuries, energy leaks, or areas of hyperactivity, such as a tumor. I can also sometimes feel distortions by running my hands through the person's energy field a few inches above and around their body.

It is my practice to attempt to extract such intrusions and deposit them in a bowl of water that I prepare ahead of time to serve as a repository. I also try to help restore normal flow to the person's energy body and to seal up any places from which the person's life force is leaking. I then attempt to gather a large supply of power and transfer it to the sufferer in a healing capacity. In many cases, I also search for a spirit to come into relationship with the individual, one who will continue to provide that person with power and support.

I should add here that I believe it is inadvisable to direct power into a woman's abdomen if she is pregnant, nor do I ever attempt to invest a tumor with energy. I know that not everyone will agree with this, especially practitioners of Qigong. In my own practice, I attempt to extract as much of the energy from the tumor as possible, and then try to reverse its energetic relationship with its host. In this way, the sufferer progressively drains the tumor of energy, rather than allowing the tumor to continue to derive its energy for growth from the one afflicted.

As I prepared to work with Sister Anne on that morning in Wisconsin, I focused on the shimmering blue presence of the water woman who was watching me from the other side of the circle, explaining what was required and inviting her to merge with me. My ears immediately filled with a rushing sound, and a whisper of affection appeared in my mind, accompanied by a sweeping feeling of coolness that conveyed an incredible sense of intimacy and benevolence. The associated surge of power was immense, and I was momentarily staggered, shaking uncontrollably for several long moments and clutching my stomach reflexively as a wave of nausea seized me.

When I recovered control of my body, I turned my eyes to Sister Anne and could perceive the dark intrusions on her bright field. I seized my rattle and shook it over the length of her body, opening her energy field with cascades of sparkling light for the work to follow. Within my mind, I heard the watery murmurings rise in pitch and volume until they took form once again as the beautiful song I had heard in the golden oasis.

I put down the rattle, focused on the dark stains, and flexed my fingers, preparing to do the extraction. As I began to extend my hands toward the dark mass in the woman's upper back, something completely unexpected occurred. A second set of hands appeared in my field of vision, and I looked up, startled. I had momentarily forgotten about the luminous presence of the newcomer standing behind me. He had kneeled down on the other side of Sister Anne and was also reaching toward her.

As my gaze swept up his luminous figure and took in his bearded visage framed by his long hair, my first thought was that it might be the spirit of someone from the nun's past, an ancestor perhaps. Then, our eyes met and shock ricocheted through me. Intuitively, I knew that it was the spirit of Jesus of Nazareth, and he had come to heal Sister Anne!

The certainty was so strong that I was stunned into immobility.

How long my eyes remained locked with his, I do not know. It seemed like an eternity, one within which I sensed portals opening—doors within doors within doors. And through these now-unconcealed interfaces, the vastness beckoned, that radiant immensity of moving golden dots whose power is simply indescribable. Then the eyes looking into mine smiled, and I felt tranquility and harmony flow through me, providing a deep sense of ease and utter goodness in those moments. As I looked full into his face, I also realized that none of the renderings of Jesus of Nazareth have ever captured his likeness. None.

His luminous gaze shifted to look down at Sister Anne, breaking the connection. I returned to myself, and my hands, arrested in their motion, continued to move toward her, as did his. I ran them through the woman's energy field, inches above her body, extending my fingers of light into her thorax like a rake, gathering the dark mass lodged between her shoulders. I watched, entranced, as the hands of the Judean healer followed mine. We worked for what seemed like a long time, extracting bands and knots of etheric substance from the woman's body, then depositing them in the bowl of water.

Our hands were also drawn unexpectedly to her eyes and ears, and to the bright wings of her lungs and the luminous roots of her bronchi in her chest area. More extraction followed, of a sort of dark, rubbery plasmic substance from her lungs and bronchi, and of minute particles like sand from her eyes and ears. When I saw her energy pattern flowing unobstructed once again, I stopped, and began the next phase of her healing, the augmentation of her personal power supply.

I looked once more into Jesus' alert gaze and mentally explained the nature of what I was going to do. Then I put out the call for a helping spirit to come into association with Sister Anne. I was half expecting a Catholic saint, but an animal spirit appeared immediately, one I knew well. I asked it if it would come into relationship with the suffering woman, infusing her with power and protection in a healing capacity. The spirit animal agreed. I gathered it into my arms, condensing its power into a golden ball between my hands, then used my breath to blow it into Sister Anne's sternum.

Throughout this procedure, the spirit of the Judean healer watched what I was doing, and to my astonishment, he leaned over and used his breath to augment my own, expelling a cloud of visible vapor like minuscule sparkling snowflakes of light that sank into the woman's body.

Then I took up my rattle and swept it down the length of the sister's energy body again and again, encouraging the flow of her light and "sealing her up." When I felt that the healing was done, I mentally extended my thanks to those who had assisted, including the one across from me. His smile and the goodness flowing out of his eyes will live in my memories forever.

I held up my hand, and the group stopped rattling. My awareness shifted in response, and the water woman's song within my mind ceased as the world became ordinary once again. I glanced at the place where the spiritual master had been kneeling, but he was gone. Words are inadequate to describe how I felt at this moment.

I looked down at Sister Anne. She was smiling up at me sweetly, and I helped her to sit up. I glanced at the group and wondered if anyone else had seen him. I was very much aware of how incredibly presumptuous it would sound to say that I had just participated in a healing ritual with Jesus of Nazareth. I could imagine the lurid headlines of the tabloids having a field day—"Anthropologist sees Jesus in Wisconsin!" I shook my head and sighed. Perhaps this one had just been for me . . . and for Sister Anne. I decided that I would only share with the group what I had done and how I had done it. I would talk privately with the sister at lunch perhaps. I felt a great stillness within me.[5]

As the morning session came to a close and we all left to walk toward the building where meals were being served, I was still quite altered. I had goosebumps all over me and could still feel the power flowing strongly in my body. Although I was walking across a college campus with new friends, I felt as though I was more connected to the spirit worlds of the dreamtime. As I looked at the leaves of a nearby tree, I could see them as small solar panels, drinking up the light and converting it into carbohydrate molecules. I could see the details of each green grid and could feel the dreamlike consciousness of the tree itself.

I entered the dining hall and passed through the lines in much the same state, aware that my *ku* was operating on automatic pilot, selecting foods that it liked from the self-serve buffet without conscious input from my decision maker. When I came to the end of the line, my inner director noted with amusement that my *ku* had gone heavily for the desserts. I looked around the room and spotted Sister Anne. I sat down at her table, and listened while she told me what she had experienced.

I do not recall much of what she said, but I do remember that I was just about to tell her what I had experienced, when another of the workshop participants sat down across from me. I glanced at him with a friendly nod, then felt myself sober with a jolt as I saw the expression on his face.

Bob, as I will call him, stared directly into my eyes in silence for long moments, then opened by saying, "Do you have any idea who came to the healing circle this morning?" I smiled and waited, my eyes locked with his. The room seemed to dissolve, the background noise evaporating into stillness as my smile crept into his eyes and understanding grew between us. I knew that he knew. And he knew that I knew.

"I have always been a seer," he began, turning his attention to the sister. "Even as a small child I had psychic awareness. My parents and friends had a lot of trouble accepting my gift, so I, like most psychics, learned to keep it to myself." He glanced at me again and continued.

"Today at the healing ritual, I saw the shadow of a bearded man with long hair and white robes come into the room. Maybe *shadow* is the wrong term because this man's spirit was so blindingly bright. I knew immediately who it was . . ." his words drifted off as he turned to regard the nun sitting with us. "You must have an inside track, sister," he went on, "because the Big One came to work on you today. It was Jesus himself, if I'm not mistaken, and how could he not come? He's your spirit husband, is he not?"

With the man's words, the vastness opened once again, and I felt myself being drawn into the dream worlds where all things, all beings, and all times exist simultaneously. I continued to watch Bob talk with the sister and could follow what he was saying, but my "strong eye" was open, looking into eternity, searching for the one who had come into the circle that morning. Gold dots everywhere, filling the cafeteria with light . . .

Perhaps this act of intention contributed to what occurred in the second medicine circle we did that afternoon. This time, two individuals approached me to be healed. The first was a young woman afflicted with systemic lupus erythematosus, a serious inflammatory autoimmune disorder. The second was an older woman with active cancer in her viscera. When the moment came to put out the call for my spirits to approach, I made a specific appeal to the spirit of Jesus of Nazareth to participate in the healings.

Once again, the white-robed spirit came into the room, appearing behind me as he had that morning. Once again, he used his hands with mine as we did the extractions, and once again, he used his breath to help augment the sufferers' personal power. I was simply stunned by these events, my amazement growing as the workshop came to an end.

This time, I was approached by several women with psychic awareness. They had all seen him clearly, a tall, bearded man with long hair, and once again, there was absolute certainty among them as to who he was. I sensed with deep humility that I had acquired a new healing master.

As the workshop came to a close and I left the building in a daze, I saw one of the women sitting on the lawn outside the big doors of the building. Her hands were plunged into the grassy earth, and there were tears streaming down her face. She was looking up into the sky, and following her gaze, I saw a double rainbow encircling the sun.

I got a written report from Sister Anne a month later and learned that the pain in her back and shoulders had left entirely, allowing her to freely turn her neck from side to side. She decided not tell her chiropractor of her healing experience, but his comments when he worked on her several weeks after the workshop were revelatory. "This is unbelievable," he proclaimed to her. "Your neck has *never* been so flexible, pliable, and easy to manipulate. This is a great improvement that I never expected to see."

What Sister Anne didn't tell me on that day in August was that she also had failing eyesight due to cataracts, failing hearing, and chronic obstructive pulmonary disease. When I saw her again a year later at the same conference, she informed me that she had been scheduled for cataract surgery until it was discovered after the healing ritual that her cataracts had mysteriously vanished. Her hearing had also returned almost to normal, and she had not experienced any more of her chronic bronchial asthma attacks. She was absolutely convinced that a healing had taken place and that it was still in progress.

The woman with lupus also communicated with me, expressing gratitude, saying how she, too, felt transformed by the ritual. After an initial flare-up of her condition a few days after the conference, she had felt steadily better physically, and her inner sense of fear, self-worthlessness, and hypervigilance had shifted enormously, allowing her to feel joy in her heart and excitement about her future for the first time in her life. She came to pick me up at the airport when I returned the next year and informed me that her condition had continued to improve.

I learned by phone that the woman with active tumors was holding her own, and that the cancer seemed to have gone into remission. I had no more news of her until the next year when someone told me that they had seen her at a gathering in Montreal and that she had seemed to be in good health.

Without claiming that I do or accomplish anything, let me observe that the positive changes experienced by many sufferers in response to such a healing ritual can be dramatic and immediate, but more often they are subtle and cumulative over the next several weeks or even months.

For example, I led a similar healing ritual earlier that same summer on behalf of a young woman who lives in northern California. She was in her early 20s and had been suffering from endometriosis since she'd been 12 years old, a serious condition involving aberrant and invasive growth of the lining of her uterus into her body cavity. The cause of her endometriosis had not yet been determined, but I was aware from my brief talk with her that she had internalized some deeply personal issues stemming from her relationship with her family. And there was, of course, the stress of adolescence from which she was just emerging. Whenever she had a menstrual period, she suffered great pain, and her doctor had discussed the possibility of surgery with her, including the likelihood of a complete hysterectomy. When the young woman showed up in one of my workshops, she seemed a good candidate for a spiritual healing. I worked with the waterspirit on this occasion.

The woman wrote to me several weeks later and expressed that she felt much better. She also revealed that she'd had a menstrual period completely free of pain for the first time in five years. She came to see me in the fall and seemed visibly changed, projecting a kind of joyous radiance that made her appear to be in great health. She informed me that she believed her body was healing in response to the ritual.

My understanding of how spiritual healing occurs has also been greatly enhanced through learning that the transcendent self of the sufferer can also be the source of formidable healing power.[6] While I was still living in Hawai'i, the *kahuna* Morrnah Simeona revealed to me that when a person is suffering from an illness that is difficult or impossible to cure, they must first be made aware of their relationship to their *aumakua*. They must then be shown how to connect with this spirit aspect and how to enter into close, conscious relationship with it. Simply having the strong desire to do so is the first step.

The sufferer can then ask their *aumakua* to send down its *ha*, its healing "breath" of power. This is received through the *ku*, and since this soul aspect is where the inner healer is located, understanding how this level of the self functions is critical to the healing process. As has been discussed, the *ku* is much like a living computer or servant in that it does what it is told. It performs best when it is given clear instructions by the conscious ego/inner director.[7] If these instructions are accompanied by a physical stimulus, so much the better, because the *ku* is very impressed by anything physical. This is why the drum, the rattle, the healing songs and ritual provide such a powerful assist in shamanic work. This is also why the physicality of lovemaking can open the inner doorway to transcendent experience.

When the person's *ku* is sufficiently impressed by the healing ritual and by the presence of the power-filled medicinemaker, it goes to work with an enhanced sense of purpose, using the infusion of energy coming in from the higher self or from the attending spirit helpers to correct any distortions or negative thoughtforms held within the pattern of the energy body.

Such distortions can come from the objective realm of everyday ordinary reality as a result of a physical injury, for example, as in the case of Sister Anne's whiplash. In such an event, the injury to the physical body is reflected into the energetic aspect, distorting the pattern. Distortions can also originate from the subjective realms, as in the case of the girl under psychic attack mentioned previously. Most of us have been on the receiving end of others who "have it in for us" and who direct hostile thoughts and feelings toward us. These thoughts, in turn, can be picked up and internalized by our *ku* much like spiritual poison darts. Among the traditional peoples, this practice of directing harmful thoughts at someone is known as negative witchcraft or sorcery—the use of power backed by heightened emotion combined with focused intentionality to inflict harm.

It is worth noting that individuals can also produce their own energetic distortions by generating unwholesome and negative thoughts within their own mind, or by experiencing negative emotions such as fear or anxiety in response to traumatic life situations. When the traumas are extreme, as in cases of combat stress; a dreadful car accident; a serious surgery; a bitter divorce; a shocking betrayal; the death of a loved one; a rape, sexual molestation, or incest experience; or some other form of physical, mental, or emotional abuse, the distortions can be equally extreme and can result in the fragmentation of the personality and the dissociation of parts of the self—a phenomenon known generally as *soul loss*.[8]

Since the physical body is formed around and within the energy body, it is not surprising that distortions to the pattern can affect the way in which the physical body functions, producing the symptoms we recognize as illness. This reveals that the causes of virtually all illnesses are ultimately to be found within the life experiences of the sufferer. This also conveys that the primary problem is not the illness, but rather the distortions caused by the loss of personal power or soul part that allowed the illness to invade the body and manifest itself.

Morrnah Simeona told me that when the energy body receives an infusion of healing power from the *aumakua* or from the helping spirits working with the *kahuna* shaman, the *ku* must then be clearly told to use this power to erase the distortions and replace them with light. This will allow the pattern of the energy body to flow normally once again. And since the *ku* uses the energy body as a psychic-energetic blueprint to make the necessary repairs, the restoration of the energy pattern will allow the renovation of the physical body to its former undistorted state.

The implication: True healing begins at the spiritual level of the self and is transcribed into the physical through the *ku*. Those suffering from incurable illness must become aware of how the self is put together and how these separate aspects operate in relationship with each other. They must accept that they have the power to heal themselves, as well as the spiritual support that makes it possible.

If my fieldwork in these inner realms of awareness, experience, and reality are valid, and I believe that they are, only 20 percent of our available energy is manifested as the life force associated with our physical embodiment. Eighty percent of our power resides in association with our *aumakua*, and this is considerably more energy than we need to cure anything. This suggests that there are no incurable diseases. When one understands the true nature of the self as well as the true nature of reality, everything becomes possible. But it doesn't always work out that way.

In the summer of 1999, I learned to my dismay that Terence McKenna, the well-known ethnobotanist, mystic, and explorer of nonordinary reality, had been diagnosed with brain cancer. I had read several of his books with great interest, and the year before, I had met him briefly at a Whole Life Expo in Texas where we were both presenters.

In late September, I was doing an evening presentation for the local member-group of the Institute of Noetic Sciences (IONS) in Sacramento, California, when Bob Blackstone, a close friend for many years, asked if we could do some long-distance healing work on Terence's behalf. I smiled and rubbed my hands together. This is an area where shamanism works well.

Let me interject here that ordinarily, one never does healing work on behalf of another unless it has been requested. There is a spritual protocol, and it is not acceptable to inflict the art of healing on the unwilling. In this case, however, I knew that Terence had requested healing through Art Bell's well-known radio program, so I smiled at Bob and said that we could try.

Let me also add that although Terence and I had actually met, I knew that he had a much stronger connection with Susanne and Sandy Sims, the directors of the New Millennium Institute, where both he and I now taught workshops. It was my understanding that Terence was in residence on the Big Island, and so I decided to gather a large supply of energy with the assistance of the IONS group and send it to him in a healing capacity, using the Simses and their Institute as a magnet for the remote healing. I also had the sense that this had to be done with great care so that the power did not augment the tumor in his brain.

I discussed this with the group and outlined the procedure we would follow. I placed the Hawaiian bowl in the center of our circle and suggested that each person access mystical power through their spirit helpers and teachers, then visualize filling the bowl with the energy. When the timing seemed right, I would convey the bowl of light in a healing capacity toward Terence through my connection with Sandy and Susanne Sims.

Everyone began to drum and rattle together, and as my awareness shifted, I could perceive the bowl brimming with light. When it seemed to reach its maximum intensity, I visualized the Sims' Frank Lloyd Wright house, activating my own connection with that place and with them, sending the energy toward Terence through that terminal, so to speak. When I got home later that evening, I e-mailed Susanne and Sandy, informing them of the ritual and suggesting that they buy a wooden bowl and some candles, a symbolic way through which they could then convey the power to Terence as soon as possible.

Susanne's reply arrived the next morning. By chance, Terence was at the Frank Lloyd Wright house that very evening, and at the exact moment we did the ritual, a small portion of the tussocky lawn immediately in front of the tall wooden and glass doors suddenly burst into fire. No one could figure out how it started, and of course, no one at the Institute knew of the ritual. So they all rushed to put the fire out. Then came my e-mail.

Terence subsequently decided to come to San Francisco and have brain surgery, a risky procedure for him, as he had been diagnosed as terminal, his cancer inoperable. He survived the surgery, his faculties intact, but his cancer recurred. Six months later, on April 3, 2000, Terence passed into the dream world for the last time.

What role the conveyed power of the IONS group played in all this cannot be ascertained, of course, but I had a chance to share this strange story at a conference with the founder and president of IONS, Dr. Edgar Mitchell, one of the Apollo 14 astronauts and the sixth man to walk on the moon. Ed is also an accomplished scientist with an extensive background in theoretical physics, and he expressed great interest in response to my account of the lawn bursting into fire, proclaiming the event to be a genuine example of nonlocality. He added that nonlocality is to the physicist what interconnectedness is to the mystic, and that of the 150 studies on remote healing that have been published, over half report positive results. In the long conversation that followed, I also learned that quantum physics is in the process of confirming virtually everything that the mystics have told us over the centuries.

With the end of the second millennium and the dawning of the third, science and spirituality are coming together.

CHAPTER EIGHTEEN

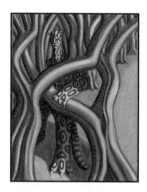

The Message

T HE UNUSUAL ACCOUNTS recorded in my autobiographical books now have an existence and a value separate from myself, and I have offered them for what they are, nothing more, nothing less. In the late summer of 1995, I was approached in a bookstore by a man who was attempting to write a review of *Spiritwalker* for a scholarly journal.[1] In the course of our conversation, he asked me to qualify my work as fiction or nonfiction, and to say where one stopped and the other began. I smiled and answered without hesitation, "There is no fiction in my book," to which he looked completely puzzled.

I understood his quandary, and I sympathized with his dilemma. The reviewer was looking for a clear-cut boundary between my dreamlike shamanic experiences and the waking world with which he was familiar, and in my books, such a carefully patrolled border is elusive. Westerners tend to be very objective in the way they define reality, and they believe that there is an unbroken line between the subjective regions of the mind and the objective plane of material physical reality. This division is, in fact, an artifact of European literate culture.

The separation between a supernatural realm of the spirits and the natural realm of the everyday world does not exist for the traditionals, nor can it be applied to their experience of reality. The traditional sees the world as made up of things seen and things hidden, and draws no distinction, no boundary between them. It is understood that they present themselves together, as two halves of a whole, woven into one common, seamless fabric.

The degree to which I have been able to accept this truth is the degree to which I have been able to successfully practice *cultural relativism,* one of the fundamental principles of anthropological research. This is the ability to view the beliefs and customs of other peoples within the context of their culture, rather than judging or defining them from the perspective of one's own. Through the practice of cultural relativism, we acquire the ability to set our own culturally determined preconceptions aside and put ourselves in someone else's skin so that we can see, hear, and feel their ways of being in the world from their viewpoint—and understand them from their perspective.

This ability does not come naturally to Westerners, nor to anyone else for that matter, and as I watched the man in the bookstore struggle to understand, all this passed through my mind in a flash.

Many years ago, the Hawaiian *kahuna* Nelita Anderson said to me, "You may never fully understand why you were chosen to have these experiences, Dr. Hank, but it is tempting to say that you have been given them for a reason. You are a trained anthropologist with impressive academic credentials. You are also an accomplished teacher with strong skills of communication." She was the one who listened to my story, validated my spontaneous visions, directed me to write them up as nonfiction, and gave me "permission" to share them with the world at large. In the spring of 1995, Kahu Nelita passed into the spirit world and did not return, but her legacy to all who knew her has been considerable, and Jill and I sometimes sense her presence working behind the scenes.

Woven into the fabric of these unusual books is a message that can be perceived at several levels. The first definitely falls into the category of prophecy. I seem to have been given a look at the future—an extended and experiential overview of a slice of time roughly 5,000 years down the road in which Western civilization and its high technology, as well as virtually everything that we all take so much for granted, is completely and utterly gone.

Since the publication of *Spiritwalker* in 1995 and *Medicinemaker* in 1998, many have asked me if I believe that the future is fixed, if what I have perceived in my visions through Nainoa is now an inescapable given. I usually reply that we are in the process of creating the future through the decisions each of us makes in the here-and-now, that there are virtually limitless numbers of potential futures, and that nothing is fixed. But it is also quite clear that if we choose to follow the path of denial, if we allow ourselves to be driven by greed and continue to follow the strategy of short-term gain at the expense of the world's resource base, the collapse of our civilization is inevitable, and the future we are walking straight into is Nainoa's world.

Is this partly why I was given these experiences—as a clear warning to the world at large to change our ways or face the consequences? I do not know, but this part of the message certainly casts light on the well-known fact that we live in perilous times. In addition to all our social, political, religious, and economic issues, there is an enviromental emergency of truly epic proportions. Curiously, our governmental and corporate institutions are seemingly unwilling or unable to accept the potentially catastrophic nature of our current situation and act on it.

The mounting body of scientific evidence suggests overwhelmingly that we are in the process of destroying our life-support system, and by association, our civilization—a direct result of the manner in which humans have been living since the first city-states were established more than 5,000 years ago.[2] There are, as well, the dangers caused by more recent human cultural changes, such as the relationship between our industrial technology and the current worldwide climatic warming trend whose intensity and rate of increase have taken weather forecasters completely by surprise.[3]

The evidence reveals that the global warming trend is having a much more dramatic effect on the planet's polar regions than on the temperate or equatorial zones, supporting the hypothetical scenarios that were presented in my first two books.[4] It is no longer a question of "if" the ecological catastrophe will happen, but "when." The informed citizen and scientist alike now have enough background information to clearly see the signs of the impending crunch. The question is: "What do we do?"

The second level of the message deals with this question, and conveys information about the magnitude of humanity's sins—as well as what we must do to rectify them.

First, the relationship between our runaway population growth and our social, political, economic, and environmental problems is quite clear. In October of 1999, the world population of human beings surpassed six billion, with three billion of us enduring lifeways in which stark poverty and starvation are part of the given. There are simply too many of us, and we must control and reduce our population size immediately or suffer the consequences. Studies of the contemporary population dynamics in natural ecosystems reveal that species engaging in catastrophic overpopulation inevitably crash. There seems to be no built-in evolutionary mechanism to keep organisms from reproducing too rapidly. This means that there is no built-in safeguard against extinction—and the extinction of humankind is a real possibility.

Second, we must stop exploiting and degrading the environment that feeds us. As an informed citizen, I feel great unease at the monumental waste being generated at every level of the world's capitalist system. As an anthropologist, I understand that our problems are arising out of Western culture's mechanistic view of that world. It is also quite clear that most of the solutions that our think-tank specialists have conjured up simply won't work because they are based in the same worldview that has produced the problems. So where do we look for answers?

As a graduate student at Berkeley, I was able to immerse myself in the journals, accounts, and ethnographic field studies recorded by the missionaries, travelers, and early anthropologists who made contact with the indigenous peoples over the past two centuries. These Europeans and Euroamericans had great faith in their own culture's ability to conquer and control nature, and not surprisingly, their sentiments toward the so-called primitive peoples' emphasis on living in balance and harmony with the natural world often reflect an attitude of condescension mixed with disdain.

Today, with the environment under siege from a hundred fronts, the views of the indigenous peoples are beginning to look a lot less like superstition and a lot more like wisdom. Their lifeways kept their people and their cultures alive and well for a thousand times longer than Western civilization has existed, and the average person had far more leisure time than most citizens today will ever enjoy.

The indigenous peoples have important lessons to teach us, lessons that may ultimately save us. In my opinion, our corporate, religious, and political leaders would do well to stop exterminating them and changing their lifeways, and instead approach them with the understanding that they are living treasures. We Westerners simply must change our ways of seeing and understanding reality if we are to create real, meaningful, and lasting resolutions to our problems, and the wisdom of the indigenous peoples holds the key.

Third, we must assess the planetary resource base—water, air, soils, agriculture, livestock, forests, metals, petroleum, energy, and everything else upon which we depend for our continued survival. We must determine the carrying capacity of this resource base, and we must determine exactly how large the human population can be to remain within this limit. To exceed this number means that we are spending our savings with the inevitable result—bankruptcy.

There exist planetary laws that will not accept the limits imposed by religious dogma, nor do these universal principles of living systems have the slightest regard for the legislated rights of special-interest groups or the corporate businessman's profit margin. In a sentence, we can no longer afford to pursue the strategy of short-term gain at the expense of long-term sustainability. We do so at our peril.

Fourth (and paradoxically), it is quite obvious that those most capable of assessing the resource base and the managing of it are the multinational corporations. These economic giants have created a privately run world economy in which they control the global flow of materials, energy, and capital. Unfortunately, they have been pillaging and plundering like pirates who lack a disciplined and ethical captain. These multinationals simply cannot continue to do business as usual, because if they do, they—and we—will lose everything.

The Modernist paradigm that came into being during the Renaissance with the rise of science, intellectualism, and the business world is failing to solve the problems it has created. We are now in transition between what was and what will be, and the decisions that we make or don't make today will affect the entire next stage of human evolution, a truly awesome responsibility. Seen in this light, the prevailing mythologies of our organized religions and our political, economic, and scientific ideologies simply must change if they are to provide humanity with the necessary tools to build a sustainable future.[5] The time has come for the corporate sector to take responsibility for the survival of the human species.

There is no time to question, no time to debate. We must promote worldwide understanding and awareness of these issues through public education and through the media, and we must do so immediately. Jill and I talk constantly about the enormity of our problems and what to do about them. As she put it recently, "It is much like trying to turn around an immense aircraft carrier at full steam ahead—how do you do it?" The decision obviously falls to the captain, and herein lies the key.

The captain is not only responsible for the carrier and its overall mission, purpose, and safety. The captain is also responsible for the well-being of everyone on the ship, from the highest-ranking officers and military specialists to the lowliest crew member. It is much the same in traditional villages. The chiefs are responsible not only for the safety and success of the village, they are also responsible for the well-being of everyone in it, from the highest-ranking political and religious leaders to the lowliest streetsweeper or dung carrier and their families.

There is a crisis of leadership at virtually every level of the Western world. Our directors and administrators possess the power, but with rare exceptions, they have forgotten what is means to be true chiefs. The time has come for our political, military, religious, and corporate leaders to take up the responsibilities that come with the job and act accordingly.

Tom Hurley, the former educational director of the Institute of Noetic Sciences, recently put it this way: "What if the purpose of business was to nurture and sustain life?" This is a valid question and deserves immediate consideration. It contains the seeds of humanity's ultimate survival.

This brings us to consider another most important question: If our directors and administrators accept their responsibilities and truly lead, will the public, hypnotized by the glitter of our gadgets and by the endless distractions provided by television and our entertainment industry, respond? I believe they will.

The 44 million people of Paul Ray's American Lives Survey have revealed themselves to be environmentally aware, socially concerned, and spiritually focused individuals who are carriers of more positive ideas, values, and trends than in any previous period of history, and this number appears to be growing.[6] This unexpectedly large population of enlightened citizens, representing about 25 percent of the adult population in the United States alone, reveals that we should take heart, for we are traveling in the company of an enormous number of allies.

In summary, the first two levels of the message reveal that a test of unbelievable magnitude is upon us, and if we fail it, neither the sanctified misunderstanding of our mainstream religions, nor the misguided ideologies of our political and economic systems, will save us. We must reevaluate all our priorities. Failure to do so will hasten the demise of Western civilization and will clearly place the future of humanity at risk.

The next level of the message reveals the path of salvation—one that has the potential to change the directions of world history.

A major spiritual reawakening is currently going on within a growing and important sector of the population of North America and Europe. It is occurring among well-educated and well-informed people who are often in social, professional, and political positions of power from which it is possible to influence the larger societies' ideas, values, and trends.[7] These individuals represent a distinct group that holds a set of beliefs that differ from those of the general public, beliefs that often reflect the influence of non-Western traditions.[8] They are unified by their search for the direct, transformative experience of the sacred that defines the mystic.

Accordingly, there is a resurgence of interest in the ancient, time-tested practices of the shaman, perhaps because of the ease with which these methods can be learned and utilized, and because shamanism is intensely democratic. Everyone, no matter what their ethnic and cultural background is or their socioeconomic station in life may be—can learn the methods pioneered by the traditional shamans for accessing the inner realms to acquire power, knowledge, support, protection, and guidance.[9] In the process, a new religion is coming into being.

And just what is this new religion? Simply knowing and accepting that it is possible to have transcendent experiences is where it begins. If you believe that the accounts documented in my books are impossible, then that is the first obstacle that has to be removed before you, too, can have them. Of course, there is also the possibilty that your own "inner hard drive" will spontaneously present you with "the program" in response to some physical stimulus. This is the way in which it began for me. Until that initial ego-shaking experience with the guardian of the threshold recorded in *Spirit-walker*, I was very much "Hank the nonbeliever."

Once the expanded state of visionary consciousness became available to me and I learned how to access it through my intentionality, it enabled my subsequent investigations of the spirit worlds as well as my relationship with Nainoa—a man who may be my descendant and possible future self. This unusual, nonlocal connection across time and distance offers oblique confirmation for the reality of reincarnation and strongly suggests that we are truly immortals.[10]

If what I have perceived is valid, and I have come to accept that it is, we are all traveling through time, continually growing and developing as we progress toward the end of our evolution. At that point, we will re-merge with the mysterious Source, entering into an entirely new level of relationship with the composite, evolving mind-spirit of the Universe. Then we will truly be gods.

Whether or not we achieve our destiny, both personal and collective, depends on the choices we make on our long journey toward the future. One of my goals in writing these books has been to inspire others to give themselves permission to find that inner doorway and embark on their own hero's journey. Only as players of the Master Game can we become truly superior beings, and only then can the ascent to true power begin.

For the past century, material education in the Western world has focused upon providing men and women with a working knowledge of history and mathematics, business and the sciences, engineering and the arts; and most recently, fields such as computer technology, molecular biology, and advanced theoretical physics. This goal has succeeded, as far as it goes. The problem is that modern education has not provided us with any knowledge of our own inner selves. The nature of the soul cluster and the inner levels of reality find no place in our educational system, not even in traditional Western psychology.

The result is evident. Our material culture, corporate successes, high technology, and scientific miracles have not provided us with happiness; they have not resulted in honesty; they have failed to inspire integrity. The wisdom of the mystics is clearly necessary to complete our education, providing us with a deep, inner security by investing us with a sense of moral courage and revealing the path toward spiritual illumination.

We live in a time when the old mystery schools of the past are being re-created in response to need. Contemporary explorers can now attend workshops and seminars at places such as the Omega Institute near New York, or the Esalen Institute in California,[11] or they can enroll in training programs offered by the Foundation for Shamanic Studies or the Nine Gates Mystery School (through the IONS), to name only a few.

These institutions, and others like them, are founded in the realization that the average person now possesses the power to analyze and estimate their own character, and it is no longer necessary for an organized priesthood to provide us with an understanding of the forces of right and wrong. Each of us now has the potential to become a player of the Master Game through which we rediscover that the source of all truth, power, and knowledge lies within us.

Paul Ray's survey reveals that a new sense of the sacred has appeared in the world, one that incorporates spiritual realization, personal growth psychology, and being of service all in one orientation. This general spiritual reawakening, proceeding from the personal to the global, has the potential to assist the human species in its transition into a more expanded, more aware life form. A real change in attitudes, and consequently in the directions of world history, is being achieved as individuals move into and rediscover their own spirituality.

The modern mystical movement has the potential to radically shift the beliefs, values, and attitudes of Western society. The so-called New Age is not a fad, but rather heralds the emergence of a true Transmodern Culture. In this knowledge, I find hope for the future.

Let me conclude this chapter of my life by saying that I have returned from my inner fieldwork with a very clear understanding of what people in monotheistic cultures call God.

At a personal level, there exists the *aumakua*/oversoul, which is one's own individual God-self. This transcendent self is alive as well as immortal. It is the source of our intuition and those hunches and ideas that appear within our minds at odd moments, revealing that it functions for us as the spirit teacher. In this capacity, my own oversoul seems to be the source of my dreams and visions from which I have learned so much.

I suspect that the oversoul can also manifest effects into our daily life, bringing us into connection with someone we need to meet or even ensuring that we are present at some event or location where something is about to happen—something we need to know about. This insight implies that guidance from the spiritual dimensions is not only real, but an intimate part of our personal evolution—that it is part of the given.

This personal oversoul or higher self is, in my opinion, the God-in-Heaven (the Upper World) who watches over us and listens to our prayers. It is the spirit who works in mysterious ways, provides us with power, protection, and support, and who sometimes engages us in uncommon dialogue.

I have also come to understand that all of the six billion human oversouls or higher selves are, in turn, aspects or holons of a singular greater God-aspect that is sometimes thought of as The Human Spirit. This greater human God-aspect is also alive and immortal, and it seems to include within itself a collective memory field that contains the composite history and knowledge of our entire species. This revelation suggests that each individual human mind is like a computer terminal connected to a giant database—a phase resonance that transcends space and time and carries the collective consciousness, wisdom, and energy of the entire human species pooled into one holographic field.

Our oversoul, or personal God-self, serves as the extension cord between ourselves and this greater human God-source, an insight that implies that separation is truly an illusion—as mystics across time have always affirmed. It reveals that each of us has always been, and will always be, in relationship with the greater Human Spirit. It also conveys the certainty that each of us possesses the potential to access the unlimited information and energy carried by the database, and in my experience, this access can occur in split seconds, and at any time or place.

As a scientist studying the evolution of body and mind on the physical plane of existence, I have stumbled into the realization that there also exists an evolution of spirit, of God if you will, at both the personal and collective levels. By becoming who and what we are on the physical plane in each manifested lifetime, our personal God-self changes and evolves. And since the personal oversoul is in relationship with the greater God-source, as we grow, increase, and become more, so does the database.

I suspect, as have countless others before me, that this is going on everywhere in the Universe, and that this is the great goal of the evolutionary process—the transformation of raw matter, power, and awareness into the great mind-spirit of the universal matrix of the Source. Within that golden, luminous cloud, the evolving human mind-spirit complex is already woven into the fabric, a knot in the pattern, a spot of light in the transcendent nerve-net of the great grid.

As humans, our evolutionary lineage is now known to stretch back at least five million years into the past. But as we turn our attention toward the future, it is obvious that we are destined to become something else, and that this, too, is part of the universal pattern. When the physical level of reality is transcended and humanity makes its final transformation to exist purely as *aumakua*, as spirit, as microcosm within the macrocosm, the human species will become the light, rejoining the luminous Father-Mother of which we have always been, and will always be, a part.

The universal mind that infuses the vast golden radiance of the Source, the most inclusive holographic field that could be called God, is being co-created through the evolutionary process, through the actions taking place on the objective level of physical reality and through the subjective level of thoughts, feelings, and dreams. And we humans, as actors and as dreamers, are the creators of our part of the pattern. That, as Nainoa would say, is our *kuleana*, our responsibility, our great task.

And beyond . . . ? Does an ultimate God-like Creator-Being exist somewhere out there beyond the edges of the known? This issue will always be the great question, the *mysterium tremendum*. Only as players of the Master Game can we, as individuals, have direct experience of the Source, and only then will we know the answer.

As players of the Great Game, we also rediscover something well known to all our indigenous ancestors, a universal principle of life that served them well:

> *There is no room*
> *for set decrees*
> *or specific laws*
> *in a sea of grace*
> *which knows no boundaries*
> *and has no shores.*[12]

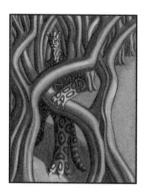

Postscript

I HAVE COME TO SUSPECT that there are countless numbers of "evolutionary sleepers" out there in the mainstream of humanity at large, each a holon containing within itself an extraordinary biological-energetic program that can reveal who and what we may all become as the human species continues its ascent toward the culmination of our evolution.

There appear to be higher functions coded into the personal mind-body matrix that can remain dormant throughout life—but once awakened, they can transform us. The inner fieldwork of the Eastern mystics suggests that these timing mechanisms involve the ductless glands, the brain, and the heart—and once activated, these centers can enlighten the whole body, which, in turn, often undergoes striking changes.[1]

At the time of this writing, the human species as a whole has not experienced the triggering of these higher functions. But those rare individuals who have, stand before us as markers, as signposts, as prototypes of what humankind may become when the whole population awakens and makes the jump. At that point in time, we will cross an evolutionary threshhold and become a new species.

This is not fantasy, but is, in fact, a real phenomenon known to students of evolutionary theory as punctuated equilibrium. Unlike most of my scientific colleagues, however, I suspect that this evolutionary goal may have been predetermined before the dawn of humankind—that it is part of a universal imperative or evolutionary probability that is drawing us forward like a magnet toward that which we are destined to become.

This statement does not throw me into the political sphere of the religious creationists and their limiting concept of a fatherly creator-God. Rather, it implies that evolution is a co-creative process, in which everything everywhere is in relationship, united by a biophysical-energetic prospectus—a common program in which everything is both driven by evolutionary impulses from the past and drawn toward evolutionary probabilities that exist in the future. The related fields of geology and paleontology, and now molecular biology, reveal that this push-pull dynamic has been going on for truly immense amounts of time.

This is a heretical statement for a scientist to make, yet a full comprehension of its implications reveals the place where science and spirituality can truly come together. The key lies in understanding the true nature of reality and the true nature of the self, topics examined from the Polynesian perspective by Nainoa and Kahu Sala earlier in this book.

When we as individuals, as holons, become aware of the biophysical-energetic program that exists within us, each of us can use it as a map to navigate our way through the forests of illusion and across the plains of experience toward the next stage of our uniquely human evolution. When we awaken from the consensual slumber of culture-at-large and remember that we were once seeds of light, traveling among the stars, accompanied and protected by spiritual guardians, we become aware that we have truly fallen from grace into a world of shadows through our preoccupations with the gods of materialism—money, power, sex, and status.

Postscript

With the closure of the old millennium and the beginning of the next, recent surveys have unequivocally revealed that as many as one in every two of us has had an involuntary paranormal experience at some point in our lives—one that has carried us across some unknown inner threshold into the more expanded realms of consciousness. These sudden, unexpected glimpses through the portal often change the whole direction of our lives, and as a result, we come to an inescapable conclusion—that the everyday world that we all take so much for granted is not at all what it appears to be on the surface.

As we awaken, our life experiences can begin to manifest themselves as an evolutionary hero's journey, as an upward quest that leads us inexorably from the world of the senses into the direct experience of spirit—a journey that becomes possible for us only through the doorway of the heart. It is through our heart that we finally return to the garden, and once there, we discover that we can use it as a gateway through which we can personally experience the spiritual worlds of the mystic.

This quest, this hero's journey, can only be discovered by each one of us operating alone. As we explore the world of sensory experience and investigate the limitless dimensions of our own mind, we come face-to-face with our strongest abilities and our highest qualities. We also discover our ignorance, our self-indulgence, and our egocentrism. When we recognize these personal demons to be the source of our suffering, despair, and violence, we can look at ourselves with honesty and with truth, for we know quite clearly then that we have choices. And it is at this critical crossroad that we begin to sense the immense energy and universal intelligence working through each one of us.

When we personally experience connection with this unlimited power and God-like mind within ourselves, we know with certainty that no holy words or books, no secret ceremonies or rituals, no spiritual leaders or gurus or faiths can do this for us. In order to experience true initiation, we have to know who we are, and only when we are willing to accept this unrelenting awareness of our own true nature can we find our clarity and our light once again.

And once we do, the rest will take care of itself.

I, like many others, have come to believe that the evolutionary sleepers awakening among us are the bridge to the next stage of human evolution. Like countless others out there on the trail, my visionary experiences have drawn me into a completely new lifeway, one that has led me to suspect that the experience of *en-light-enment* is actually our natural state.

And as we move into it, reexperiencing it once again, our body and brain changes at the cellular and molecular level as it adjusts to the power, to the energy that then becomes available to us. Once the higher evolutionary functions are triggered, it seems that a predetermined schedule is set into motion, a program that cannot be given to the spiritual seeker by any religious belief system or esoteric practices, or even by any accomplished spiritual teacher. This is because each of us already has it.

The Buddhist teacher Joan Halifax recounts a conversation in which she once asked a Zen master the following question: "Going to the temple, you take the path; entering the temple, you leave the path. What does this mean?" Without a pause, the Roshi's response came: "Joan, the path is the temple."[2]

The paths that each of us take as we negotiate through life toward the temple are the vehicles through which we awaken. This is why we must each find our own way. If we choose to walk the path already pioneered by someone else, we usually get lost. As old Pali told Nainoa by the pool in the forest, we are already that which we seek. This reveals that the one contribution that the true spiritual teacher or discipline has to offer is to help us step onto our path. And once that is accomplished, their job is essentially done. A person who is in thirst needs water, not the faucet. And the water is everywhere, in everything, as Tehura so wisely revealed.

Knowing this, it is up to each of us to live our lives in ways that contribute to the greater good—to the greater good of ourselves, the greater good of our families and friends, the greater good of our colleagues and communities, and the greater good of the environment that nourishes and sustains us. By doing so, we will ultimately acquire the power to transform ourselves, our societies, and our relationship with our world.

This is our true work. This is the ancient teaching of compassionate action found at the center of all the world's great mystic and religious traditions. As players of the Master Game, we are the exploratory consciousness of our species. So as each of you proceeds on with your lives, growing, increasing, and becoming more, please take these thoughts with you.

A Hawaiian friend of mine who lives far away in the future would close with a prayer and a blessing. He would begin by addressing his spirits and his ancestors . . .

E Akua	High Gods and Goddesses
E na Aumakua	and esteemed ancestors,
Ia kahina'kua ia kahina'alo	you who stand behind us and before us
Mai ka la hiki a ka la kau	from the sun's rising to the sun's setting,
Mai ka ho'okui a ka halawai.	from the zenith to the horizon.
E ho'omaikai keia honua mea	Blessings on this sacred Earth,
E ho'omaikai keia wai ola	blessings on this water of life,
E ho'omaikai keia ea	blessings on our atmosphere,
E ho'omaikai keia ho'ola-(eia nei)	blessings on this medicinemaker—(you)
E ho'omaikai keia imi pono.	and blessings on your endeavors.
E Akua	High Gods and Goddesses,
E Aumakua	Revered ancestral spirits,
E Kupua	and spirits of Nature,
Mai ka Po wai ola	bring forth from Po the water of life,
E ho'omahuahua	create abundance without limit,
E ho'o'olakino maikai	give us good health,
E homai i ka ike papalua	grant us spiritual insight,
E homai i ka maopopo pono.	and grant us true understanding.
E ola mau ka honua.	May the Earth continue to live,
E ola loa au i ke Akua	may the spirits grant you long life,
Ho'ike a mai i ke ola.	and may these blessings be manifested.
Amama,	The prayer has lifted,
Ua noa.	It is free.

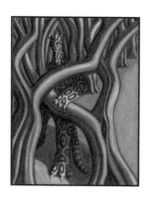

Endnote

ON JUNE 2, 2000, I was in New York to lead a workshop and decided to go the Metropolitan Museum of Art to see Paul Gauguin's painting of the "Two Tahitian Women." Knowing how much Tehura loves flowers, I wore a small rose boutonniere in the buttonhole of my jacket.

Upon my arrival at the gallery, I studied the picture carefully. Tehura's resemblance to the bare-breasted girl was striking, and for long moments, I stood there awestruck, wondering if she could see me. I noticed the label fastened to the wall to one side and leaned forward to read it. I learned that the painting was done in 1899 and that the woman holding the tray of lychees has been identified as Gauguin's mistress "Pahura"—a bit of art history that was unknown to me until that moment.

I turned and sat down on the bench across from the painting where I remained for an hour, my focus upon Tehura undistracted by the crowd that surged around me. Toward the end of this meditation, a chunk of information spontaneously appeared in my conscious awareness. It was almost as though the painting itself possessed a field of information, or perhaps emotion, that I was able to receive in those moments of heightened lucidity. Quite suddenly, I knew with absolute certainty that Gauguin had loved her. Broke, ill, and nearing the end of his life, the disillusioned idealist had loved her. There was no question, no doubt in my mind that this was so, and I determined to tell her this the next time I saw her.

When the time came for me to leave, I waited until the guard was in the next room, then took the rose from my lapel and placed it on the narrow ledge just below the painting where she could see it. I felt a surge of emotion in response to this small offering, but whether it was Tehura's or my own, I could not tell.

Notes

CHAPTER 1

1. On a semantic note, let me say that I continue to use William the Ennu's term for this formidable spirit simply because I know of no English equivalent word. See *Spiritwalker*, ch. 22.

2. See *Medicinemaker*, ch. 18.

3. Joseph Campbell, *The Hero of a Thousand Faces* (New York: World Publishing, 1968).

4. Roger N. Walsh, *The Spirit of Shamanism* (Los Angeles: Jeremy P. Tarcher, 1990).

5. Robert S. De Ropp, *The Master Game: Pathways to Higher Consciousness Beyond the Drug Experience* (New York: Delta Press, 1968).

6. Ibid., p. 18.

7. Walsh, p. 24.

8. De Ropp, p. 19.

9. Ibid., p. 21.

CHAPTER 2

1. In my previous books, I have discussed the nature of the language that is used by Nainoa's people, a *patois* much like the pidgin English spoken in many parts of the world. Nainoa's language is quite unlike any spoken

today, although it includes some near-Hawaiian and near-English words. Because of his interest in history and his training with his adoptive father, a scholar, Nainoa is familiar with what he calls Old English, a literary language in which the most ancient historical accounts of his society were written. This is most fortunate because it allows us to communicate directly in a somewhat modified conversational mode—but only when both of us are in the shamanic state of consciousness simultaneously.

2. I have followed the custom of translating occasional key words and concepts from Nainoa's language into their nearest available equivalents in Hawaiian, utilizing terms that are still in use in the islands today. Nainoa's people do this themselves, drawing on what they call Classic Hawaiian in a literary sense, much like Westerners draw on Latin and Greek, and Indian scholars on Sanskrit.

As a verb, *moe* means "to sleep" or "lie down," and as a noun, it is the word for "sleep" or "dream." The *uhane* is the aspect of the self analogous to what we might call the conscious mind, the intellect, the thinker, the analyzer, and the decision maker. In short, the *uhane* is the inner director, the "spirit that speaks to us" in some translations. *Ala* means "awake"; it also means "the path." So the term *Moe'uhane'ala* might be literally translated as "dream or soul sleep taking place with conscious awareness." The word used by Nainoa is somewhat different and sounds close to *Muyanala,* but I may have misremembered the term or written it incorrectly.

3. Curiously, although there are many terms for the different aspects of nature in Nainoa's language, there seems to be no general word for *nature.* I don't know if this is a correct assumption, but it also seems to be true in contemporary Hawaiian, hence the term tacked on the end of the phrase "*o waho,*" literally meaning "outdoors."

The whole phrase might be thus translated as:

Au lilo—I have become   *mea*—a person   *punihei*—ensnared or captured
i na—belonging to   *aiwaiwa*—the mysterious   *o waho*—outdoors.

4. As I have mentioned in my previous books, when I journey to Nainoa, I both perceive and understand through his body-mind complex. I have total access to his thoughts, memories, desires, and knowledge while we are in connection, so I record these events of his life and time from his perspective. Therefore, when I relate Nainoa's thoughts about *me*—for he is sometimes as fully aware of me as I am of him—I do so in the third person. He knows me as "the American," and thinks of me using that term.

5. On a semantic note, let me say that I am aware that many use the term *sorcery* to describe a form of traditional spiritual practice devoted to the gathering and use of mystical power in the stage of life sometimes called "the way of the warrior." In a like manner, many use the term *witchcraft* to describe the positively focused spiritual practice devoted to healing associated often with the "wise women" of Europe. In a similar vein, the term *witch* is often used to describe such medicine-people and healers.

In anthropology, the term *shaman* has been specifically chosen to describe certain individuals within traditional societies who function on behalf of members of their group as spiritual healers and gatherers of power in the postive mode. The terms *sorcery* and *witchcraft* are used to describe the practice of magic with the intent to inflict harm or misfortune on others. *Magic* refers to the ability to access the realm of the sacred in order to control, influence, or persuade supernatural power to assist in achieving some given end in ordinary reality. *Sorcery* is distinguished from *witchcraft* in the sorcerer's use of material substances—the classic voodoo doll or juju object, or the bone pointing of the Melanesian peoples. *Witchcraft* normally does not utilize "material aids," but operates solely within the psychic levels of reality, accomplishing the same ends through intention combined with ritual and energy (*mana*), gathered and released with the intent to inflict harm. In this sense, Nainoa's inadvertent use of power, which resulted in the death of his adversary, would technically be called *negative witchcraft*.

Semantic bickering over which terms should be regarded as positive or negative, with honor or dishonor, etc., frequently results in confusion and negative effects. In my opinion, the terms *shaman* and *shamanism* lack such negative associations. The adoption of these terms with reference to the spiritual healer, spiritual healing work, and other positively focused, life-enhancing, community-oriented activities would seem to be a way of resolving such academic disputes.

6. Much of this data is included in chapter 22 of *Spiritwalker*. The fact that this information was repeated suggests that this spirit being possesses a kind of recorded message that it repeats, with variations, from the beginning, much like replaying a tape from the start, or the way humpback whales restart their long, complex songs from the beginning each time they communicate them. This message from the *dorajuodiok* was considerably longer than the first, however, providing entirely new data not received previously.

7. An important review of some of the traditional *kahuna* teachings shared by David Kaonohiokala Bray can be found in Laura Kealoha Yardley, *The Heart of Huna* (Honolulu: Advanced Neuro Dynamics, 1990).

CHAPTER 3

1. Computer graphics have clearly demonstrated the designs of these attractor fields. See G. Mandelbrodt, *The Fractal Geometry of Nature* (New York: W.H. Freeman & Co, 1977); and also David R. Hawkins, *Power vs Force: An Anatomy of Consciousness* (Sedona, Arizona: Veritas Publ., 1995) for an interesting overview of how attractor research in the field of nonlinear dynamics has been used for developing a map of human consciousness.

2. Much of this information is derived from a conversation with Dr. Edgar Mitchell, theoretical physicist and Apollo 14 astronaut, who is also the founder of the Institute of Noetic Sciences. He is a pioneer in efforts to expand science toward understanding consciousness and inner experience.

The recent discovery that all matter emits quanta of energy that are coherent, nonlocal, and carry usable information about the material object, demonstrates that quantum physics pertains to all matter, not just particles. Furthermore, these emissions can be modeled by the same mathematical formalism used for laser photography, thus the term *quantum holography*. Nonlocal information about the physical universe, which is the core of what Nainoa and I received from the *dorajuadiok*, provides the missing link between objective science and subjective experience, including the mystical experience. Experimental validation for these claims now exists from magnetic resonance imagery (MRI), and it is thought that quantum processes underlie all classical processes (the ghost in the machine).

This means that when we are talking about intuition as well as psychic/parapsychological processes, there is a quantum hologram underlying the process. Nonlocality is to the physicist what interconnectedness is to the mystic, and the quantum hologram is the foundation through which to understand virtually all psychic phenomena.

3. I highly recommmned Jeremy Narby's *The Cosmic Serpent: DNA and the Orgins of Knowledge* (New York: Jeremy Tarcher/Putnam, 1998). The beginning of Narby's exploration lies with the Peruvian Indians, who claim that their scientifically confirmed knowledge of chemical reactions has its origins in the preparation of certain drinks that contain plant DNA, through which they gain information that human beings could not

acquire by traditional methods of trial and error alone. Looking at what we already know through the eyes of the molecular biologist, Narby suggests the seemingly impossible: that specific knowledge might be transferred through the DNA. Since every living thing on this planet's surface shares the same molecular-genetic source, written in the same molecular alphabet, his conclusion is that every thing is minded and interconnected at the consciousness level.

4. The Omega Institute for Holistic Studies, 260 Lake Drive, Rhinebeck, NY 12575 • (800) 944-1001.

5. For an interesting look at this fast-growing religion, see Diana Degroat Brown's *Umbanda: Religion and Politics in Urban Brazil* (New York: Columbia University Press, 1994).

6. See Edith Fiore's *The Unquiet Dead* (New York: Ballantine Books, 1987) for a classic work by a traditionally trained psychologist that has led to serious consideration of depossession work in the West. See also William Baldwin's *Spirit Releasement Therapy* (Falls Church, Virginia: Human Potential Foundation, 1992); Irene Hickman's *Remote Depossession* (Kirksville, MO: Hickman Systems, 1994); and Eugene Maury's *Exorcism* (West Chester, PA: Whitford Press, 1988). In addition, an excellent manual on healing and depossession work is available from George K.W. Yim called *Chakras and Mind/Body Healing*—contact him directly at 724 Essex Street, West Lafayette, IN 47906.

7. At that time, I knew next to nothing about depossession work. I have since done some reading and some training in this area and would probably not do this in the same way now. See above references for information and resources.

8. See *Medicinemaker*, ch. 16.

9. See Paul H. Ray, "The Rise of Integral Culture," in the *Noetic Sciences Review*, Spring 1996, pp. 4–15; also, "The Rise of the Cultural Creatives," in *New Age Journal* (January/February issue, 1997, pp. 74–77).

10. A large number of investigators have written interesting review papers about this movement. See, for example, Jeffrey L. MacDonald, "Inventing Traditions for the New Age: A Case Study for the Earth Energy Tradition," in *Anthropology of Consciousness* 6 (4): pp. 31–45, (1995); and Joan B. Townsend, "Neoshamanism and the Modern Mystical Movement," in *Shaman's Path: Healing, Personal Growth and Empowerment,* edited by Gary Doore (Boston and London: Shambhala Press, 1988, pp. 73–85).

CHAPTER 5

1. See Narby, ch. 9, and Fritz-Albert Popp, "On the coherence of ultraweak photon emissions from living tissues," in *Disequilibrium and Self-Organization*, edited by C. W. Kilmister (Dordecht: Reidel Publ., 1986).

2. Narby, pp. 126–131.

3. See, for example, Joan Halifax, *Shamanic Voices: A Survey of Visionary Narratives* (New York: E.P. Dutton, 1979).

4. See *Medicinemaker*, ch. 7.

5. For information about the Institute of Noetic Sciences: their membership services, opportunities, conferences, travel program, etc., as well as the Nine Gates Mystery School, please contact them at: 101 San Antonio Rd., Petaluma, CA 94952 • (707) 775-3500 • www.noetic.org.

6. I believe that this is an important point. From my ongoing discussions with others engaged in spiritual work, I have learned that most seem to be aware of the existence of this hidden agenda—of the actuality of an ongoing program over which we as individuals have little or no control but within which we are sometimes drawn to be active participants. For the mystic, the existence of this agenda is confirmed by direct experience, and suggests, as well, that the spiritual dimensions have an existence and a value quite separate from the one who perceives them. This assertion may disturb the philosophical materialist, but it is very much a part of traditional shamanic cosmology.

CHAPTER 6

1. See *Spiritwalker*, ch. 24.

CHAPTER 7

1. For information about the Foundation for Shamanic Studies, please refer to the last section of this book: Shamanic Training Workshops.

2. *Welina*: (the phoneme <w> is pronounced as a <v>) is an ancient Polynesian greeting of affection similar to *aloha*.

CHAPTER 9

1. This glimpse was quite different from the one reported in the last chapter of *Medicinemaker* and may represent a clearer image of how the transcendent self actually appears once it has taken up permanent residence on the "lotus throne" within our hearts. It is also possible, of course, that this image was generated by my creative imagination in response to old Pali's use of the term *illumination*. However, as has been observed, the aspect of the self that perceives (and visions) is the *ku*, and this aspect is not creative. This leads me to conclude that what I perceived was a bona fide glimpse of my own higher self aspect—a glimpse of my own seed of light, unfolding and growing and becoming more.

2. See *Medicinemaker*, chs. 17–20.

3. I have written about the nature of the evolutionary relationship between the leopard and the human lineage in *Medicinemaker*, ch. 11.

CHAPTER 11

1. Yardley, pp. 77–79.

2. Ibid., pp. 82–83.

3. Ibid., pp. 90-91.

4. See *Medicinemaker*, ch. 5. See also Walsh, pp. 59–69, for an overview of shamanic dismemberment from a Western perspective.

5. See *Spiritwalker*, ch. 4.

CHAPTER 13

1. For those interested, see R. Fischer, "A Cartography of the Ecstatic and Meditative States," in *Science,* vol. 174: pp. 897–904 (1974); and E. Gellhorn and W. F. Kiely, "Mystical States of Consciousness: Neurophysiological and Clinical Aspects," in the *Journal of Nervous and Mental Disease*, vol. 154, no. 6: pp. 399–405 (1972).

Fischer has mapped a perception-meditation-hallucination continuum, encompassing the hypoaroused states of Zazen and Transcendental Meditation at one end of the scale; and the hyperaroused creative, psychotic, ecstatic, and mystical rapture experiences at the other.

Gellhorn and Kiely have reviewed the hypo- and hyperarousal systems of autonomic-somatic integration and their relevance for the study of a variety of levels of consciousness, and have addressed the neurophysio-logical basis of both meditation states and the yoga ecstasy. Interestingly, their study reveals that the patterns recorded in EEGs during meditation, and experiences of ecstasy, are compatible with full conscious awareness. In addition, a remarkable parallelism exists between the state of yoga ecstasy and that which occurs during REM sleep and dreaming, revealing that a state of cortical arousal is common to both, as is the associated inhibition of skeletal muscle tone. A quote from their paper further states: "A loss of distinctiveness in the sense of time and space, and vivid perceptual imagery with condensation of imagined persons and events, are physio-logical correlates of both dreams and the state of ecstasy."

2. See N. N Das and H. Gastaut, "Variations de l'activite electrique du cerveau, du coeur et des muscles squelettes au coeurs de la meditation et de l'extase yogique," in *Electroencephalography and Clinical Neuro-physiology*, supplement no. 6, pp. 211–219 (1957).

3. See M. Eliade, *Yoga: Immortality and Freedom*. (New Jersey: Prince-ton University Press, 1958).

4. See N. S. Don, "Topographic Brain Maps of the Abductee, Sueli," in *Alien Discussions: Proceedings of the Abduction Study Conference*, A. Pritchard, J. E. Mack, P. Kasey, and C. Yapp, editors (Cambridge, MA: North Cam-bridge Press, 1994); and N. S. Don and G. Moura, "Topographic Brain Map-ping of UFO Experiencers," in *The Journal for Scientific Exploration* vol. 11, no. 4: pp. 435–453 (1998).

5. While living in Hawai'i, I did some training with an accomplished hyp-notherapist named Marga Zack and discovered that I am an excellent hyp-notic subject. Moura was able to utilize long-distance hypnosis over the telephone from Brazil to extract this memory.

6. Yardley, p. 78.

7. See *Spiritwalker*, ch. 5.

8. See Richard Katz, *Boiling Energy: Community Healing among the Kala-hari !Kung* (Cambridge and London: Harvard University Press, 1982).

9. See *Spiritwalker*, ch. 1.

10. This is an enormous topic, beyond the scope of this book. It is known that although the size of the brain is genetically determined, the process of learning actually alters the morphology of the cerebral cortex, reveal-ing that the physical structure of the brain changes in response to what

is learned. Current research has shown that the brain can essentially be rearranged in 15 minutes. See, for example, Daniel Weinberger, Douglas W. Jones, and Alicia Bartley's paper, "Genetic Variability of Human Brain Size and Cortical Gyral Patterns," in *Brain*, vol. 120: pp. 257–269 (1997). For an interesting review of this subject, see P. M. H. Atwater's *Brain Shift/Spirit Shift: A Theoretical Model Using Research on Near-Death States to Explore the Transformation of Consciousness* (1998). This self-published paper is available from Atwater at: P.O. Box 7691, Charlottesville, VA 22906-7691

11. See Charles Tart's *States of Consciousness* (El Cerrito, California: Psychological Processes, 1983); and Walsh, p. 164.

12. The reader is again referred to Narby's *The Cosmic Serpent*, referenced above.

13. For those interested, Norman Don and I wrote a paper together detailing our work and reporting on the results of the EEG recordings of my brain waves during the ecstatic trance state. I delivered the paper, titled "Hyperaroused States as a Gateway to Transcendent Experience,"at the annual conference of the Society for the Anthropology of Consciousness, a section of the American Anthropological Association, held at the University of California at Berkeley on March 30, 1997. My presentation (Don was in Brazil and couldn't attend) included a brief overview of the nature of my hyperaroused trance states and what I perceive within them. I also presented overhead transparencies clearly demonstrating the EEG data and showing my recorded brain waves, both in the baseline resting state and during the hyperaroused trance. The reaction of my esteemed colleagues was predictable. Few asked questions, for a theoretical model or paradigm for such extraordinary human abilities such as those reported in my books simply doesn't exist yet. But all the Xerox copies of my written paper were picked up. This paper will eventually find its way into published form.

14. See note 1 above.

CHAPTER 15

1. The Hawaiian spiritual warrior society, Na Ao Koa o Pu'u Kohola Heiau, is like a woven body of people "braided with the cords of *aloha*," to use the *kahuna* elder's words. Unlike the old Western initiation myth in which the quest usually includes the overcoming of some enemy such as Nature, the initiation of the Na Ao Koa involves understanding the rela-

tionship between the self and the Universe with a special attunement to the Earth. In seeking this harmonious resonance, the Na Ao Koa become record keepers and the custodians of spiritual power. On November 6, 1997, these spiritual warriors performed a sacred *Awa* ceremony on the 21st floor of the Fairmont Hotel in San Francisco at the State of the World Forum.

CHAPTER 17

1. When I recounted this visionary episode to Michael Harner several months later, he told me that when the Spaniards invaded the Andes in the 1500s and sacked the Inca cities, they found an entire garden that was made of gold that belonged to the Inca king. Like the garden in my vision, it had even included golden birds in the golden trees. In the name of their Christian God, the invaders destroyed the golden garden, melting it down into ingots for transport back to Spain.

Such monumental avarice combined with such barbaric insensitivity and extraordinary lack of vision continues in our own time as our multinational corporations pillage and plunder both the biosphere and the geosphere of our planet, drastically diminishing the resource base upon which the continued survival and well-being of the human species now depends. The rights of these corporate giants to pursue this strategy of short-term gain at the expense of long-term sustainability are currently both socially condoned as well as protected by laws that were created for them by their political supporters.

Until they, and we, understand that with their legislated rights come moral responsibilities and begin to act accordingly, it could be argued that the term *civilization* is an ideal state that has yet to be achieved. Indeed, when one casts an informed eye over the history of Western civilization, including our current political, economic, and environmental problems, as well as our often overwhelming issues of humanitarian concern, it could be argued that our species, despite the admittedly miraculous achievements of our high technology, is still very much ensconced in the barbarian stage of human evolution.

2. Lew Welch, *Ring of Bone: Collected Poems 1950–1971*, edited by Donald Allen (Bolinas, California: Grey Fox Press, 1973).

3. Readers of my second book, *Medicinemaker*, will recall Nainoa's experience during the ritual in which he facilitated the healing of his mentor Chief Kaneohe in just this way (ch. 8).

4. I must include here that what I perceive and how is state-dependent and determined by how deep the shamanic trance is. In doing healing work, I must still be able to function, so I rarely go into the full-fledged cataleptic trance accompanied by paralysis that typifies my trans-temporal connections with Nainoa. For an interesting overview on how the energy body is perceived cross-culturally, see David V. Tansley's *Subtle Body: Essence and Shadow* (New York: Thames and Hudson, 1977).

5. The article titled "Healing with Jesus—the Shaman's Breath," was written by Connie Bickman and published in a periodical called *Turtle River Press*, the October-November 1997 issue, pp. 14–15. Inquiries can be directed to *Turtle River Press*, 218 Mill Street West, Cannon Falls, Minnesota 55009 • fax: (507) 263-0166.

6. See *Spiritwalker*, p. 160; and *Medicinemaker*, p. 165.

7. As I have written elsewhere, I experience strong misgivings every time I hear a spiritual teacher say something like, "You've got to get rid of your ego," or "The ego is an expert at destroying love." The presence and correct functioning of the conscious mind/ego aspect, or what Nainoa would call the *uhane*, is absolutely essential in achieving a harmonious balance between the three levels of the self, as well as gaining access to the shamanic state of consciousness.

8. Soul loss is considered to be most dangerous among indigenous peoples and is regarded as the primary cause of premature death and serious illness. Curiously, it's not even mentioned in our Western medical textbooks. For those interested, please see Sandra Ingerman's books: *Soul Retrieval: Mending the Fragmented Self* (San Francisco: HarperCollins Publishers, 1991); and *Welcome Home: Following Your Soul's Journey Home* (San Francisco: HarperCollins, 1994); as well as her novel *A Fall to Grace* (Santa Fe, New Mexico: Moon Tree Rising Productions, 1997).

In traditional societies, shamans who are accomplished in retrieving lost souls and soul parts and returning them to their owners are often called "soul catchers," and are usually considered to be in a class of their own as healers. Let me also reveal that my wife, Jill Kuykendall, RPT, has become an accomplished shamanic healer who specializes in soul retrieval work in her private practice. Those wishing to connect with Jill for soul retrieval work can do so through the contact numbers for SharedWisdom on page 323 of this book.

CHAPTER 18

1. See the *Noetic Sciences Review*: Summer 1996, pp. 42–43. The book review begins: "If *Spiritwalker* had been written by anyone with less powerful credentials than Wesselman's, it might leave the reader wondering about just where to draw the line between 'reality' and a well-written adventure story. But Wesselman is a respected professional anthropologist who works with an international group of scientists exploring the mystery of human origins in East Africa's ancient Rift Valley. Trained in observation and fieldwork, he has spent years living a day-to-day existence within cultures completely different from his own. Perhaps this, more than anything, equips him to observe and report with clarity and detail his unexpected excursions into the realm that shamans have called the 'spirit world.'"

The review ends with the observation: "It took considerable courage for Wesselman to risk revealing his experiences. His carefully crafted story is . . . a unique opportunity to explore an altered dimension of consciousness as seen and experienced through the eyes of a trained anthropological explorer."

2. For example: In the 24-hour period since this time yesterday, more than 200,000 acres of rainforest will have been cut down, 13 million tons of toxic chemicals will have been released into our environment, 45,000 people will have died of starvation—38,000 of them children—and more than 130 plant or animal species will have been driven to extinction by the actions of humanity, a loss that may exceed in both rate and volume the mass extinctions at the end of the Mesozoic Era, 65 million years ago, best known for the disappearance of the dinosaurs. See Thom Hartmann's *The Last Hours of Ancient Sunlight: Waking Up to Personal and Global Transformation* (Northfield, Vermont: Mythical Books, 1998), for an informative and ultimately hopeful overview of these most important subjects.

3. As of this writing, global temperature averages for 1998 reached all-time highs, achieving a whopping 0.25 degree Celsius increase above the same value for any previous year, strongly suggesting that the activities of industrialized humanity are contributing to a potential ecological catastrophe of truly immense proportions. *Source:* Report issued by the office of Vice President Al Gore and by the National Oceanic and Atmospheric Administration (NOAA) in June 1998. Reviewed in *Science News*, vol.153, p. 399 (June 20, 1998).

The year 1999 has followed suit. An analysis led by Tom Karl, the NOAA climatologist, and published in the March 1, 2000, issue of *Geophysical Research Letters,* reveals that on average, global warming throughout the

1900s occurred at a predicted rate of just over one degree per century. Since 1976, however, warming has quadrupled to a rate of nearly four degrees per century, a trend that is unprecedented, Karl confesses. Such a steep warming rate was not expected to occur until well into the 21st century.

A historical analysis of this climatic trend reaching back to the time of William the Conquerer was published by Michael Mann and his colleagues at the University of Massachusetts at Amherst in the March 15, 1999, issue of *Geophysical Research Letters*. This study confirms that planetary temperatures are steadily rising and are now considerably higher than those of any period during the past 1,000 years.

Not surprisingly, scientists studying the Arctic pack ice are seeing changes that are nothing less than dramatic, and the possibility that the perennial sea ice is in the process of disappearing has become a reality. In the December 1999 issue of *Geophysical Research Letters*, Andrew Rothrock and his collaborators presented data collected by sonar aboard nuclear submarines, revealing that the ice cover of the Arctic Ocean is now 40 percent thinner than it was 20 years ago. If thinning continues at this rate, the ice thickness will reach zero in only a few decades, converting the Arctic Ocean from a brilliantly white reflector, sending 80 percent of solar energy back into space, into a heat collector, absorbing 80 percent of incipient sunlight, with effects extending to mid-latitudes and possibly beyond.

Another study published in the December 3, 1999, issue of *Science* by a team led by Dr. Ola Johanssen of the Nansen Environmental and Remote Sensing Center in Bergen, Norway, presents satellite data that reveals the lateral extent of the Arctic ice sheet has diminished by 14 percent in the same two decades.

In 1998, scientists reported that the southern half of the Greenland ice cap was melting back by about two cubic miles per year, enough ice to cover the state of Maryland with a sheet one foot thick. See William K. Stevens' article: "Arctic Thawing May Jolt Sea's Climate Belt" in the December 7, 1999, issue of the *New York Times* for an overview.

Similar research at the other end of the planet has revealed that the West Antarctic Ice Sheet seems to be in the process of a dramatic meltdown. Radar photography has uncovered a network of ice streams under both the West and East Antarctic Ice Sheets that are considerably larger, faster, and more ominous than expected, revealing a disquieting mechanism for moving ice rapidly from the interior of the continent to the coastal ocean and raising sea levels.

In August 2000, passengers aboard the Russian icebreaker Yamal on a cruise to the North Pole, discovered a mile-wide lake of open seawater at 90 degrees north, with gulls flying overhead. In an article in the *New York Times*, Harvard oceanographer James McCarthy proclaimed this as "totally unexpected," and paleontologist Malcolm McKenna of the American Museum of Natural History said that "the last time anyone could be certain that the pole was awash in water was more than 50 million years ago." Taken together, the existing evidence confirms that an accelerating worldwide environmental shift is very much in progress and will define much of the politics of the 21st century.

4. See *Spiritwalker*, ch. 15; and *Medicinemaker*, ch. 13.

5. See Paul Hawken's *The Ecology of Commerce: A Declaration of Sustainability* (New York: HarperCollins, 1993). It contains the seeds of survival of both the business community and ourselves. It is required reading.

6. See ch. 3, note 9.

7. The fact that *Spiritwalker* has been translated into more than a dozen languages, with *Medicinemaker* following suit, suggests that this spiritual reawakening may be a far more widespread phenomenon, perhaps even worldwide.

8. See ch. 3, note 10. Many investigators are now beginning to ally themselves with the few remaining traditionals to explore the interface between scientific knowledge and traditional wisdom. In addition to Narby's *Cosmic Serpent*, I wholeheartedly suggest Thomas E. Mails' *The Hopi Survival Kit: The Prophesies, Instructions, and Warnings Revealed by the Last Elders* (New York: Arkana/Penguin Books, 1997).

9. In addition to those noted above, the reader might find the following useful: Michael Harner, *The Way of the Shaman: A Guide to Power and Healing* (San Francisco: HarperCollins, 1990); Shirley Nicholson, *Shamanism: An Expanded View of Reality* (Wheaton, Illinois: Quest Books, 1987); Tom Cowan, *Fire in the Head: Shamanism and the Celtic Spirit* (New York: HarperCollins, 1993); Piers Vitebsky, *The Shaman: Voyages of the Soul, Trance, Ecstacy, and Healing from Siberia to the Amazon* (London: Duncan Baird Publishers, 1995); Mircea Eliade, *Shamanism: Archaic Techniques of Ecstacy* (New Jersey: Princeton University Press, 1964, 1974); and Michael Winkelman, *Shamans, Priests and Witches: A Cross Cultural Study of Magico-Religous Practitioners* (Phoenix, Arizona: Arizona State University Press, Anthropological Research Papers No. 44, 1992).

10. For an important review of the "time-traveling" phenomenon, see: P. M. H. Atwater's *Future Memory: How Those Who See the Future Shed New Light on the Workings of the Human Mind* (New York: Birch Lane Press, 1996).

11. The Esalen Institute, Highway 1, Big Sur, California 93920-9616. For catalog requests: (831) 667-3000.

12. In the fall of 1998, I was invited to a book conference in Tennessee, and while there, I accompanied my hosts to a Sunday-morning gathering of Quakers in the suburbs of Nashville. As we sat in silent meditation, I happened to glance at the back cover of one of their newsletters I had picked up in the lobby, and it was there that I read these words.

POSTSCRIPT

1. Many others have also explored these interesting insights. See, for example, Yatri's *Unknown Man: The Mysterious Birth of a New Species* (New York: Fireside Books, 1988).

2. Joan Halifax, *The Fruitful Darkness: Reconnecting with the Body of the Earth* (San Francisco: HarperCollins, 1993, p. 51).

GLOSSARY

HAWAIIAN TERMS

ailona	Symbol, sign, portent, or omen.
aka	The primordial energetic "stuff"' out of which everything in the universe is made; in contemporary usage, shadow, image, or reflection.
akaku	Vision, trance, hallucination.
akua	God, goddess, supernatural deities, ghosts, or spirits; *atua* in Tahitian.
akua ko'o	A carved stick that can serve as a repository for a spirit; the shaman or *kahuna* mystic may invite the spirit to inhabit the stick so that he or she can converse with it.
akua kumulipo	The mysterious origin or source of life; the creation chant; the godhead.
ali'i	Chief, chiefess.
ali'i nui	High chief or chiefess.
aloha	Love, compassion, greeting, kindness; literal meaning: to be in the presence of the "divine breath" or "divinity."

Ao Aumakua	The place in the spirit world occupied by the human *aumakua* spirits.
atua	Tahitian equivalent of *akua*; deity or spirit.
Aumakua	Personal ancestral spiritual aspect; high self, god-self, angelic self; immortal, spiritual source self.
awa	Ceremonial Polynesian drink also known as *kava*.
ha	The breath; an aspect of the self received at birth and released upon the death of the physical body.
haku	Master or captain (of a voyaging canoe).
hala	The pandanus or screwpine, whose long, flat leaves form an important source of thatch, mats, and basketry.
hale	House.
hale mana	The "house of power" used as a repository for power objects and sacred relics; usually located on temple platforms.
hale pe'a	House of seclusion for menstruating women.
heahea	A hospitable greeting of welcome.
heiau	Sacred place of power and spiritual practice; usually surmounted by a temple platform including sacred buildings and symbolic images of deities and/or aspects of the self.
ho'okalakupua	To make magic.
Ho'omana	The spiritual knowledge and practices of the mystics and shamans of Hawai'i; literal meaning: to empower, to place in authority, to worship.
Huna	Literally: hidden, secret, to hide or conceal; colloquial term sometimes used by non-Hawaiians for *Ho'omana*.
IAO	The sacred source of all being; also the planet Jupiter.

Glossary

ike
Spiritual power; knowledge; awareness.

ike papalua
Psychic awareness; extrasensory perception; also used to describe the second level of reality, awareness, and experience.

I'o
The great all-generating void.

Io
The hawk.

Kahiki
Term for the Middle World of dream.

kahu
The honored attendant, keeper, or caretaker of a *heiau,* sacred object, or body of knowledge.

kahuna
Literal meaning: expert; in colloquial expression: a priest, shaman, or mystic.

kahuna kupua
Kahuna mystic, shaman, master of spirits.

kahuna la'au lapa'au
Medical *kahuna,* herbalist, master healer.

kahuna la'au kahea
Psychologist.

kahuna pale
Expert in counter sorcery, in warding off spells or evil magic.

kahuna pule
Priest or ceremonialist, master of prayer.

Kai
The spiritual Lower Worlds, also known as Milu.

Kane
In its outer aspect, one of the four major *akua* of old Hawai'i with over 70 recorded names, the creator god; in its inner aspect, the dual-natured god-self (Kanewahine) or high self of the indivdual; the *aumakua,* the personal ancestral spirit; also the ordinary term for *man* or *male.*

Kanaloa
In its outer aspect, the *akua* of the ocean, the progenitor and sustainer of life; the essence within everything; in its inner aspect, the fully awakened or enlightened state in which all aspects of the self are fully formed, fully aware, and fully experienced; *Tangaroa* in Tahitian.

kaona
Hidden meaning, metaphor.

Kapo'e'Aumakua
The collective gathering of all the human *aumakua* higher selves; the composite human spirit.

Kapohaku'ki'ihele Hawaiian name of the spirit stone; literally: the stone that travels.

kapu Forbidden, taboo, sacred, holy, under restriction.

kaula Prophet; one who can achieve expanded states of awareness in which the future can be seen.

Ke'aka Literally: the shadow; the formidable, dark spirit that functions as the guardian at the threshold into the spirit worlds.

kino The physical body.

kino'aka The energy body; includes what Westerners would call the etheric body and the astral body.

Koko'aka The great energetic grid or net formed of *aka* substance within which everything in the mani-fested universe(s) is interconnected across space and time; the great pattern.

Ku In its outer aspect, the *akua* of rain, fertility, sorcery, war, and business; in its inner aspect, the subconscious mind or body mind of the individual; also known as *unihipili*.

kukui Candlenut tree, light; inner light of illumi-nation.

kupaianaha Marvelous.

Lanikeha The spiritual Upper Worlds of the major gods, goddesses, heroes, and heroines and spiritual teachers; the place of the human *aumakua* spirits; Heaven or Paradise of the Judeo-Christ-ian-Islamic traditions; also known as *Uka*.

lei A wreath or necklace of flowers.

lele Altar for offerings to the spirits.

limu Seaweed, algae.

lokahi The establishment of balance and harmony within and between the different aspects of the self; unity or peace.

lomi To press, rub, or massage; a spiritually focused bodywork practice.

Glossary

Lono	In its outer aspect, one of the major *akua* of old Hawai'i; the *akua* of agriculture, medicine, navigation, and science; in its inner aspect, the conscious mind; the thinker, inner director and decision maker, the ego-intellectual aspect of the self also known as *uhane*.
lua	The number two; also hole or pit; also toilet or outhouse.
maka'ike	Psychic sight; the ability to see supernatural phenomena.
mala	Garden.
malo	The ubiquitous loincloth worn by most men.
mana	Supernatural or mystical power or force.
marae	Tahitian equivalent of *Heiau*.
mauli	Life force, heart, life.
milimili	Favorite, beloved.
Milu	The spiritual Lower Worlds to which the traditional shaman or *kahuna* mystic journeys to make contact with mystical power and the spirits of nature; also known as Kai.
moe'uhane	Dream, dreaming.
moe'uhane'ala	Dreaming while awake; visioning or shamanic journeying; a learned skill practiced by *kahuna* mystics.
mo'o	Water spirit, lizard.
na'au	Heart wisdom, gut feeling (*na'au.ao*).
nani	Beauty, beautiful.
noho	Spirit possession.
nohona	Existence, residence.
oki or **okolehao**	Alcoholic drink made from the roots of *ti* plants.
ola'hou	Reincarnation, resurrection.
olelo	The everyday speech of the commoners.
palena	Interface, border.

pali	Cliff.
Palianu	Literally: cold cliff.
papa hana	Plan, agenda, strategem.
Pele	The spirit who currently lives within the active volcanos of the island of Hawai'i; also may be generally present in association with volcanic stone.
Po	The spirit worlds; the realm of darkness.
pohaku	Stone, rock; literally: lord or master of the spirit worlds.
pohaku kupua	Spirit stone.
pu'olo	An offering tied in a bundle.
pu'uwai	Heart.
pu'uhonua	A place of refuge; a spiritual training center.
siti	A word for "city"; probably borrowed from old English.
Tangaroa	Tahitian equivalent of Kanaloa, the spirit of the deep ocean and ancient progenitor of life.
taro (kalo)	Starchy tuber that is a staple crop plant in Polynesia.
ti (ki)	Plant whose broad leaves are often used to wrap ritual offerings.
Uhane	Literally spirit, soul or ghost; another term for the conscious mind, the intellect, or *Lono* aspect of the self.
Uka	The spiritual Upper Worlds; also known as *Lanikeha*.
ulu	Breadfruit.
Unihipili	Alternate term for the *ku*, the inner subconscious or body mind; also the spirit of a deceased person or one able to be conjured up by a shaman.
Waena	The Middle Worlds of dream; also known as Kahiki.

welina A greeting of affection, similar to *aloha.*

OTHER TERMS

dorajuadiok Ennu name for spiritual entities of vast intelligence, composed of pure awareness in association with dense concentrations of energy or universal power; function as activators and conductors of power and are without material, physical form.

phosphene Visual hallucinations perceived in the initial phases of trance; frequently appear as flashes or spots of light, rows of dots, lines or meandering curves, nested sets of curves, zigzags, vortices, or grids; entoptic phenomena that can be seen with the eyes open or closed.

sesshin A Japanese term for the Buddhist retreat, usually lasting seven days.

ACKNOWLEDGMENTS

MANY FAMILY MEMBERS and friends have contributed greatly to the quality of my life as well as to this book. My feelings of gratitude to my wife, Jill Kuykendall; to our daughters, Erica and Anna Wesselman; and to Kahu Nainoa Kaneohe and Ali'i Maraea Kahalopuna, are matched only by the great affection that I feel for them. The same holds true for my ancestors and for my friends and allies on the other side of the mirror. . . .

Other worthies include: Kahu Nelita Anderson, P. M. H. Atwater, Hedy and Mario Baldassarrini, Michael Baldwin, Carolyn and Bob Blackstone, Tahdi Blackstone, Marguerite Craig, Norman Don, Larry Dossey, Michael Fleck, Kathleen and Peter Golden, Michael Harner, Tom Hurley, Sandra Ingerman, Marilyn Jasper, Bokara Legendre, Ted Mallon, Leslie Meredith, Edgar Mitchell, Lynn and Michael Nelson, Judith Orloff, Carolyn Lee Precourt, Marilyn and John Rossner, Kahu Morrnah Simeona, Susanne and Sanderson Sims, Christina Stack, Brian Tart, Lili Townsend, Cynee and Bill Wenner, Chris Wesselman, Tim White, Sandra Wright, Laura Yardley, and the members of my three-year training group with the Foundation for Shamanic Studies.

A me ke aloha pumehana a mahalo nui loa to the Na Ao Koa o Pu'u Kohola Heiau, the Spiritual Warriors of the Mound of the Whale, among whom deep gratitude and great affection are extended to Nina and Kahu Hale Kealohalani Makua.

My homage and appreciation are offered to Jill Kramer, my editor at Hay House; to my literary agents, Candice Fuhrman and Linda Michaels; to my publicists, Cate Cummings and Cor van Heuman; and to Louise Hay, Reid Tracy, Jacqui Clark, Tonya Toone, Jeannie Liberati, Shannon Todd, Jenny Richards, Summer McStravick, and Margarete Nielsen at Hay House.

Finally, I would like to acknowledge Ato Tadesse Balcha and the staff of the Central Shoa Hotel, Addis Ababa, Ethiopia, where I wrote part of the manuscript for this book in the winter of 1998, and where they cared for me while I recovered from a broken leg suffered in an accident in Nairobi, Kenya— almost ten years to the day from the time that Nainoa broke his.

To all of them I offer my very warmest *aloha*.

SHAMANIC
TRAINING WORKSHOPS

Interest in Dr. Hank Wesselman's schedule of lectures, presentations, and training workshops in core shamanism and shamanic healing can be directed to:

SharedWisdom
P.O. Box 2059
Granite Bay, California 95746
(916) 553-2951 • Fax (916) 797-4914
Website: www.sharedwisdom.com
E-mail: hank@sharedwisdom.com

Information and schedules of training workshops in core shamanism and shamanic healing with Dr. Michael Harner, Sandra Ingerman, and their associates are available from:

The Foundation for Shamanic Studies
P.O. Box 1939
Mill Valley, California 94942
Telephone: (415) 380-8282 • Fax: (415) 380-8416
Website: www.shamanism.org
E-mail: info@shamanism.org

ABOUT THE AUTHOR

NTHROPOLOGIST HANK WESSELMAN, PH.D., has worked with an international group of scientists for much of the past 30 years, exploring the ancient, eroded fossil beds of East Africa's Great Rift Valley in search of answers to the mystery of human origins. In the 1970s, while doing fieldwork in Ethiopia, Dr. Wesselman began to have spontaneous altered states of consciousness similar to those of traditional shamans. Years later, while living with his family on a farm on the island of Hawai'i, he began to experience a series of classic visionary episodes that continue to this day.

Dr. Wesselman's first book, *Spiritwalker: Messages from the Future* (Bantam Books, 1995), has been translated into more than a dozen languages and presents an account of how these experiences began. In *Medicinemaker: Mystic Encounters on the Shaman's Path* (Bantam Books, 1998), his ongoing explorations of the spirit world and the nature of the human soul are disclosed, leading us ever deeper into the heart of the Great Mystery.

Visionseeker: Shared Wisdom from the Place of Refuge is the third remarkable volume in the series and reveals what it means to be a mystic and a medicine man in an age of high technology and super science.

Born in New York City in 1941, Dr. Wesselman received his bachelor's and master's degrees in zoology from the University of Colorado at Boulder, and his doctoral degree in anthropology from the University of California at Berkeley. He served in the U.S. Peace Corps in Nigeria and has taught for Kiriji Memorial College in Igbajo, Nigeria; Adeola Odutola College in Ijebu-Ode, Nigeria; the University of California at San Diego; the West Hawai'i branch of the University of Hawai'i at Hilo; and California State University at Sacramento. He currently resides in northern California where he teaches anthropology at American River College and Sierra College.

◊ ◊ ◊

We hope you enjoyed this Hay House book.
If you would like to receive a free catalog featuring additional
Hay House books and products, or if you would like information
about the Hay Foundation, please contact:

Hay House, Inc.
P.O. Box 5100
Carlsbad, CA 92018-5100

(760) 431-7695 or (800) 654-5126
(760) 431-6948 (fax) or (800) 650-5115 (fax)

Please visit the Hay House Website at: **hayhouse.com**

◊ ◊ ◊